Zen Tapes

TALKS ON THE ESSENCE OF ZEN AND ENLIGHTENMENT

Rama - Dr. Frederick Lenz

LIVING FLOW

Contents

Personal Power..1
Career Success..23
Happiness..38
Overcoming Stress...55
Enlightenment..78
Reincarnation...108
Karma...142
Psychic Development...165
Zen: Concentration and Meditation.................184
Tantric Zen...208
Developing Willpower..225
Managing and Increasing Your Energy............240
Overcoming Fears..254
Rapid Mental Development...............................271
Advanced Meditation Practices........................288
The Zen of Sports and Athletics.......................314
How To Be A Successful Student......................330
Winning..352

Also By the Author...369
Copyright..370

CHAPTER ONE

PERSONAL POWER

(Zazen music plays in the background, and Rama speaks to the beat of the music.)

This is Zen Master Rama, and you're in search of personal power today. Must be—that's why you picked up the tape. Personal power. You want to know what it is or how to get it, or get more of it or stop losing it. And it's a feeling, my friend. Personal power is a feeling, like life.

So for the next 45 minutes or so, take off your mind, put it on a table, look out the window and watch out! You're in the magical world of Zen! In search of power.

Today we're here on radio station WZEN sending out your favorite songs to all you *bodhisattvas* and *dakinis* out there in Lokaland. Power is everywhere. It's in your nose! (Rama laughs.) It's waiting for you to discover it. It's under rocks, in trees, in people, and the wind and the sky and fire when it burns. Nuclear fission and fusion. The power to love, the power to avoid those who would gain power over you. The power to be free.

Power. People are obsessed with it. They can't get enough of it, the ultimate addiction. You can take a nice person and turn them into a slob, into an insane being, craving power, destroying anything that stands in their way. Or it can be guided with wisdom, light and knowledge, to be used to benefit others and oneself—power.

(Rama sings with the music.)

Anyway, enough of this nonsense. Let's shut the music off here (Zazen music ends) and stop singing and get down to what matters—power!

What is power anyway? Power, as I define it—personal power—is something that's not necessarily visible. We can see its effects, but we cannot see power itself in the same way that the wind blows, and we can see the effect of the wind. We can see it moving a wind turbine or perhaps blowing the trees. If it's strong enough, a tornado or hurricane can blow a house over, capsize a ship. We can feel the wind against our bodies and in our hair. But we can't actually see the wind. We see its effect. Because we can't see it, that doesn't imply that it's not there. Of course it's there.

So power is very much like the wind. It comes and goes; no one really owns it. Some people are foolish enough to think that they possess power. You don't possess power; power possesses you. Power uses you. And you can't exactly see, unless, of course, you have very advanced inner seeing, if a person is powerful. A person can seem to be not powerful and be quite powerful. Oh, there's physical power and the ability to lift large amounts of weight. There's mental power, the ability to get an A on an examination or to give an examination. There's political power, power to make decisions that affect the lives of other transient beings.

Power is the big obstacle, or one of them, that you have to overcome and learn effectively to deal with before you can reach enlightenment. There's no way around it. You can't just ignore it and pretend it's not there and avoid it. It's something that at some point in your life you're going to have to tackle. So you shouldn't be afraid of it.

Power has destroyed many, many people? Not really. Power doesn't destroy anyone. People apply it poorly and it can ruin their lives, of course. Power is like fire. If it's controlled, it can be beneficial to your life. If it's uncontrolled, it can destroy you. But fire is neither good nor bad;

it's how you use it.

Personal power then, is not necessarily sexual power, political power, intellectual power or physical power. Yet all these attributes of power certainly come from having personal power. The ability to get down to that gym and work out on a regular basis is a reflection of a certain type of personal power. The ability to be President of the United States, the ability to win in the karate match, the ability to get the job, the ability to survive when there are those who would like you not to survive. There can be hundreds and thousands of people who would like you to die, and if you have enough personal power, you can keep them all back.

Personal power is the reflection of a person of knowledge. A person of knowledge, an enlightened person, a person even close to enlightenment, has a great deal of personal power. But they don't use that personal power to the disadvantage of others. As you know, when we look around at the world we see people in different states of evolution, of mental development. And some people are further along, clearly. They no longer want things just for themselves. They want things for the benefit of others. Some people want things just for themselves, and then even lower on the scale there are people who want to injure others. They derive an enjoyment from that.

We can really chart a person's evolution by how they react to the world around and within themselves, in the sense that those whose primary concern is to destroy others are at the lowest level of development. They don't understand much. They're very blind. Those who don't want to injure others particularly but are only interested in their own satisfaction are further along. Those who both do things for their own satisfaction primarily and for the satisfaction of others, who put energy back into the system, are even farther along. Then there are those whom we would call saints who just constantly live for the welfare of others and really only do a minimum of what is necessary for their own self-preservation so they can continue to work for the welfare of others. They're even further along. Then, beyond that, is enlightenment—an enlightened person who is not bound by any system. They've already gone through all those stages, from probably the worst to the best in one lifetime or another, and now, having passed through the saint stage, they've become something else. They're off the map. But that's a topic for another time.

Power. Personal power, as I suggested, is something that is invisible. And in my opinion, everybody, including you, my friend, everybody wants it. Now, you might think to yourself, "Well, gosh, I've never really sought power." I would disagree with you. What is power? Power is a feeling, a feeling of satisfaction, a feeling of being in control. And I believe everybody wants that, everybody wants to be in control, and everybody wants satisfaction, fulfillment. It's a basic drive. Two basic drives.

While you may seek that feeling in other things—a good dinner, going to bed with somebody you like, pulling off a coup in a business deal, appreciating some art in the art gallery, being alone in solitude and just enjoying your mind, going dancing, competitive sports, noncompetitive sports, intellectual achievement—whatever it may be that you get a kick out of, that feeling that you enjoy when you have those experiences, where the feeling you seek—which you may or may not get through those experiences—is the experience of power, of satisfaction.

Now, most people don't realize it. They assume that that feeling can only come through experiences that they enjoy. They don't realize that that feeling is the reflection of personal power, and you can really get that feeling from absolutely anything when you know how. It's not specific to one thing or another. The feeling of power comes from within you. Something is triggering a release in you.

So personal power, then, is invisible. It's something everybody wants. We can see its reflection, while we can't see it directly. We can see it in someone who has a powerful life, someone who is able to get what they want to get or avoid what they want to avoid. And the more a person is able to do this, we say the more power they have. That's one level of personal power. Now naturally, there's an entirely different level of personal power. That's when we enter into the world of the psychic, the world of the occult, the world of the spiritual and so on. Here, personal power is the ability to enter into different planes of reality.

There are many, many different worlds. Just as there are different continents on the earth, just as there are different universes, there are different dimensions, dimensional planes. And you can move from one dimensional plane into another. You can go into them; you can stay in them. There are thousands of them. Each one is a different—"universe" isn't even the right word. Some are much more enjoyable, some are less enjoyable. There are dimensions of power, there are dimensions of knowledge, there are dimensions of confusion. The universe is a very, very big place and to think the universe is only composed of the physical universe is to be rather shortsighted. All of the physical universes put together, stretching out endlessly, are only a fraction of the totality of reality. In other words, all of the physical universes are only part of the physical dimensional plane, and there are thousands of dimensional planes. In different lifetimes, you incarnate in different dimensional planes, let alone in different universes in the physical universe.

Personal power is the ability to go into those other planes, to cross that threshold from one dimension to another. It takes a lot of power to do that. Why do that? Why go down the street to the local supermarket? Why go to the art gallery? Why ever deal with another person? Because it's there to do. Because knowledge lies in those other dimensions. Power lies in those other dimensions. Beauty. Everything that's here, and more. It's part of your world, that's why. It's part of the universe. It's part of you. Everything that is, is part of you. And as you pass through the other dimensions, you get an education, and you change and you grow; just as you received an education in grammar school, high school and at the university; just as you receive an education if you take a trip to Japan, or go to Hawaii, or go to London; just as you get a very different type of education if you go out to the desert, to the places of power, places where it's easy to cross over from one dimensional plane to another. Where power hovers, so to speak.

A great deal has been written about personal power by a fellow named Carlos Castaneda, and I find his first four books are valuable, in this sense. After that they don't make much sense to me. But I think that based upon my own experience, the first four books that he's written in his series about don Juan and don Genaro make a lot of sense, the principles in them. Of the experiences themselves, who knows? Fantasy? Reality? But the principles that are presented via the teachings of don Juan and don Genaro in those first four books, *Tales of Power, Journey to Ixtlan, A Separate Reality* and *The Teachings of Don Juan* are quite valuable for one who seeks power.

The big problem with power, of course, is obsession. Once you begin to get some of it and feel it, it dominates your whole life and it's all you can think about. That doesn't have to happen. But as a person progresses along the path of power, you attract certain forces and beings to you from other dimensions, who feel the power that you're storing. Sometimes they want some of it; sometimes they want to ruin you. We call these beings *entities*.

Today it's very popular to do a thing we call *channeling*. There are all these groups out there, and people are trying to channel entities and have these beings come through them at little séance sessions, which in my estimation is downright ridiculous and dangerous. I mean, anyone who had gone and seen the movie *Poltergeist* would know that, right?

Entities are beings that are dead, and they're the lowest beings on the evolutionary scale because they don't even know that they're dead. (Rama laughs.) You see, the universe is made up to work in a very specific way. OK, the systems design is great. The idea is that when you're alive, you're alive, and when you're dead, you're dead. When you're dead, you're not really dead, but you go into another dimension for a while, where you have different experiences. And then when it's time, you reincarnate, and you're alive again. This process goes on forever, unless you attain enlightenment and you're able to go beyond this circle of birth and death. Which doesn't mean that you're not alive and it doesn't mean that you might not die, but you're no longer affected by birth and death. Your personality doesn't dissolve at death. You're always conscious, you might say. The two don't really seem like different states to you because you can see beyond both.

In any case, entities are beings, ghosts, whatever you want to call them, who don't know they're dead. By that I mean that they have died, but what they seek is life again, and they don't realize—they're so-o-o stupid—they don't realize that they should be dead for a while and enjoy being dead. They'll be alive again, they'll reincarnate. So what they do—they're very confused, they don't even realize that they're dead—they come into the world of the living, where they don't really belong, and they seek to have experiences that they had while they were alive. They miss it. They're so bound to experience. They want to experience sex again, they want to experience food again, usually pretty basic things because they're pretty basic beings. That's why they're so low on the evolutionary scale. They want to experience the joy of destroying something. They're usually from that first spectrum I talked about before, those who enjoy destroying others.

So entities come to people, they approach them in their dreams, and they make them all kinds of promises. They promise them that they'll give them power, that they'll get them sexual partners, that they'll, you know, do all these things. They really don't have the power to do anything. They don't even have the power to be alive again. But they can see a certain amount because they're outside of the physical dimensional plane. So they might see that you're going to meet a beautiful woman or a beautiful man, or that you're going to be successful at something. And they will come to you in dreams and they will tell you that this is going to happen because of them, and then when it happens, you think that they helped you and you listen to what they say. When you listen to what they say, they gradually work their way into your thoughts and after a while you'll start thinking their thoughts, and you won't know that they're your thoughts and soon you'll be fully possessed.

Channeling is a practice that's very popular right now. All kinds of people are doing it, and Shirley MacLaine is writing about it, and it's very dangerous. It's a process in which you are opening yourself up to astral entities and inviting them to come into you, speak through you and give you knowledge and power. Now this is silly. Knowledge and power doesn't come from an entity, it comes from within oneself. Now, what can these things tell you? To put five bucks on Snowflake in the third race? They can't give you anything. They can't really teach you anything because they don't have enough personal power.

An enlightened teacher has personal power, and sitting and meditating with an enlightened teacher in a meditation hall or out at a place of power can change you forever because the teacher has so much power that when they meditate, when they stop their thoughts, a tremendous aura builds up around them. That aura will open up your own aura; it will increase it so that you will move into a higher plane of knowledge, see things you would have never seen and feel things that you would have never felt. And you will gain a new view of the world. Then, when you're not with the teacher, this experience will fade, naturally. But it will encourage you to pursue these experiences on your own.

In other words, if I took you to Europe because I had enough money and you didn't, and if you really liked it there, once we came back, then you could go again on your own. You would have to make the money. But obviously, if I have learned to make enough money to get there, I could also teach you how to make the money. So a teacher of knowledge and power shows you or gives you experiences in other dimensions. They show you that the universe is much bigger and much more fascinating than you had ever imagined. They don't do this with verbal descriptions. Those are worthless. How can you describe the other worlds? They give you direct and immediate experiences in other realities. Then, they teach you the things that they had to learn on the path of knowledge and power to be able to do that.

They teach you how to make your life efficient, organized, powerful, fun and happy—and how to learn and deal with the forces that abide in those other dimensions, just as your parents taught you how to cross a street so you wouldn't get run over, things that were good to eat, things that you shouldn't eat, like the things under the kitchen sink—bleach, Drano. You learn the ropes of this world. You got a description of the world and you functioned through it, and you function, obviously, somewhat successfully. You're alive today.

So in order to pass into the other dimensions, you really need to understand what's out there, the different beings, the different forces—good places to go, places to avoid and so on. A teacher of knowledge and power—which is the subject that I label mysticism—is able to provide the student with these experiences and to explain how to deal with these other worlds and other universes. I conduct a number of desert excursions, and on the desert excursions I expose people to these other dimensional planes—out at the places of power. I do it at other times too, sometimes just in a seminar. But particularly, that type of education, the education in mysticism, occurs out in the places of power where it should. Most of the rest of the time, I'm just teaching Zen, enlightenment. Mysticism is certainly a part of the enlightenment experience, but it's a variant part. Enlightenment is a very big subject and it has many component parts. One aspect of enlightenment is dealing with the different dimensional planes.

So a person who seeks power usually goes into other dimensional planes to find it. Then they bring that power—once they network with it—back into this world and they use it to enhance their life.

Now, everybody goes into different dimensional planes. You do it every night when you go to sleep, when you dream. You're journeying into other dimensional planes. Dreams are not just functions of the cerebral cortex. Oh, no doubt some are, but there are dreams, and then there's "dreaming." Dreams are just the silly things that pass through your mind at night. "Dreaming" is out-of-the-body experiences where you are traveling through the different dimensions, most of which you don't remember. You meet beings, have conversations, have experiences, all kinds of things.

Personal power is a feeling. It's a feeling that everybody is looking for called satisfaction. It's different than enlightenment, but you need personal power to become enlightened. But personal power is not the end of the process. It's another step in it. It's a tool that you use to get someplace. It's like a car; it takes you someplace. The purpose of the car is not to live in the car, it's to drive you someplace you want to go. So power is an operative force. It's a component part of the universe. You need power to listen to me, the power of awareness. You need power to walk down the street.

We see power operating constantly in this world because the particular dimensional plane that we're in is a plane of power. The beings who are here, who are incarnate on this planet, the vast majority of them, are at the stage of their evolution where power is the dominant theme. They're learning about power. That's why we live in a world where there are so many wars and so much destruction. Because people are gaining power over others and using that power to destroy anyone or anything that doesn't agree with their point of view. This is an arena of power that we live in. It behooves a person to know as much about personal power as they can because anything that you want to do in life—if you want to be a winner, if you wish to be successful—you need power to do that, to accomplish anything. There's a science of power and that's the science of Zen. How to gain control of your time, life and mind.

Where does personal power come from? Well, it's hard to say. Who knows where it comes from? Where does the wind come from? Where does the light come from? Or you could say the sun—where does the sun come from? And so on. But I do know—I can tell you in words—it comes from "the absolute reality." I can tell you that there are places that you can gain power, there are things you can do to gain power, and they're pretty simple and a great deal of fun.

The place that you gain the most power is within your own mind. When you have the ability to stop thought, which is meditation, when you practice meditation and you become good at it, stopping thought generates power. That's why people meditate. The longer you can stop thought, the more power you gain. That's the ultimate way to gain power. Even just the practice of meditation which we call *zazen* in Zen—sitting, concentrating, doing concentration exercises to gain control of your thought and learn how to focus—that creates a lot of power. Then when you move to the next stage, which is not only being able to focus thought, and say, focus on a candle flame for 15 minutes or a pretty colored rock, or one point, a *chakra,* or something like that—when you move to the next step, which is not just to focus, but then to stop thought completely without having to focus, you gain a tremendous amount of personal power. It comes into your life. It's like a bank account.

You have an inner bank account and there's a certain amount of power in it. If you lead a sloppy life, if you indulge in your emotions, if you're always upset and freaked out, if you're stressful all of the time, if you're not happy, you're wasting power and your power level will get very low. When your power level gets low, it's dangerous; your mind doesn't function clearly, you make mistakes. And if your power level gets low enough, you'll die. You'll get in a car accident, you'll pick up a disease. That's why it's very, very important to keep your power level high, just to be a happy human being, let alone a human being who's seeking to develop their mind and enter into other dimensional planes and gain self-knowledge.

Someone who really wants to unfold and see what they're all about and discover themselves, has to be particularly careful about the use and abuse of power. But even your average human being just passing through another lifetime has to be careful because when your power level gets too low, you die. So it's important to keep your power level as high as possible—to survive, to be happy—let alone to truly gain control of your time, life and mind, to become enlightened and free and filled with knowledge.

A great deal of time then is given in Zen to considering where you lose power. Not just where you gain it. You gain it through practicing zazen, meditation and concentration. You gain power by doing anything that you like that makes you feel good. You gain power by being happy. You gain power by going to places of power. There are certain places in the earth—the earth is alive—and there are places on the earth that are very powerful. Again, it might look like one piece of ground, which doesn't look necessarily so different than another piece of ground 500 yards away, but some places have more power than others. Meaning that on a second level or a third level, on another dimensional level, there's an interfacing dimension there where there's a crossover point between dimensions and a tremendous amount of energy is passing back and forth.

When you go to such a place, if you're receptive, if you're able to quiet your thoughts and concentrate, a lot of that power can enter into you. Conversely, there are places that are very draining. There are places where there is another dimensional crossover but to a dimension that's not powerful at all. And at these crossover points, there are a lot of beings, nonphysical beings that cross over back and forth constantly. If you go to a place of power, the beings are higher, magnificent beings of light. They're not from our world, necessarily, but they pass through it—the place where the dimensions touch, where there are many worlds present.

If you go to another place, a lower crossover point, a negative place of power, then the beings there are very unevolved, very demonic, crazy—lower than the people in this world. If you spend too much time in a place like that, you can get dragged down and your power level will be lowered and these beings will annoy you. And of course, if you go to a higher power level, a higher place of power, you can gain power there, and you might even encounter some beings of knowledge and light who might help you, aid you in some way.

So if you want a suntan, go out in the sunlight. If you want a suntan, don't stay inside. If you're seeking power and knowledge, you need to go to places that are healthy and happy and radiant. And you avoid places that aren't. If you must go to them, you go to them in a very conservative way. You go to them when your power is up and your energy is tight. It's like going to war. You've got to be ready if you're going to survive, if you're going to win.

So power, then, comes from doing zazen, meditating, leading a controlled life, being conservative, not wasting all your energy on drugs, alcohol and sex or other pastimes. That doesn't mean you can't have a drink once in a while. That doesn't mean you can't enjoy having sex. But the guideline for all experience is—how do you feel afterwards? Not ten minutes afterwards but the next day or several hours later. When you've been with a person, is the person raising your power level or lowering it? Oh, we meet people all day long in business and so on. But that's not so much the question. We deal with people. But people you are emotionally open to can drain your power level or raise it tremendously, depending upon what their intentions are.

Some people, they're like psychic sponges and they just drain power from others constantly. They lower your awareness because they're at a lower level. If you spend too much time with them and you're open to them all the time, and you never associate with people of your own power level, let alone a higher power level, you get pulled down. It happens.

It's necessary to examine your experiences, to examine your associations with the people you know, if you seek personal power. And just see how you feel. If, after being with someone, going to bed with someone, going hiking together, going to a movie together; if afterwards you don't feel very good, if your attention level is lower than it was to start with, this is a person who has drained your power. Now, that doesn't mean they necessarily took power from you for themselves. It just means they're operating at a lower attention level and you got pulled down by it because you're not sufficiently strong enough, at this point, to be with someone and be unaffected. So it would behoove you not to spend too much time with a person like that—as little as possible. And if you have to spend time with someone like that, or if, at the office or in different exchanges in daily living you have to spend time with people who are at lower power levels, then you have to be aware of that and keep your awareness very much within.

Keep some of your attention centered on your navel center. The primary power center, one of them, is around the navel area. When you're in a situation in which you feel your power is being drained—you know, you're in a good mood and suddenly you're just being pulled right out of it, and it's not because you're doing anything. But you're in a physical operative situation where you're walking, you're in the grocery store, you're talking to someone—if you can put a little bit of your attention, focus your mind a little bit, feel the area around the navel center, at times like that you'll find that you'll keep your power tighter, you won't lose as much. Because you don't have a limitless supply of power. It's something that you need to be conservative with—not stingy, not afraid.

Oh sure, everybody loses a little bit every day and you pick up a lot. Don't be afraid of losing a little power in daily association. Sit down and do your zazen in the morning and then in the evening, and you'll pick up enough power to not only be in the world all day and lose a little, but you'll gain a lot. Then, by leading a strategic life, in which you're not wasting power—you know, people who seek power and knowledge aren't misers, and they're not afraid. "Oh God, I'm gonna talk to this person and lose power"—that's a paranoid. But at the same time, there are people who will impact our lives in a very negative way, and they're not necessarily good or bad, but if you're an Olympic athlete and you're in training, you don't spend your time hanging around in bars all the time with people who are just not doing that. They don't have to be in training. That's not what they want to do. They don't get a kick out of it. They like hanging around bars, drinking beer, getting fat and getting in fights. That's their power level, that's where they belong.

The trick in life is to find out where you belong. Once you find out where you belong, you'll be happy there. If you're trying to be an Olympic athlete because someone told you you should be when you were little, and it's making you miserable, then that's the sign. Your body is telling you that there is no power in that for you. You should do something else. Those guys down in the bar may be having a great time, and you may say that's a terrible world. Not necessarily. For them that is their world; that is their place of power. The events that take place in that bar every night, the conversations; there's a little world of power in there too. That's their spot. It's different for everybody.

But if you're a person with a more altruistic nature, if you're interested in developing your mind—which I assume you are, that's why you're listening to this tape—then you have a different nature. Oh, you are a part of everybody. You're like the guys in the bar, and a part of you is like that gal in the corner with the red dress. We're a little bit of everyone. Let's not get too fancy here. We all have desires and emotions and feelings. But you may be at a stage in your evolution now where your mind needs to be developed—mind, spirit, same thing from my point of view—and that's a lucky place to be, I guess. I think in a way every place is a lucky place to be. It's all eternity.

But when you enter into the plane of mental development and you start to increase your personal power level, your life becomes quite wonderful and very happy. You move beyond delusion. You begin to see that life is very, very complex. It's made up of thousands of dimensions—of wonder.

The average person just sees through their senses—hearing, smelling, feeling, tasting, touching. That's all they know. And they think and they feel some emotions, and that's their life, and then they die. But the world is filled with wonderful mysteries and beauty, knowledge, experiences to be had. It's a great place. But you need the personal power to open up to all of that. Without it, these are just words. If you have it, it's your everyday experience, as it is mine.

Naturally, along the way, there are beings and forces that will challenge you. If you're the fast gunfighter in town, "Somebody's gonna come a-lookin' for ya, pardner." I meet people all of the time, and beings, that come to me, that challenge me. They feel a level of personal power, which one gains through the practice of Zen, and they come and they seek to challenge me. They want to try and get some of your power, take it away from you, all this nonsense, and of course, you just defeat them.

Whereas a person of knowledge and power never goes out looking for battles. All their battles are within. They don't need to get in a battle of power with someone else. How ridiculous. Only deluded beings seek that because they think there's something they can gain from it, which is their sense of ego. They think if they get in a battle with the Zen Master or with a don Juan or whoever it might be, that in some way that's going to enhance their life if they win. They think—they're deluded and vain—they think they can take someone else's power. You can never take power from someone else any more than you can take sunlight. If you get in a battle with someone, you don't get their power if you win. You might beat someone, but power doesn't transfer like that.

Power is something that you have to acquire yourself, through self-inquiry; through going inside yourself and finding out who you are and what you're all about through the practice of zazen, of meditation—by learning to lead a happy and controlled life, by mastering your thoughts and your emotions and your desires. This is what lends power to your life—not beating someone else.

The bully on the block who beats up somebody doesn't become more powerful because they beat somebody else up. All they do is walk around inside their own mind with an inflated ego, thinking how powerful they are because they beat somebody up, because they won a battle. The warrior on the battlefield who defeats someone else doesn't become more powerful because they defeat someone else. A good warrior, a seventh or eighth-degree black belt, will tell you that there's no victory. There's winning, but there's no victory in winning. You might as well win. But it doesn't make you more powerful to win. It's just what you do. It's an expression of your personal power level. Only the fool wants to go into battle to beat someone for the satisfaction of beating someone.

In the world of power, as you gain more of it, people will come looking for it. If you're a movie star, you know what I'm saying. You've gained a certain level of power to get a part to do a good job—or a rock star, a politician, or anyone in the public life. Now there are people who will come around you, little groupie types, who want to be around you because they think by being around you they can get something. What they should do is learn to do what you do. Learn to control their life, learn discipline, learn to work hard, learn to be creative, funny and balanced. Then they should go do it themselves and get themselves a part in a film, or get themselves elected, or whatever. But the world is filled with beings who don't want to do the work, they just want to try and be around others. The danger is, if you are a successful person and you let a lot of people like this in and around your life, they can drain your power. It won't go to them, but it will leave you.

So as you become a powerful person, it becomes increasingly important to have periods of solitude. One of the best things you can do, and I recommend it highly, is once a month take a weekend by yourself. Go up into the mountains, check into a little cabin, or out into the desert. There are lots of places you can go and they're not necessarily expensive. And go by yourself. Go alone. Spend a weekend by yourself, two, three or four nights. And just walk around in the desert, walk around in the mountains, go swimming, go jogging, but don't bring anyone. Bring a good book as a companion, some tapes. Just drive around. We live in a great and beautiful country. There's lots to see. But you should do that at least once a month. You will find that you won't be lonely and you'll come back feeling much better. Your mind will clear out. You'll feel great. Go camping, same thing. But don't go to a place where you're going to be surrounded by people. Oh, you don't have to avoid them. You'll go out to the restaurant and eat; bring your book so you won't feel lonely. But it's important to have a certain amount of solitude just to clear your circuits.

You'll find that you can be very happy just being by yourself. And then four days later, wham! Or three days, or after the weekend, you're back in the middle of the world with everyone around you. But you'll find those little sabbaticals will tremendously aid you. You don't have to just sit around—get out, walk, hike, see the world! Go to new places. It will cleanse your spirit. Then when you come back into the world, you can, for the next three or four weeks, have a great time. But then get out again. It's very, very important, if you seek power, to be on your own for a number of days, at least once a month. That's only 12 times a year, and you only have a few years in your life, you know? Those are important times. Naturally, you'll do a lot of meditating when you're up in the hills, or at the beach, or wherever it is. But that time is time invested and it will pay off for you.

There's a grace and an ease to power when you have it. It's very comfortable. You feel good about yourself and your life. It's well worth having, and it's certainly miserable not to have it, because what personal power really gives you, in my opinion, is a sense of mental equilibrium. The real reflection of personal power is control of thought. When I said earlier that a person who has power doesn't seek to challenge others, their battles are within, by that I mean that the person of power uses their power to open up their mind to higher and newer levels all the time, which creates tremendous happiness inside oneself. It's a very personal matter, as all things ultimately are.

A person with power has control of their emotions. Most people, when depression comes along, which is a force, they get depressed. When fear comes in, they can't stop it and they're terribly afraid. But a person with power can stop fear, can stop depression, or they can augment a positive emotion. When joy comes, happiness, love, bliss, ecstasy, a person can focus on these qualities and increase them. Most people don't have any control of their time, lives and mind. Just minimal control. They don't even understand how life works. They're not privy to those mysteries of the universe that create success.

A person who has power has an open mind. They're not just a liberal, that's not what I'm saying. But their mind is open and they can see on other levels. Right now you may be in a room, and there's power. It comes out of the outlet where the tape machine plugs in, or where the light plugs in. But you can't see the wiring. Or if you were blind, perhaps you couldn't even find the outlet, let's say. But a person who can *see*, who's developed the facility of *seeing* into other planes can do so. They can see the wiring in the walls. They can see where power comes from, how life works. They have a great advantage in daily living over the individual who can't *see*. *Seeing* is a quality that comes to a person who has personal power.

Thought control is the primary interest of a person who seeks power because most energy and power is not lost simply in associations with others or by going to a place that lacks power, but most power is lost in one's own mind by thinking negative thoughts, by worrying about the future, by focusing on the past, as opposed to thinking positive, strong, happy thoughts, creative thoughts, new thoughts, thoughts you never thought before.

A person without much power is easily influenced by others, whether they're physical or nonphysical beings. Their life is easily ruined. They're blown around like a leaf in the wind. A person with power, on the other hand, controls their life and their destiny. They have a mastery. Their moments are aware moments in this world, never wasted. That control in life, that's what you admire—that ability to control one's mind—not to get angry if you don't want to get angry, not to be unhappy if you don't want to be unhappy, or to be happy; to be powerful when its necessary to engage in a challenge, if someone comes along and they want to screw around with you, to be able to win. That's a reflection of power. That power comes from leading a controlled life, a happy life, a perky life. I'm not talking about moving into the local monastery and giving everything up. You can move into the local monastery and give everything up and be miserable and have no power. Power doesn't come so much from what is around you. It has to do with how you use your mind.

The study of Zen is a retraining. It's a series of new ways, not just one way, to learn to use your mind more efficiently. This efficiency will cause you to increase power and not to lose power. And it is my belief that if you practice Zen or something similar, you will become a much more powerful person than you are now. Naturally, the challenge of power is how to use it and not abuse it. When you abuse it, it reverses on you and it hurts you. If you've gained some powers by your entrance into other dimensions and you use them to attack others or to make others miserable, then power reverses on you and it pulls you apart because it's not supposed to be used that way.

Such people are unhappy, shallow beings who become more and more unhappy. They lower their power levels. Nonphysical beings are drawn to them, take them over and all kinds of things happen. The only way out of such a situation, of course, is to stop doing it. How do you stay out of jail? You stop breaking the law. How do you overcome the negative karmas and problems and misery that occur to people who abuse power? You stop abusing power, of course. But some beings are so deluded that they think that—well, who knows what they think? Who cares, that's deluded beings. But you, my friend, on the other hand, can use power in positive and creative ways to enhance your life. And that's what I suggest.

Power is mostly gained through the practice, again, of meditation, which I've described on other tapes and in books and others have described it. If you practice it on a daily basis, you'll become powerful. Then, if you have a good teacher, the teacher will show you the ropes in the world of power. They will not only provide you with experiences in other dimensions via their own personal power, but also they will give you the wisdom—they can't give it to you, but they will present you with ideas and knowledge which you can look at and examine and see if it makes sense to you. They will give you the wisdom that is necessary to be able to use power. You don't just give a kid, on his 16th birthday, a new Ferrari. You teach him how to drive it.

Naturally, you need someone who is versed in the ways of power to teach you a thing or two about it, and then you have to go experiment with it on your own. And then, when you reach your next power level, they'll teach you a little more, and so on and so forth. Again, it's very much like the study of martial arts, where you're moving from belt to belt and as you've gained more power, and you've become a black belt, then the teacher will teach you how to get to your second level and third, and so on. But before that can happen, you have to practice and become competent at a certain level. Then you can learn something new and move to the next level. The study of self-knowledge and gaining personal power is very much like that. It's a wonderful study. I teach it; I enjoy it and practice it. I recommend it highly.

If you are a person who wants an uncommonly fine life; if you are an individual who wants to lift yourself up in this lifetime beyond the common misery and pettiness, unhappiness, frustration and delusion that most beings here experience; if you seek something more, control of your time and life and mind, and you're willing to put in some time each day to do that, to give yourself a wonderful life—then that will happen to you. And you will become quite different than you are now. You will become a more developed being. You will learn the ways of knowledge and power.

(Zazen music begins.)

So, my friend, power is everywhere when you can see it and know how to find it, and it's nowhere when you can't. (Rama laughs.) And you know, when you have power, you can do nice things for people. Like stay out of their way, right? (Rama laughs.) You could do whatever it is you want to do—which of course is another subject for another time.

What is it that you want to do and just what do you want this power for? That's what I want to know. I think I can guess. And you will find out what that's all about, right? Getting power and going out and doing what you want. Oh God! What an experience you have ahead of you! What things to learn. What an awesome responsibility it must be to be you! Gads! I can't imagine.

(Rama sings to the music.) So here we are, singing along with Zen Master

Rama, in search of power, knowledge and experience. On the planet Earth, or wherever you might be hearing this tape. They've imported it into your dimension; you might gain something from it. The operable rules are the same wherever you are. So have a good time out there.

(Zazen music ends.)

CHAPTER TWO

CAREER SUCCESS

(Zazen music plays in the background, and Rama speaks to the beat of the music.)

Zen Master Rama here today with you, discussing career success.

Next to meditation itself, next to the practice of zazen, I really can't think of anything more important than the development of your career—because nothing has a greater effect on your awareness level. Whether your career is in the work force or your career is retirement and hobbies, looking after a family, a nation, a universe, it's all the same. We're talking about the major focus of your life, your time. Whether it's 40 hours a week, 60 hours, 80, 20, your career affects your awareness far more than you realize.

It is very important to be successful, successful in the sense that your career raises your awareness. It adds energy and power, clarity, beauty and stillness to your life. And it's not a distraction from your enlightenment. If your career is lowering your personal power or your approach to it, then it's got to change.

Let's face it, you just can't go on like that. It doesn't make any sense. Plus, you've got to pay the bills, maybe buy that new dress or that latest hot car, or help provide funds to aid others in their enlightenment. I mean, it's up to you.

For the next 45 minutes or so, we'll be talking about ways you can become more successful in daily life—here with Zen Master Rama, Zazen in the background, from their album, *Urban Destruction*.

(Zazen music ends.)

Today is the 8th of January, 1987. I'm in Los Angeles, second largest city in America, land of many careers. New York, Los Angeles and Chicago are the major metro centers of America where people work and live. There are many others. Boston is an interesting place at the moment in terms of career success because it has the lowest unemployment in America—because of the computer industry.

Careers—what we do with our lives. My career—I'm a teacher. I teach people the arts of enlightenment—how to become conscious, powerful, successful, at peace with themselves; how to move from one world to another, through different dimensional planes, and to explore and experience the different parts of this vast creation; how to become selfless; how to become everything or nothing, or just to be the moment; how to reach that still point between the turning worlds, where everything is one, or to play in the multiplicity. I'm a trainer. I train people at different levels, depending upon their interest and their natural talents for studying perception and the various arts related to perception—one of which is Zen Buddhism.

It has been my observation, having been teaching for about 18 years now in this particular lifetime, that one of the greatest mistakes that people make who pursue self-discovery, in my opinion, is they neglect to work on and develop their careers. There is a popular notion that those who seek enlightenment, self-discovery, empowerment, should abandon the things of this world, the pursuits of this world—careers, cars, homes, clothing, material possessions, associations with others, relationships—and that they should withdraw from the world and only meditate and attain enlightenment, that all these other things are a hindrance to enlightenment. I disagree with this. It is not correct.

There are different pathways that lead to enlightenment. We could say that everyone's life is one of the pathways that lead to enlightenment. Your life is a pathway that leads to enlightenment. Sometimes you may walk in the direction of enlightenment—conscious enlightenment. Sometimes you might walk away from it. The path runs in different directions. But each life and each lifetime that we go through is a journey, a search, an experience, a struggle, a success, a failure. Different things. Different words we use to describe that which is beyond description.

In my travels over the last 18 years of teaching different forms of self-discovery—Zen, mysticism, jnana yoga, bhakti yoga, Tantric Buddhism, different forms of self-discovery that I've taught in different lifetimes—I've met many people, as I said, who neglect career. I meet them, and their lives aren't centered at all. They're all over the place. They don't have much money. They're undisciplined. They have a spaced-out look in their eye, and they're interested in enlightenment. And their chances of becoming enlightened in this lifetime or any future lifetime are very small, unless they change the way they live and look at life.

It is possible, of course, to renounce everything and attain enlightenment. But most of the people that I have encountered really don't want to renounce; they wish to run away from responsibility and hard work. Or they are simply misguided souls. Somebody told them that is what you're supposed to do, and they believed it.

There are lifetimes where one does go off into the Himalayas and meditate in a cave and not have many material possessions—no tape players to listen to tapes with, and so on. But this is not really one of those lifetimes for most people who are in self-discovery on the planet Earth. Our earth has changed, and our time of retreat is still there. There is a time to get away from things, to go up into the mountains by yourself for a few days, or to walk in the desert or the forest, or to be at the beach in the winter when there's no one there.

You can be alone, too, in the city streets, among the crowds. We are all alone. But we pick up so many vibrations from others that it's hard to still the mind and to know what are our feelings. It is good to get away. I think at least once a month you should take a weekend by yourself with no one else and just be by yourself—preferably not in your home because we set up so many patterns in our homes. We need to step outside of that.

Sometimes it's good to go away with others or to spend some time at home alone. It is good to take a weekend and just you, or you and your dog, head out into the wilderness. Rent a cabin someplace or go camping. Stay in a hotel on some nice, warm, secluded island, whatever it might be, but around no one you know. And don't spend too much time talking with others—walk by yourself. Be by yourself. It is important. It will help you in your search for stillness and perfection. That is absolutely true.

We live in a world of careers. We live in a world of billions and billions of people. And work, as Sri Krishna points out in the *Bhagavad Gita*, is a necessary path for everyone in attaining enlightenment. Because it's something that we all do. Some people work very hard at not working. That is still their work. We all work. Work is what you do when you're not sleeping (Rama laughs), or actively engaged in sports, unless sports is your line of work, how you pay the bills. I would say, after you're retired, you're still working—you're working at not being bored, you're working at being bored. And if you're smart, you never retire. Oh, you may retire from that job you've had for many years, but you'll pick up another career for yourself of some type, whether it's volunteer work or writing a book, doing something.

It is necessary to be occupied almost all the time, to have your mind focused on something because otherwise, you get very spaced out. There are many variant psychic forces and powers that roam through the worlds that are just like bacteria. You can pick them up. If your immune system is in a very low state of power, you can pick up things that would never bother you otherwise, and you'll get sick and perhaps die. If your immune system is very strong, of course, you can walk through worlds of microbes, which we all do all the time, and not become sick—our immune system is helping us.

The immune system for a person who seeks enlightenment is focus. Focus is absolutely necessary. There are times when we go beyond focus, in deep meditation or in our activities, where the *suchness* of something, the *nothingness* or *everythingness* of something becomes manifest, and we are one with it—we see our *oneness* with all things and all beings.

The path, the fast path, the short path that leads to that, is focus. The power of focus is absolutely essential. To stop all thoughts, you have to have tremendous power of focus, to reach the still point between the turning worlds, *nirvana*. You must have tremendous power of focus, tremendous concentrative power, to direct your life and not allow all these variant forces, different vibrations, to enter in you. If you're just spaced out and you have no purpose in life, you pick everything up. Everybody else's thoughts will come into your mind. Everyone else's desires, psychically—you'll attract them. You'll be drawn to things that you could care less about and think thoughts, disturbing thoughts, that you don't need. So it's necessary to be focused. This is the raison d'etre of career.

Intent is all-important. Your intent determines what happens to you inwardly, in a karmic sense. Two people can be working at the same job, side by side, at an office. One person is working just for a paycheck. Another is working because they see work as a way to develop the power of focus, to perfect their being, to pay for their life here on earth, to fulfill whatever their earthly needs are, and also to make more money to utilize to aid others in their search for enlightenment, or to donate to the United Way or Audubon or the National Geographic Society, Amnesty International, whatever your favorite cause might be. My favorite cause, of course, is the enlightenment of others. I think that's the best place to put money. You get the highest "yield" in terms of karma (Rama laughs) on your money.

One person is just working for themselves, for their own pleasure, or to avoid unpleasantness—not having a place to live, not having clothes. Some think that the material world will make them happy. They think that if they can buy more and have more—a bigger house, a bigger car, fancier clothes, better trips—that it will make a difference. It doesn't make a difference at all. You can be rich or poor; it doesn't make a bit of difference. Everything depends upon your state of awareness. If your state of awareness is low, then all the material success in the world won't help. If your state of awareness is high, then in poverty, you'll know no poverty. Naturally, the Zen Master Rama philosophy is—have a high state of awareness and material success. The two really, in my opinion, go together because if you're in an empowered state, then you should be able to draw the power of material success through you.

Material success is not something that will bind you—unless you become attached to it—any more than poverty will liberate you. But some people have a very strange idea that material success does not coincide harmoniously with self-realization, which is absurd. Material success is as much a part of this universe as anything else. The aversion to material success, or the clinging to it, is an attachment that brings about pain and suffering and separates one from the natural realization of enlightenment. Those who seek poverty or who avoid wealth, or who are afraid of poverty and exclusively seek wealth—they're equally hung up.

We live in a world where money is necessary. You can't just go out and roam the forest and the cities, at least in America. Money also helps you, as I said. Naturally, you can use it to aid others in their enlightenment process, or in any way that you choose, but money is also very useful in this particular world to buy you space. In the old days, there were not too many people on the planet, and you could roam around in the forests and woods. Today everybody owns the forests and woods, and there are "No Trespassing" signs.

Some of the highest vibratory places one could visit to renew and recharge one's spirit, places where the earth's energy is very strong, have become very expensive. They are the domains of the rich. Because the rich figured out a long time ago that certain neighborhoods have more power and by living in them, more power comes through you than in other neighborhoods. So true! The earth is not the same everywhere. Certain powers are available in one part of the earth that are not available in another part of the earth. The rich realize this, and they live in these places and they use that power to stay rich, or become wealthier, or for their children to be wealthy.

People who seek enlightenment can live in those neighborhoods and use that same power, not simply to become wealthy, but to advance their awareness field. The power is not simply the power of material success. It is plain, strong power that can be used for any purpose—to become rich, to become famous, to become notorious, to become enlightened, to become selfless. It requires money to live in these places.

Also, there's a certain beauty and refinement that is often found in our world, and it's expensive, in a sense. It shouldn't necessarily be so. Beautiful clothes shouldn't necessarily be more expensive, but they are. It is just the way our economic system is. In other words, clothes can have a refined vibration. An ochre robe can be extremely refined, and so can a wonderful satin gown or a silk brocade coat.

What matters is the vibration. The way our world is set up, a higher economic priority is given to things that bespeak a greater refinement. That's just the way it was decided. It could be the other way around. It is just a determination that was made, to make money.

There are certain things that are nice to have—a nice car that will get you where you need to go, that has a nice vibration so when you ride in it, you don't feel terrible. A nice place to live with good energy, the best that's available. Clothing that's refined and will suit your purposes. The ability to travel and get away from your area and go out into natural areas to renew yourself. And, of course, money to study enlightenment.

Some people wonder why one charges for the study of enlightenment. They harbor the idea or belief that all teachers should teach for free. Obviously, these people have never been teachers and don't know too much about teaching, particularly in the twentieth century. Teaching meditation is a very expensive hobby, I must say. To book halls, security services, accounting services, advertising, insurance, on and on and on, it costs hundreds of thousands of dollars, millions of dollars, just to do a couple hundred nights of meditation a year. To make it available to people is very expensive.

If you don't really care about anybody knowing, then you can just teach meditation and put up a couple of little posters around your block. But if your aim is to open the door to as many people as possible, then you need to step into the world of advertising, which is a very expensive world.

In my own budgeting of my corporation, our largest budget issue is advertising. Because that is how we let people know that they can learn to be enlightened and become aware. So it is necessary to have a certain amount of money to study enlightenment. When you go to Japan and you visit the monasteries, the Zen monasteries, one of the first things that is required is that you bring a donation. They even have special envelopes. It reminds me of the Catholic Church. When I was in Japan recently, visiting some other Zen masters, it was necessary, even as a visiting Zen master, to bring the proper offering for the monastery—because they have to pay for those monasteries. The upkeep is fantastic. The monks have to be fed, and so on and so forth.

Only in America do people seem to have this funny idea about enlightenment and money. Most teachers, of course, have a charge, an admission fee, a seminar fee, something. They don't try to become rich with the money—how absurd. They use it just to pay the bills. Money expresses a level of commitment. In other words, as you work and you pay the bills, the bills for your car and your clothes and your insurance and the place you live and your medical bills and some entertainment money and travel money—you should also be working to pay for your enlightenment.

Studying enlightenment is like going to a university. You don't think for a minute about paying tuition to go to the state university, let alone an expensive school like Harvard or MIT or Stanford or the University of Chicago. To study enlightenment requires a commitment. Part of that commitment is a person's willingness to go out and work to make money to pay for their own way. An exceptional person, of course, will pay even more, will give even more because they not only want to just pay for their own way, they wish to make enlightenment more available to others.

Another good reason for working is so you can make some money to help pay your way in your study of enlightenment. There are lots of good reasons to work.

Career success depends not only on having the right intent, which from a spiritual point I've just gone over, but once you've come to these realizations, you say, "Yes, there are very good reasons to work and have a career. Even if I have enough money, I could always make more and aid others."

When you're traveling in the Orient, there are the *sutras* of Buddha placed in your hotel room, just as in a local hotel or motel there's a Gideon Bible placed by the Gideons free of charge. They are placed there by a wonderful man who decided that it would be very nice for people to be able to read the works of Buddha. He dedicated his life to creating a very large corporation in Japan, and he works many, many hours, more than he needs to, personally, just to have those books printed and placed in hotel rooms for travelers through the *bardo,* voyagers through eternity, so they can read the words of an enlightened one.

Focus. It is necessary to have a strong, strong focus. Work will give you that focus. Naturally, a person who approaches career for these reasons will draw from a deeper level of their being. In other words, if your intent is not just to work to make money to pay the bills and to avoid the pain and suffering that would come from not having money, but your intent is to work because it will aid you in perfecting your awareness, make you strong, teach you more about concentration, enable you to live in the environment you need to succeed in the study of enlightenment; if your motive in working is to work for the welfare of others, to make money for your own enlightenment process; if your motive for working is because you get a kick out of it, because it's fun to work, it's exciting—it doesn't really matter what your work is. It is exciting to do well at something, it empowers you, it is an enjoyable feeling—then you will be working from a very deep level.

In other words, your intent is most important. You will pull a very deep level of power when you're working not just for yourself per se, in the way that most people do, but you're working for your enlightenment, to make it possible, to pay your way, to pay the bills while you study enlightenment, to pay for your enlightenment classes, to aid others in their enlightenment, to have the things you need to enable you to refine your awareness and exist happily and to further your self-discovery. You need a job. You need a career. You need a focus. Otherwise, you'll just pick up lots of strange psychic energy all the time because you're not focused.

There are billions and billions of people on the earth, and they're all like radio transmitters and they're transmitting thoughts and energies and impressions, most of which are not directed towards enlightened states of mind. If you're not focused all the time, if you don't always have a task before you, you will pick up these energies—unless you're meditating. Career, then, is absolutely essential. It's a wonderful way to develop all kinds of good karma and to perfect yourself.

What I'm saying is, what is most important is your intent. Think about these things and see if they make sense to you. And if they make sense to you, adopt them as policies in your inner life. If you do, you'll find that work will no longer be a four-letter word. It will be a three-letter word—fun. It is not what you do, it is why that determines the karmic result. The karmic result, meaning if you work for these reasons, you'll find that your work will be pleasant. You'll go into a very high state of consciousness while you're doing it. You'll actually enjoy it tremendously. And you'll do better at it because you will seek to bring a level of perfection into your work that others don't. Most people want to do minimum work for maximum money, and then they want to get away from work and go "enjoy themselves." Of course, they really don't enjoy themselves, do they? They are pretty unhappy most of the time.

On the other hand, people who work because they want to bring about perfection, not just to their work but to themselves, see their work as an extension of themselves. They are not worried about running as soon as 5 o'clock comes. The point is to do a good job because that will empower you. To do a poor job will make you weaker.

Sometimes you have to draw a line. You don't want to work all the time and neglect your meditation, neglect your athletic development, neglect the practice of martial arts or other arts, neglect just going out and having a good time, going hiking, going to a movie, having fun, being with people you enjoy. But if you seek enlightenment, if you wish to raise your mind into other worlds, worlds of light, peace, perfection, power, joy, knowledge and balance, then career is a very important item on your agenda. And as I've indicated, the place to start is [asking] why we do something.

You need to think this out in your own mind. I have given you some ideas. If they make sense to you, adopt them as policies and start to dwell on these reasons. Feel them out. Write them down. Make them part of your life. Then approach your career from that standpoint, and you'll see—you will have a very different career. You are much more apt to be successful. You will be successful.

In other words, just to adopt these ideas and live them is career success. Your career now will bring about a high level of empowerment. That is the success. The success is not promotions or making lots of money. That, of course, inevitably will happen to someone with this attitude because the best workers in the world are people who are studying enlightenment, who are using their careers as vehicles for their enlightenment. They are going to do a better job than anybody. Because, of course, you meditate each day and you're developing your mind in ways that most people can't imagine, you bring a full mind and one-pointed focus to your work and a level of creativity that comes from your meditation, which will make you absolutely great at what you do.

Now, the next question that comes up, of course, is what to do, what to do. Now that you know why you need to work, and, obviously, you know how to work, and that's perfectly—giving it your very best without attachment to results, just doing it for the sake of the work and having a ball doing it, drawing the power from your zazen practice, your daily meditation, the clarity from that practice, from your study with the teacher, with the Zen master, and from your daily experiences in life—and bringing it all to your work. Obviously, that's how one works. Now you know how and why, what do you do?

It really doesn't matter, but it does. You can do anything. You can be doing housework, you can be lifting boxes all day, you can be running the government, teaching people to be enlightened, teaching college algebra, composing music, it doesn't matter. But it does. It doesn't matter in the sense that all work is the same. If your motives are high and noble and your work is hard and you do a good job, then whatever the task is in your life—whether it's doing your laundry, working out, singing, dancing, playing or, of course, your career focus, whatever it is will benefit you. It doesn't matter what you do—but it does, in that there are some careers that will develop your mind more than others. And in the study of enlightenment, it is most important to develop your mind and your body.

Some people are professional athletes, professional dancers. They use the body. Working on their bodies continuously will aid them in their enlightenment because the discipline of the body and the focus required will also aid them in developing the mind and their focus of the mind. In other words, the mind is a muscle, in a sense, and as you exercise it, it becomes stronger. There are certain exercises that will make your mind stronger and will enable you to direct your attention in more specific ways so that enlightenment will be easier for you. Work with the body helps. If you don't work with the body, if that's not your profession, then it's a very good idea to become involved with sports and athletics in your free time. It really helps you develop a power of concentration, and it makes you strong, and you need to be strong to deal with this world and the powers and forces of this world that block enlightenment.

In addition to this, it's nice to pick a career that really taxes your mind. As you use your mind in new and creative ways, not just doing routine tasks, you'll find that your mind will develop and become stronger, which will aid you in your meditation and your self-discovery. Also, it's good to pick a profession that will give you enough money to give you the economic freedom to go where you need to go and do whatever you need to do and have whatever you need to have. [You are] setting up your life as a field of energy or power so you can go to the seminars, travel when you need to, have the kind of car you need—all the things that I discussed with you earlier.

I recommend for many people the study of computer science. Obviously, it's a smart career choice. It is our country's number one business now, and it will only become more so in the coming times as the economic climate of the world changes. Our natural resource, in America, is the mind. It is certainly not cheap labor. The mindset used in computer science is very similar to the mindset we use in Zen and in the more advanced stages of self-discovery. Programming will aid a person in developing their mind and will aid their meditation, in my opinion. If you're not familiar with the world of programming, you might take a simple course in it. Then there are two ways to plunge into it. One is to go to a short-term computer school where you go for six months or nine months or a year, either during the day full time or in the evenings. They usually train you in business programming to get your first job. The other approach is the traditional academic approach, and that's to go out and get a B.S. in it [computer science] or a master's or a doctorate, or whatever.

I find that people who have pursued programming are doing much better in their meditation. Also, I'm very fond of law, the study of law, the study of medicine and the arts—in other words, music, dance, things like this. In each of these instances, the mindset, the developed mindset necessary—along with the arts, I would include sports—is very helpful to one who is practicing meditation. It can be anything. It can be clerical work, it can be sweeping the floor, it can be absolutely anything. But in my opinion, if you seek to develop the mind fully, which is necessary for the enlightenment process, you will be even more benefited if your career is related to computer science, law, medicine or the arts.

Again, under the arts I classify acting, sports, martial arts, dance, singing, all of those things—the creative arts. In the creative arts, you draw a special power. The discipline required is awesome—to be an actor or an actress, to be really good, not just another one waiting on tables. To be a singer, to be a musician, to be a professional football player or basketball player, to be a karate teacher, to be a painter and to be successful at it, to be able to pay your way with it—in other words, to have that level of discipline in your art so you don't only enjoy it personally, but you can market it. To be commercial requires a lot of discipline, to be successful in the competitive world of the arts.

Obviously, teaching is another profession that aids one to develop the mind—all types of teaching. Writing, any field where you're really taxing the mind, science, naturally, of all types. I just happen to be partial to computer science. But any type of science—architecture and so on—any study where you're using the body or mind intensively and constantly pushing yourself forward to new forefronts of knowledge—these will aid you the most. But pick anything. It doesn't matter. Pick whatever makes you happy and will fulfill your economic necessities.

What is most important is your intent. If your intent is proper and you pick from among the choices available to you what seems most exciting and also practical—one that you can actually go out and do and succeed at—then you will find career success. Career success will come to you. Career success is an inner feeling, a stillness that will come to you. Not because of what you do—that is important—but because of why you do it and how you approach it.

Use that career to develop yourself. Have fun with it. Dedicate your activities and your career to eternity, to enlightenment.

So this is Zen Master Rama, encouraging you to make money and to become enlightened. The two are not necessarily different. And most of all, to have fun with whatever you do because we're only here for a while, and then we're someplace else. So you might as well be perfect. There is really not all that much else to do here that's exciting, except to become perfect in every possible way, shape, manner and form.

Good luck. You'll have it.

CHAPTER THREE

HAPPINESS

(Zazen music plays in the background and continues throughout the talk.)

Zen Master Rama here. Today our topic is, guess what? Happiness! A warm puppy, right? (Rama laughs.) Could be! We'll find out!

Our subject today is happiness. And the koan is, happiness is a warm puppy. As opposed to a cold duck? You're in the magical world of Zen, where anything can happen and usually does because it's your life! And in your life, just about everything happens all the time.

So sit back if you're driving in your car, or your car's driving you, or your mother's hitting you on your head, or, just about anything could be happening, I mean it usually is. Your wife left you, your kid just went to jail, you went to jail, they smuggled you in a Zen Tape. The Russian missiles are on the way and you haven't finished dinner. You're lying in the hospital and you've got two days to live. You've just made your first successful movie and everybody wants a part of the action, which is you. Your team just lost, and you missed the shot and the papers said it was your fault—and it was.

Happiness. How can you be happy in a world like this? I mean you've got to be crazy to even attempt something like that. How can you be happy in the midst of delusion, when everyone around you doesn't know what they're doing? They're all trying to make each other miserable and themselves miserable. Happiness? You've got to be kidding. Happiness? Happiness is a warm puppy! Happiness is simple.

I am an expert in the world of the supremely happy because I am happy. I'm probably the happiest being you'll ever meet. You become as happy as I am, and you've done an amazing thing. I've never met anybody as happy as I am. That in itself should make you unhappy. I mean what can be more miserable than someone who's happier than you? (Rama laughs.)

So sit back and be cool. Let's talk a little bit about how to be happy from someone who really knows. Enjoy the music. Be happy! In the background is the rad sound of the music group, Zazen. And happiness is a warm puppy, isn't it, Charles Schulz?

Happiness is your life, when you let go of it a little bit more. Happiness is everything in the whole universe. It's a state of mind. Like everything is a state of mind. Your whole life is a state of mind. So be happy. Why not?

Now, how do you become happy? I just feel like leaving the music on for a while, if you don't mind today. How do you become happy? (Rama talks in the tone of a desperate person) "Oh, God! There's got to be a way! There's gotta be a way to be happy! I know there's a way! If I could find a way, I'd give anything! I'd sell my soul to the devil, anything!" (Back to normal voice.) Because who wants to be miserable? Why live, why exist, why be? Why, why?

Maybe if you stopped asking "why" all the time, you might be happy. Leave it alone, you know? I mean life is happy! Go look at a tree. You look at a tree, what do you see? You see leaves. It's nice. Palm trees out here in California, we have palm trees. You may not live in California. Of course you're not happy if you don't live in California! We all know the beautiful people live in California because we have palm trees. They have them in Florida—it's not the same.

Life is happy. Trees are happy. They don't have to do anything to be happy, except just be trees. And maybe if you were just you, you'd be happy. But of course, you don't know who or what you are. So how can you possibly be happy? That's why you've got to study Zen. Or something. I mean call it what you want to, but it has to be a way in which you can discover "you," so you cannot distinguish yourself from anything or anyone else. Because you, as we both know, think you're somebody, and that's where the problem begins—because you're really not somebody, you're everybody. And because you're somebody, you objectify yourself into thinking that you are a particular state of being or mind with a past history, a future identity, things you want, need, plans.

"Oh God! Things that you can get! Experiences to have!" You think that you're all that. Well, no wonder you're not happy. What an awesome responsibility to carry around all the time. You. Yuck! I mean, how could you possibly be happy if you think you're a person? Because we all know, just by definition, that people are definitely not happy because they take everything so seriously. I mean, I don't know if they take everything seriously, but they take themselves seriously.

Ah! But in Zen we have a secret. The secret to happiness. Happiness may be a warm puppy, as opposed to a cold duck, but the way you become happy is by realizing that there is no "self." Nope. No self at all. Not a half of self, not a quarter of a self, not an eighth, not a sixteenth, not a silly millimeter of self. "No thelf whathsoever," as Daffy Duck would say. No self. There is no self. You don't exist. And when you know this, you'll be happy. Like I'm happy. Happy in all states of mind, in all conditions, on all occasions, even somebody else's birthday. Happy at the Mad Hatter's tea party, happy in the office, happy under pressure, happy when you create pressure for others, happy when there's no pressure. Happy. Because life is beautiful all of the time. And just to be alive and to perceive that beauty of life all around you and within you is just the best that there is.

What more could there be, but the absolute beauty of our lives? Look around you, for heaven's sake and stop thinking. It's only in your thoughts and in analytical processes that you lose yourself. Sometimes you find yourself there; there are days like that. I mean, my God! Life is beautiful. Look at the colors! And if you're blind, look at the colors of your mind.

Just to exist, just to be, to take a breath, to feel that. Whether it's pleasure or pain, loss or gain, just your experience in life is unique to you. No one sees life like you do. Because you're no one. You change constantly, like the light outside the window. The sun comes up, the sun goes down. The puppy is warm. Your life is warm. Happiness only comes when you let go of who you think you are. Because even if you think you're wonderful, if you think you're enlightened, if you think you're wealthy and powerful and noble and truthful or horrible and demonic, or whatever it may be, however you conceive of yourself, it's all a waste of time. Take it from the Zen Master. He knows.

You are everything and everyone. You're in all things. You exist in all conditions. You are the universe. You just think of yourself as existing inside a temporal body. You believe you were born at a certain time, and the experiences you've had from then until now have created the sum total of you. You feel that you'll probably end at your death—unless you believe in an afterlife or reincarnation, in which case you just think you are older, you've had more lives, or you'll always stick around in the afterlife. But you could be miserable forever. Forever, you know, is a very, very long time.

So how do you become happy? How do you find that magic essence? It's a balance. It's inside your mind. Everything. Everything, my friend, is inside your mind. And there's a whole crazy world around you that you're born into. You can't control it, so don't even try. Because the more you try to control your environment, the more it controls you.

People think that they can tame the earth. How absurd! I mean, the vanity of human wishes is endless. It's more fun to dance with life. In all of your activities, no matter what they are—making love, making money, making friends, whatever it may be that you're doing—you can be happy, once you learn how, because you will realize that happiness is not dependent upon experience. That is to say, what you experience shouldn't make you happy or unhappy when you know how to be happy.

Happiness is separate from daily experience. If picking the right door on the game show and winning all the money makes you happy, then, of course, you know you're going to be unhappy in the future because eventually you'll pick a wrong door. If your happiness is dependent upon what occurs to you—"You got the job, you got the loan, Charlie! Congratulations!" You got the loan, now you've got the payments. This is going to make you happy? You got the house, wonderful! Now you've got the house, you've got another millstone around your neck, right? I mean, it depends how you look at it. Now you're rich and famous, and now everybody wants a part of the action. Not because they like you, but they like what you have, because they think that will make them happy. The rich aren't happy, so they try and get richer thinking it will make a difference, or they use their riches. And the poor aren't happy. They try and get rich thinking that will make a difference. Everybody is dependent upon external circumstances because people don't know the secret of life. Sad!

I do. I know a lot of secrets. I think that's because I've been around a very, very, very long time, a lot longer than you. You learn a few things in those tens of thousands of millions of lifetimes. And I'd like to pass a few on to you.

One of those secrets is how to be happy. Which again, in my opinion, is not a very difficult thing to do but requires a certain spirit, more than anything. Enthusiasm is the key word.

Now today we're talking about happiness. We're not talking about bliss, ecstasy, tranquil peace and perfection, power. Today we're talking about being happy; rhapsodically, ridiculously happy; bubbly, perky, cute; just generally happy all the time, no matter what happens, right? Ten-five.[1]

---

1. For fun, Rama says "ten-five" instead of "ten-four," meaning, OK.

How can you be happy? Well, as I said before, you've got to realize that there's no "self." There's nobody home. No forwarding address, no zip code. Address unknown. The reason you're not happy is that you've tied yourself to an identity. You identify with your "self," with your life, with your being, with all kinds of things. You have personal history. You have commitments. There are things that you like, there are things that you don't like, there are things that you want to experience and other things that you want to avoid. In other words, you're a mess. Let's face it. You don't know what reality is, where it begins, where it ends, how the universe works. You can just get through the day, get through the lifetime.

It's because you're too busy, my friend, looking around you and not inside. I mean, everything is inside—gosh, didn't your mom or dad tell you? Everything is inside you. It's true! The whole universe, everything. How do they fit it? Micro technology. We had it a long time ago when we first invented the universe. How to take a whole universe and put it inside someone's mind. It's one of our better tricks—systems design from the higher *lokas* to you.

But anyway, you want to be happy. And of course, that isn't how you get to be happy because if you want to be happy, then you're going to be sitting around being unhappy because you're not as happy as you'd like to be. Another in a series of endless Catch-22's.

So then, perhaps, the way that you become happy, first of all, is by not trying. Not trying to be happy. Not wanting to be happy, but by doing something quite different. That's Zen practice. In Zen practice, we don't directly try to do or achieve anything because we know that all doing and all achieving only binds us to an idea of our "self." In other words, you're such and such a person who likes football, basketball, young cute women or men. You don't like Ferraris, you like Lamborghinis. You don't like the cities, you like the tranquility of the country. So of course, if you're ever in a city you'll be unhappy, or you'll be unhappy in a Ferrari, or if you're with an older woman or older man you'll be unhappy. You'll only be happy in the situations and circumstances that you've set up for yourself. Of course, you won't be happy in those for very long because while you're sitting inside the Lamborghini, you're still inside your mind. If you haven't worked it out inside your mind, you're just not going to be having a very good time, are you?

There are no problems, there's only confusion. And when confusion passes away, there's only happiness. Happiness is a warm puppy. Happiness is not complicated at all. You don't need a lot of things for it. You've just got to go get yourself a warm puppy, right? And there it is.

Happiness consists of just being in a lovely, clear state of mind because if you're in a clear state of mind, a mind that isn't tormented with doubts and worries and anxieties, then naturally you will be happy. Happiness is not dependent upon outer circumstance. Happiness is falling in love with everything around you, everything inside you. You can be locked away in that prison and be free, if your mind is not a prison. Or you can be out walking around with lots of credit cards and be in a prison, the prison of your own mind, the prison of your illusions.

Today we're going to break you out. We're going to get you a pardon, here. (Rama talks in the tone of a desperate person) "Warden! Warden! I want to get out. Warden! Warden! What did the Parole Board say?" (Rama playfully imitates an Irish cop) "Sorry, Johnny, aye, they shot ye down, ye know? Johnny, ye're a bad boy, we're never gonna let ye out of here. Aye, Johnny, ye're never gonna be happy, ye're just gonna rot!" (Back to normal voice.)

It can happen—I guess. Happiness. Happiness comes from living in the moment. This moment, now, right here. "Number Five is alive," right? [Reference to the film *Short Circuit.*] Just to be. To be clear, in a clear state of mind, is to see what this moment is. Naturally, if you're in obscure states of mind, you won't see what this moment is, and of course you won't be happy in it. You won't realize its beauty.

I'm suggesting that you don't have to do anything to be happy, nor do you have to avoid anything. You can do things and be happy, you can do nothing and be happy. Happiness comes from within. Within what? Within your mind. It's already there. That's the thing you need to see, my friend. Happiness already exists. You don't have to go out and get it. No one—I can't give you happiness. I can show you where it is, but I can't give it to you. How can I give you what you already have? You have to get it yourself, inside your mind.

Your whole life is inside your mind. Your mind is the prism that refracts all of the universe. Everything around you and within you comes from your mind. Mind is not simply, of course, the collection of aggregate cells inside your brain. If you're only the gray matter, so to speak, then when that dies, you won't exist anymore. It's not that easy. You exist forever. You've always existed and you'll always exist. You move in and out of bodies like some people in Los Angeles move in and out of houses—every other week, every other lifetime.

Happiness is in the mind, and the mind is the universe. Your mind is the universe. Not just this physical universe that you're perceiving through the medium of your senses—seeing, smelling, touching, feeling, hearing, kissing.

Life is love. It is! Oh, it may look objectively cruel. You see people suffer—how can you be happy when somebody you love is suffering? Well, why not? You think not being happy is going to make it better for them? They could be happy if they're suffering too. We all experience pain and pleasure. We all die. We're all the same. But we're not as we appear to be.

Ah! Therein lies the rub, and the rub is a good rub for us. We're not what we appear to be. We're not simply beings in bodies that live in houses, that drive cars, that have social security numbers and pay taxes. We are something else. We are something other than what we appear to be. This is what makes life fun. If it was just the way it looked, it would be pretty dull.

You are awareness, perception. You are mind. You're not from this world. I mean, think about it. Could you really be from here? Shopping malls, bad TV shows. I mean, it's just too weird out there on the street. People sitting around (Rama talks like a couch potato) "108 Channels, Madge. We got 108 channels with nothing on every one." (Back to normal voice.)

Dead minds producing dead shows for dead people. Who needs to go to the horror movies? Just go outside or turn on the TV. Buddha called it "the nightmare of the day." It's all around you friends. Welcome to incarnate experience. And if you think this world is bad, you should see some of the others. Yuck!

Do you realize that the universe is endless, it doesn't end and it doesn't begin, it goes on forever? And do you realize that you can't be born and can't die, that you will exist forever in a universe that goes on forever? That's the ultimate horror from the Zen point of view. You could be unhappy forever! You could be more unhappy than you are now. And of course, most people have no idea how unhappy they are because they don't know what happiness is.

When they get a break from their total pain, they feel a little better and they call it happiness. I mean, it is what it is, but I see it all the time—in restaurants, in movie theatres, in offices, on the freeways, on the tennis courts. I mean, you've got to be kidding. This is a world of unhappy beings out here—because they don't understand how simple it is to be happy. It's very, very simple to be happy. You just have to practice Zen—zazen, actually, meditation. To meditate is to be free. To meditate is to be happy.

There are two kinds of meditation practice. One is formal meditation when you sit each day and meditate. A couple of times a day, stop the body, sit up straight, and practice a meditation and concentration exercise. Clear your mind of all the garbage that runs through it and enter into a higher level of perception. And in that higher level of perception, you will see life as it really is, and when you do that, you will automatically be happy. You will find that spot within yourself that is happiness. Then, when you're not formally sitting and practicing zazen, when you're not practicing meditation, you can do what in Zen we call mindfulness. You can be mindful, which means that the rest of the time, there's more of a passive meditation practice. It's passive when you're active. When you're shopping, you're talking to someone, you're riding on the subway, you're dodging bullets, you can be meditating. That's passive meditation when you're active. Then there's active meditation, when you're passive, when you're sitting still.

Mindfulness is passive meditation, which you practice all the time unless you're sitting still with the back straight, in which case you're practicing active meditation, meaning you're completely engaged in the practice, which you can do eventually in passive meditation—when you get good at it, it becomes active meditation. But in the beginning it's passive because your energy and your attention are divided between your actions, thoughts, your sensory data, your feelings, locomotive activities, and your practice, your meditation.

Now what is it to meditate? Well, to meditate is to be happy because meditation simply means entering into states of mind, parts of yourself or whatever it is that's in there, which are happiness. Profound happiness, simple happiness, beautiful happiness, complicated, uncomplicated—there are lots of kinds. There are ten thousand states of mind. Ten thousand to explore and pass through, and beyond all states of mind of course is *nirvana,* the endless reality, perfection beyond happiness. There's something beyond happiness.

But happiness is not bad in the meantime, I think, if you're even around the total absorption of perfection. Happiness gets you through the day and through the night. And you don't have to take drugs to be happy. You don't have to drink to be happy. You don't have to have people around you who love you to be happy. You don't need anything—except your own mind, the integrity and clarity of your own mind. That's all it requires. You've got the mind part. You just need the integrity and clarity. Meaning, you have to become a master or a mistress of your mind.

As you study your mind, as you explore it, as you meditate, as you gain control of it and sometimes lose control completely and just swim in it and dissolve in it; then you'll become happy. Happiness is something that you can definitely achieve. At first it will just come for a moment or two, and then it will come for longer periods of time—hours, days, months, lifetimes. Eventually you'll be happy all the time, which is not such a bad thing to do because it's your expression or your statement of being. It's your way of celebrating life.

Happiness then, as I suggested, is a state of mind. And the key to happiness is being able to disconnect your life from your perceptions, from the way you see things now. There are only states of mind, and you need to develop the discipline and the clarity of mind to see things as they really are. If you're not happy, it's because you're in what I call illusion. Illusion means you're not seeing things as they really are. If you saw things as they really were, you would be happy automatically. You don't have to do anything to be happy.

Happiness is a warm puppy. In other words, happiness is the things around you. Just to see that puppy is to be happy. You don't have to do anything; you don't have to add anything. But if you don't see that, if you walk by that warm puppy or you want to kick him, well, you're not happy because you're in a state of delusion, like most human beings are. Your job is to raise yourself out of that state of delusion, which is done by practicing meditation and concentration, learning new value systems, rejecting some old ones, by becoming sensitive to life and strong and powerful at the same time. By learning about your mind.

Happiness comes from *self-knowledge*. Self-knowledge is not an arbitrary phrase or a series of words. It's something real. Self-knowledge means that you have understood your mind, which is not just a series of thoughts that you experience—there are dimensions and dimensions within your mind. Your mind is the whole universe. Your understanding of your mind will come about step by step. You'll unfold like a flower unfolds, but only when you begin to practice meditation and detach yourself from your thoughts and experiences.

I'd like to suggest two simple exercises that I think will greatly improve your happiness. One is passive zazen and one is active zazen. Let's do the active one first.

You should practice meditation each day, or you should start if you don't—it's pretty hard to be happy if you don't do that because meditation gives you the level of control necessary to go beyond illusion. When you sit down to meditate, which I've discussed on other tapes and at my seminars, or many books are written about the subject so you can get the basics from those sources—but anyway, you sit down to meditate. And you're concentrating, focusing on something, a visualization, focusing on a candle flame, trying to stop your thoughts and all the different things that are involved with the practice of meditation so you can move beyond the level of mind you're in now into other states of mind, which is why you meditate—sort of ungluing the glue that binds you to a particular perceptual mode, a way of seeing life or the world which is an illusory one.

Sit there and smile. This is a very simple practice, but it works. Sit there with your eyes closed or open, as you're sitting in meditation, and stop meditating for a minute. Stop trying to meditate; that's good to do. But just smile. Let your smile get bigger and bigger. Oh, you're unhappy, you're miserable, nothing is working in life, doesn't matter. Smile anyway. Practice smiling for five minutes. And feel grateful. Feel grateful for the fact that you're alive, that you can sit and feel grateful. Feel grateful just to be, to be happy. Sound simple? Sounds facile? So is a warm puppy. So is life. Hey, if you know so much, try it. Sit and smile, for five minutes a day. At some point during your zazen practice, your meditation practice each day, take five minutes and smile—for five minutes, continuously.

You will find that as you do that—and of course while you're smiling, it's not just a physical smile, but you're focusing on the feeling of the smile, of happiness—you have become much happier, that the whole world around you will glow. You're invoking a certain state of mind, which you've experienced. You've experienced happiness at one time or another in your life. You don't need to focus on the moments, just on the essence of happiness, because, you see, what you focus on, you become.

We become what we focus on. This is how the mind works. If you're just focusing on unhappy things all day long, unhappy states of mind, then you will become unhappy. But if you spend time focusing on happy states of mind, hopeful states of mind, then it will grow in you.

We aren't anything in particular. There is no "self." There are only ideas and states of mind. You can generate whatever state of mind or ideas you would like, and that's what you'll live in, my friend, that's the quality of your life—what's inside your mind. Most people don't generate it, they just experience whatever happens to be lying around. But in Zen, you're going to begin to gain control of what you experience, not necessarily externally, but internally—your reaction to things.

So to start with, I'd like you to practice smiling for five minutes a day. When you practice meditation, take five minutes of the meditation and concentration practice and devote it to smiling and focusing on happiness, while you're smiling, of course. Take five minutes of your day and practice being happy while you're sitting in meditation, which is a very powerful time. Everything you do in meditation is amplified. If you meditate for five minutes, totally, with your complete mind focused on happiness, that's like focusing on happiness for several hours as you're walking around. Everything is so intensified. And that happiness will carry over into the rest of your life.

Then, the passive form, when you're not formally meditating and sitting, is just to see beauty—beauty is happiness—and as you walk around through your day, to look at things, to feel things, to touch things, to taste things, whether it's through your senses or through your mind. To unhook from your thoughts and all the busy things you're doing and all the things you're feeling and all the emotions that are shooting through you, and just to start to look at life. This is mindfulness.

In the particular form of mindfulness I would like you to practice, which is paying attention to what's going on—that's mindfulness, minding the store, right?—I'd like you to just look at beauty. Not just physical beauty or the beauty of things you see with your eyes, but beauty—beautiful feelings, beautiful awareness. Remember, again, there is no such thing as reality. Reality is what you make it. And in Zen, you're learning how to make new realities, to build things inside your mind. So you need to start to focus on beauty more, all day long, and just realize how incredibly beautiful your life is. How incredibly beautiful it is to feel, to look around, to be, to experience all of this wonder.

Even when you're in a painful situation, look at it, and if you look deeply enough and you don't get freaked out by it, you'll see that there's a beauty in everything. You'll see there's a beauty in you. The beauty you see is just your own mind. There is no external anything. There's only the mind and the mind is endless reality. Endless perfection.

So if you'd like to be happy for now and forever, do these two things. Focus on happiness more and more in your daily meditation, and focus on beauty—and happiness of course—in just the simple things around you. The koan is, happiness is a warm puppy. Happiness is just being you where you are right now, if you would allow yourself to be you. If you shut off all the silly thoughts and desires and crazy emotions, if you forget that you are anybody and just perform the activities around you that you need to, but look at them, watch what you're doing, my God! Life is right in front of you, and it's great!

But you have to take the time to see it. So slllooowww it down. "Relax, be cool," says the Zen master. Look at the beauty. Right now, as you hear my voice, look at the beauty in front of you. Look how incredible life is, and just keep looking until you see it. You won't see it right away; you've developed some bad habits. Practice. Look at the sidewalk, look at the color of the car, look at the colors of your mind. Look at your feelings, look at all the different things you can feel. Stop taking life for granted and experience it completely. You don't experience it completely because you allow your mind and your thoughts to wander all over the place, and you don't see what's in front of you because you're so distracted by your thoughts.

Think about what's in front of you, if you must think. Look at the chair. Look at the people. Look at your hands. Feel your body when you run. When you make that business decision, enter into it completely and see that it has a power of its own. When you're running on that athletic field, it feels good. It feels good just to be alive.

Life is just a state of mind; different states of mind. Choose a happy one.

So then, in summation, happiness comes not from external things, as we're really taught as children. It doesn't come from Santa Claus bringing you a good present, nor is happiness lost in unfortunate circumstances. Happiness is not dependent upon circumstance. Happiness is from within your mind. Just realizing that in itself will change your whole life. If you just meditate on that, ponder what I've just said—happiness does not come from external circumstances, it comes from within your own mind—then you'll stop trying to do things to make yourself happy, and you'll start to see that happiness is a state of mind. Because otherwise you're a slave to circumstances.

Door Number One opens and you're happy, and Door Number Two opens and you're not. That's silly. That's the short path to hell, to inner hell. All heavens and hells are within the mind. And the mind is not just a brain. Your mind is endless; you just haven't discovered it yet. You're just living in small sections of it, and in the practice of Zen you can discover, of course, the rest of it.

Meditation is essential for that because meditation opens the mind to itself. You need to practice meditation every day and become very good at it, and then you'll be in clarified states of mind in which you'll see life as it really is, which is happy, and then during the day and at night, practice being happy. It's something that you have to work at. It's a new role for you. Conceiving of yourself—you need to start thinking of yourself as a person who is happy.

Redefine "you." Oh God, life is so beautiful. Don't let it pass you by. Don't miss it. Don't miss it.

Be happy. Dance with yourself, inside your mind. And focus on beauty all around you. Look at things, feel things. Stop worrying about tomorrow. Stop thinking about yesterday. Mindfulness is to be here now, in the moment. Focus on this moment. Hold your hand and see what it feels like. Go look at some grass. Talk to a palm tree. Outrun a Ferrari. Experience life. Keep your mind on what you're doing and look at it. Keep looking until you see clearly. See the beauty of all things, which will make you happy. And for five minutes a day, sit there and practice being happy when you do meditation, when you're practicing zazen. Smile, physically smile for five minutes, and focus on happiness. And if you do all these things, you'll get started.

Let go a little bit. Relax. Get excited. Just see the incredible beauty of who you are. You're beautiful. Your mind is beautiful. Your mind is made up of light. We call it the *dharmakaya,* the clear light of reality. (Rama playfully imitates an Irish priest) "Aye, underneath the surface of that mind, ye know, and all those thoughts and emotions and feelings, aye, Father O'Flannigan tells ye there's light. Ah, the transcendental eternal light is everywhere, ye know, and ye're it and it's ye. Aye, it's the light of God! Or whatever ye want to call it, and ye're that, so ye just got to get to that, and ye'll be happy all the time. So do it! Don't make excuses, aye! That's a good fella, that's a good gal." (Back to normal voice.)

So this is Rama, wishing you well, as always, and telling you that life is better than you know, but just take the time to explore your mind. Practice being happy. Work at it. It's a new role, I realize, but you'll get it. The auditions will be coming up very soon. So get on top of it. I'm sure you'll get the part—a happy being in a strange and crazy, mysteriously beautiful world, only here for a while.

(Zazen music ends.)

CHAPTER FOUR

OVERCOMING STRESS

(Zazen music plays in the background, and Rama speaks to the beat of the music.)

Zen Master Rama here with you today to talk about stress. For the next 45 minutes or so, I would like to talk with you about how you can more effectively deal with and overcome the stress of life. So relax. Loosen your tie. Unbutton your dress. Take your clothes off. Dance naked in the streets. Have a good time! It's your life.

This is Zen. And in Zen, as we all know, anything goes. So sit back, sit tight, fasten your seat belt, relax. And leave the driving to us as we cruise through the world of stress management. Ways for you to overcome anxiety, insomnia, tense muscles in your shoulders, stomach and other places I won't mention. Freaking out.

How to deal with the noise, the pollution, the demands of the information processing society. What to do when your pet frog, Wilbur, runs off and joins the circus. How to deal with your business that's failing, your business that's succeeding. The fact that you don't have a business. It's somebody else's business. It's none of my business. Think about it. I try not to.

Your mother-in-law is coming to visit for the next 20 years. Your pet duck just bit the mayor and the city is suing you for $20 million. Somebody found out all the things you've been doing and thinking, and they published it on the front page of *The New York Times*. You lost the big game, and everybody on the team knows it.

You're successful, and the demands are just too much. You're going crazy. What can you do? Success is no fun.

You're failing. Nothing's working out. You're depressed, discouraged. You'd shoot yourself, but you're afraid. I mean—stress! It's no fun. Everybody experiences it, what do you do? How do you handle it? The pressure building up and up. Taking Di-Gel. Ulcer preparations, Preparation H, Preparation X, Y and Z. So listen to the Zen Master for a while and let's think about all that stress and how you can deal with it.

I like this part with the guitar solo. Do you know dancing is one of the best ways to overcome stress? And laughing and loving and getting a little silly? Has it ever occurred to you that you're just taking it all toooo seriously and that it's all going to work out; you just need a little more faith in the processes of life?

You just kind of let go and unwind. Slow it down. You're only here for a while. Might as well have a good time.

Relax.

(Zazen music ends.)

Stress elimination. The koan is: "Life doesn't change, but you do." The world is the world. It's different than you suppose. It changes with every state of mind that you enter into. What is stress for one person is not stress for another. One person is engaged in a business, has a million activities, is working through the day and is not stressed. Put another person in the same position, in the same life, and they'd be completely freaked out.

There are lots of books available on stress management. Stress management—I get a kick out of that. What a concept. But in my estimation, most people fail to understand what stress comes from. What they seek to do is treat the symptoms. The symptoms, as I mentioned before, are physical pain, anxiety. [Stress] can lead to high blood pressure, stroke, heart attack, or just not having a lot of time, wasting all your energy. Missing your life. It's no fun to be in pain—mental pain, physical pain or spiritual pain.

How do you cope with stress? Well, from my point of view, from the point of view of Zen, of course, it's good to understand what it is you're dealing with. We want answers. We want quick relief. That's why we take the quick relief pills. The quick relief pills may give us some quick relief, but when the little pill goes away, the relief is gone because we didn't take a larger look at what it was we were dealing with and try to understand it. Zen is the study of mind in all of its manifestations and permutations. And the power of mind directed at any problem will eventually overcome the problem. But it's necessary for you to bring the full power of your mind to bear in an unhurried way, and [then] you can easily overcome stress.

Why does a person experience stress? Well, to begin with, there is really no such thing as "stress." In other words, stress is a popular word that indicates a condition of mind, not something that really exists in the world by itself. Oh, I'm familiar with all the popular theories, the "fight or flight" response, and all that sort of stuff. But that really has very little to do with stress. Stress is a state of mind. It doesn't exist independently of itself.

Go out in the woods and try to hunt a stress. Bring your crossbow or your shotgun and get yourself a stress. There is no such thing as stress. Don't objectify it and think of it as something that is outside of yourself. Stress is a state of mind. It's a state of mind that you enter into, like all states of mind, and it is a state of mind that you can leave. You simply need to understand how you have entered into that state of mind, and even more importantly, of course, what it will take to get you out of that state of mind.

I personally think it's nice to know what got you into the state of mind so that you don't do the same thing again. You can get out of it, and that's great, but then you can go right back into it. So in my approach to problem solving, I always think it's a good idea to have an understanding, which is not necessarily intellectual—sometimes it is, sometimes it's intuitive—of what causes a problem, a difficulty, and what the solution is. Of course, part of the solution has to be to avoid the symptoms or situations or energies that led us into the problem to begin with. Otherwise, we're just back to taking Excedrin or Anacin or Valium. Do you know that Valium is the most popular prescription drug in the United States? Stress. A lot of people are in that state of mind.

Now, if you look at stress, the first thing you're going to want to do is figure out the things in life that cause you stress and try to eliminate them. The koan is: "The world doesn't change, but you do."

Oh, the world changes in the sense that continents rise and fall, nations come and go, people are born and die, but the conditions of the world, the operative awarenesses of life are as they are, and have been for a long time and will be. The cast of characters may change and the locations, but life itself is life. You, on the other hand, change. All the time. Constantly. Your cells change in your body once every seven years. But even more importantly, your mind changes all the time. It's always moving and shifting. You would change even more if you didn't have such a fixed idea of yourself. The idea of the "self" is what causes you to be stuck in a particular state of mind.

Stress is a state of mind, and if you realize that, you'll find that it's something that you can deal with. It is my belief that stress occurs not because of the conditions of the world. Right now, I'm sitting in a big metropolitan city and I'm sitting in a tiny little apartment. Outside there are buses, noises, pollution; they're building a new building down the block. This is the urban world. I'm not sitting on some lofty mountaintop, where I do sit sometimes. No, I'm here in the middle of it all, dealing with computers, accountants, advertising, business, athletics, education, and all the myriad worlds that I touch in my life experience. And I have learned that stress does not come from being busy, nor does it come from having a lot of things to do, or from demands. That's what most people, of course, think. And if you think that way, I don't think you'll ever get out of stress—that state of mind.

Stress comes because you are doing things that you don't want to do, and you are not doing things that you would like to do.

That is the sole cause of stress.

Oh yes, there is noise pollution, air pollution, water pollution, an intensive national debt situation, an unbelievable proliferation of nuclear weapons, and so on and so forth.

These are things that you cannot do much about, as an individual. As a collective whole, when society or humanity wishes to change these things, they may change, and you may participate in that process. But today you are not going to cause all of the nations of the world to put away all of their weapons forever. Nor are you going to rid the earth of pollution. Nor are you going to stop people from being unkind to each other. Nor are you going to simplify the IRS's new tax form. Nor are you going to stop the kids from being kids, or husbands and wives from being husbands and wives. Nor are you going to stop the cancer that people are dying from in the hospitals. All of the things that cause pain will be there; all of the things that give pleasure will be there.

The koan is: "Life doesn't change, but you do." You can't do much about all of this. But you can do something—everything, as a matter of fact—about your own life and your own state of mind. That's where it starts. That acceptance is absolutely important. There will always be demands. There are always demands. Or there will always be opportunities and fun activities. Is the glass half full or half empty? It depends on your point of view.

To overcome stress, you go out to the countryside, you go out to the desert, you go to Hawaii, wherever it might be, or just sit at home. These things will not necessarily overcome stress because your mind goes with you wherever you are. People drink, they drug themselves, they pour alcohol into their bodies, they get involved with lots of kinky sex, they spend time with people they don't like, they do all kinds of things to just break out of the stress pattern. None of which, of course, work. They all just make you feel a little bit worse the next day.

To overcome stress, you have to find out something. You've got to do some research and homework. And it's very enjoyable research and homework. You need to find out who you are today. What it is that you would like to do today, and what things you really don't want to do today. This is called self-knowledge.

To begin with, as I suggested, you need to consider yourself in a new way. People like to think of themselves as being "fixed." You are born at a certain time. All of the experiences you've had between now and then—thoughts, feelings, emotion, education and basic personality traits and characteristics—are what make you, you. And you will always be you. You may change a little bit between now and the day you die, but you're you.

This is an erroneous assumption. It's false. This is a very poor way of seeing life.

You are not any particular way. You have passed through experiences, you have had a certain type of education, you have been taught certain value systems, but these are only ideas and experiences. They have nothing to do with the essence of who and what you are.

Think of yourself, for a moment, as a computer. A computer is a machine that does a lot of fascinating things. But the computer runs on software. Now, let's suppose that we have a very, very powerful computer, but we have a software package that isn't too powerful. So we have, let's say, a word processing package or a database package or an accounting package, and we put it up on a very powerful IBM computer. While the computer may be capable of working very fast, if the word processing software doesn't move that quickly, then of course we'll never get the full benefit of the computer.

Well, within you there's an amazing computer. And that's you. Your essence. You're capable of incredible things. Your mind is. Your mind is the computer. When I say "mind," I don't simply mean the analytical function of thought, and mind does not connote brain cells.

- You are mind. Pure mind.
- Your mind is made up of light.
- That light is pure intelligence.
- It is always in a state of flux, it is always changing.
- And it is in touch with all of the universes.
- That's what your essence is.
- Some call it the soul, whatever you might like to call it. That's what you are.
- That part of your being is not dependent upon the body or the brain.
- The body and the brain modify and give form to the experiences of that which you are, but *you are life itself.*

The problem occurs in identification. As you grow up, you begin to get an idea of yourself. You hold these things in your physical mind. And the more you collect and define yourself, the less you really see yourself.

You're part of everything, but the mind particularizes itself and starts to think of itself as separate from everything else. So you look at a tree, and you know, "I'm not that." You look at a house, and you know, "I'm not that." You look at the young girl or boy and you know, "You're not that."

Therefore, you're the opposite of everything that you perceive that is external, that you define as yourself. The reason you're different from Jane is because your feelings are different. You like blue best, she likes red best, and so on.

So all ideas of the self are generated through opposition.

This is a false notion.

And this is what causes all the problems in life.

There is no self.

By that I don't mean there isn't a "you." Of course there's a you, silly! But there is no self in the sense that there is no fixed Bob or Sue or Mary. There's only a fixed Bob or Sue or Mary either in Mary or Sue or Bob's own minds, or in the minds of those they know.

When people think they know you, they hold an image of you in mind. And of course, when you deviate from that, they get quite upset, and they try to hold you into a position with a kind of mental pressure because people don't like you to change. They're afraid of the unknown—which is part of the software operating package that most people run on.

Now, stress.

Stress occurs because that which is within you—which is light, intelligence, energy—wants to do certain things and doesn't want to do other things. And that changes.

Stress occurs, or is a result of, the fact that you're out of tune with your life and your inner being.

If you are doing that which is within you, what that part of you that is beyond body would like you to do, then you would not experience stress because you would be very fulfilled.

You could be extremely busy, there could be all kinds of demands in your life, but you wouldn't notice because you'd be having such a good time with your life that you would be relatively unaffected by environmental conditions and by the people around you.

In other words, if you're basically happy and your life is moving in a beautiful way, then things won't bother you. If you're unhappy, then someone next door can make a little noise and it dominates your attention, and you get really pissed off. If you're happy and having a wonderful time, you won't even hear it. Or if you do, it will sound like music. It won't matter.

Stress is a state of mind that results from a fixed idea of self.

In that fixed idea of self, you suppose that there are certain things that you want and don't want. That's what a fixed idea of self means.

A fixed idea of self is made up of memories, attractions and aversions.

The memories tie you down.

In other words, you remember what you liked at 12. Today you may be 30 or 40 or 20, and you don't like what you liked at 12, but if you remember what you liked at 12, you may cause yourself to still think that you like something that you no longer do.

When you were 19, there was a career you wanted to follow, and perhaps you followed it. Perhaps you didn't. Today you're still following it, and you're not happy because it's not what you want to do now.

Because you identify through memory with a concept of yourself, you think that you still like that, you're still doing that, when it's the last thing that the deeper parts of you want you to do. Or, you never did something that you wanted to do a long time ago and you still think that you should do it, even though you really don't want to.

Software packages come and go. They update them. You are running on a software package that was largely designed by others. Part of the package may have been designed by yourself, but it's probably terribly outdated and outmoded and it's time for a new one.

The reasons that you have chosen to be the person you are, are probably not your own.

Your parents, neighbors, friends, kids, society, peer group pressure, television shows and so on—all these things told you, as you grew up, who you should be, what you should be like, what you should like and what you shouldn't. You could have been a guy in school, and maybe you wanted to play the piano. All the other guys told you you'd be a sissy, so you decided that it was not the thing to do. Maybe that's something you'd like to do. But you decided it wasn't because of pressure—peer group pressure.

Your mother wanted you to be a doctor. She infused that idea in your head and today you're a doctor, and it's the last thing you'd like to be. You'd much rather be a magician. You'd much rather be a computer programmer. You'd much rather be a cowboy.

Your father told you that when you grow up, you should have children. They gave you dolls to play with. They told you that was fulfillment, even though they didn't seem too happy with the experience themselves. Today you've got a couple of kids, and you're not happy with them. And you don't want to admit it. Maybe they should go to boarding school. Maybe you should part company. But you feel obligated because you are brought up to feel obligated when that isn't really how you feel at all.

Maybe you don't have kids. Maybe you think that they'll hold you down because all your parents ever did was complain about having kids. That was the image that they fostered in your mind, and maybe that was true for them and maybe they made a mistake. But maybe kids would be wonderful for you, and very fulfilling.

You see what I mean? Of course you do.

The thoughts and ideas and images, the fears we have, the desires we have, are not really our own.

They were given to us by people who are not very happy.

Look at the condition of our world. Practically no one is happy. The world is poised on self-destruction. We annihilate our own species in vast quantities all the time.

Obviously, we're not dealing with a very intelligent race of beings if all they can think to do is destroy each other and gain power over each other and manipulate each other at every opportunity, which is what happens most of the time here.

There are individuals who are high-minded and we remember them and we read their books. There have been a few individuals who are enlightened, and we go to church and think about them.

But by and large, the human race is in a very basic level of evolution as opposed to other races of beings throughout the cosmos. Some are not as evolved.

But this race is not particularly evolved—they're still working on power.

[Power is} the dominant operating theme in this world—gaining it and using it, usually to oppress others.

You were raised in this environment. You were taught to think this way. But, my friend, there are other ways of viewing life. There are other ways of thinking. It doesn't matter what your age is or how much conditioning you have. You can let go of all of it and learn new ways.

Now, I bring all of this up because in order to overcome stress, you need to redefine your view of yourself, you need to update the software. You need to find out who you are today and what it is you would like to do today, what would make you happy.

You must have the courage to look at things that you are now doing, which you don't really want to do anymore, and stop doing them.

Sometimes this will involve a lot of change—change in your family structure, change in your career, change in where you live, how you live.

But remember, everybody dies here on the planet Earth. There are no survivors.

You're only here for a little while.

And how silly, not to be happy. Not to feel good.

Because I promise you, when you feel good, it doesn't help anybody else. And when you die, you'll be quickly forgotten.

You are independent. You can do whatever you like inside your own mind. You have the power to say yes and the power to say no, always. And that's what Zen is all about. Saying "yes" and saying "no" and going within to that deeper part of you, and getting in touch with it and making friends with it and learning what it wants.

Because when you are in harmony with the *Tao*, with the deeper part of yourself, that part of you that always changes, and when you follow its inclinations, then, as Henry Thoreau said, "You'll walk to the beat of a different drummer." And that beat will be the right rhythm for you.

Henry Thoreau lived at Walden Pond for about two-and-a-half years and, you know, he didn't stay there forever. There was a point when he left. As he said in the close of *Walden,* he realized, having lived there for a while, that he'd done it and that he had other lives to live. Even though it had been beautiful and wonderful, it was time to travel.

How many other lives do you have to live in this life? How many have you lived already?

Overcoming stress, then, requires that you get in touch with yourself, and that you stay in touch with yourself because you will change. You'll be very happy when you keep up with those changes, and you make them in accordance to what it is you want as opposed to what it is you think that you want.

Winning in this world is getting to do what you want to do. That's winning.

If you want to be enlightened, then winning is becoming enlightened. If you want to aid others in their enlightenment, then winning is doing that. If you want to make a million dollars, then winning is accomplishing that. If you want to marry a beautiful woman or a beautiful man, then winning is doing that. If you want peace of mind, if you like to travel, if you want to be independent economically, winning is doing whatever it is that you want to do.

When you win, you've accomplished the purpose of your life. It's not particularly selfish or hedonistic. Those are just ideas. Those are moralities.

From my point of view, which is the point of view of no illusions, there's only winning and losing. You might as well be a winner—because you're on your own journey. And if your definition [of winning] includes aiding others and contributing to society, great. If it doesn't, great.

Who's to say what's right or wrong?

Only you—and of course, the courts and the society. But they can be totally wrong. Nazi Germany. What did they say was the right thing to do? To destroy and burn Jews? That's what the courts and the society said.

So just because the courts and the society say it, doesn't mean it's right.

That's what creates social change—we get a new idea. We see things a new way, hopefully from a more enlightened perspective. In any case, whatever they're doing out there is not necessarily what you're doing or what you need to do.

What you need to do is go inside yourself and find out who you are today, this month, this year. Do the things that are compatible with that, and then you will not be in a stressful state, you will be in a happy state. You will be excited about your life, you will be actively engaged in different pursuits. That's what matters, and having the courage, of course, to do that. To not do that is to be stressed out and to take Valium and to bury yourself in a world of things that you don't care about because you don't want to handle the pain. What a waste of a life.

So then, how do you do that? Well, of course, that's what Zen is all about. Zen is about getting in touch with your life, your time and your mind. It's about gaining the energy and power to be a winner—and all of that starts with meditation. When you meditate and learn to control your mind, you will be able to get in touch with that part of yourself which knows what it wants, as opposed to the levels and layers of conditioning in your mind.

There's a deeper mind and a surface mind. The surface mind is the part that's been programmed by everyone else and is filled with ideas and images. Within you there's something deeper that's very still and very intelligent. That is what mind is, as I refer to mind. The thinking mind is a simple machine. But the mind beneath the surface is ancient and is connected with all things and all intelligence.

Meditation is the process of stilling the outer surface mind so that you can become aware of the deeper mind within, which has all the answers. There may be something very interesting 20 feet below the surface of the ocean. But if the ocean is filled with waves, we can't see it. As soon as the surface becomes calm, them we can see into the depths.

Meditation is a process of learning to still the mind, both in formal meditation—which in Zen we refer to as *zazen*, sitting down and meditating for 20 minutes or half an hour or an hour—and also during the day, as you're in the midst of activities.

Learning to be still, to be where you are now—without having your mind wandering all over, thinking a lot of useless thoughts, and getting you all stirred up and agitated—this is mindfulness. It is the other part of Zen practice. Where you will bring your mind, specifically, where you are and not have it wander all over the place, so you can bring the full force and power of your mind to bear on whatever it is you're doing.

All the while this is taking place, you should be drawing awareness from a deeper part of your being, from that deeper inner mind. That deeper mind will direct you. And if you follow its directions, once you've learned to get in touch with it, then you will overcome stress.

That is my solution to stress. It doesn't involve moving to the country, it doesn't involve not moving to the country. It's not specific to anything. It's specific to you. And if you are willing to take some time to do that, then you will find that you will have a terrific life. But you need to gain the equilibrium, balance and poise of your deeper mind.

Your deeper mind has everything already. It knows everything already. It has all the answers. And if you can gain control of the surface mind, then the deeper mind will control the surface mind. It will send it the right thoughts and inspirations and feelings. Whereas if only the surface mind is operating, it's like a tractor and the operator has fallen asleep and the tractor is just going all over the place—it may be destroying the very fields that the farmer wanted to plant. But if the operator is awake, he can control the tractor and grow a lot of food and do his job and be a winner.

Within you, the deeper mind, which is not limited by time or space, is asleep. I mean it's not asleep, it's awake, but it's not interfacing properly with the surface mind. So your life is going all over the place. You might hit one or two things by luck. You might get a break in the storm, and one day you get a few creative ideas and see your life in a new way. But then the storm rolls back in, the fog comes in and you can't see again.

Naturally, if you live in a world of people, as you do, who don't *see* —where *seeing* is not the norm but is quite unusual—then you may not even realize that this exists. But throughout the ages, people have practiced self-discovery, whether it's in the form of Zen or other things, and learned that there's something outside of daily life, which is their mind.

And your mind is your life. It's your essence and your substance. It's the part of you that has always been and will always be.

Its formation will change constantly—which is what makes you always new—unless you hold yourself down to a fixed idea of self.

So my suggestion is, if you wish to overcome stress, to take the time to learn about who and what you are now, and to let go of those things in your life which are no longer relevant, and to continue to do this process as long as you live.

You will learn to do this through introspection, through the process of meditation, by learning how to do a system analysis of your life and your energy and your time, and just by living in the moment, by living now.

By gaining control of your outer mind so you can direct it, both when you meditate—to get in touch with the deeper mind—and also to utilize it, to follow the instructions of the deeper mind so you can focus on what you're doing completely and be successful in whatever it is you choose to do, or are doing at the moment.

Zen is the program that teaches you how to do those things. As you practice it and grow into it, you will find that it works. That's my experience. It definitely works. Anything else is just another pill. It's just another Valium. It's just another drink. It's just a little more cocaine. It's just another relationship. It's just another headache. It's just another spoiled day.

Why live that way? Whether it's Zen or yoga or Christianity or whatever it is that does it, it doesn't matter what it's called. It's all the same.

The difference is, however, in Zen, very developed means of controlling the mind are taught. You might stumble upon these methods in a religion or a way or a whatever.

In Zen, of course, there are no cults and no gurus. It's for an independent person who lives in the world and is active, who wants to gain control of their time and life and mind.

Now let's consider meditation for a minute. I don't at this time wish to explain meditation completely. That is done in books that people write, or I've written some books and made some tapes about meditation. It's a very vast subject, and certainly in the time allotted to us in this little tape, I can't possibly explain it all. It's like explaining how to be an eighth-degree black belt in 45 minutes. You can get somebody started, but it's a very, very deep subject, and you grow and develop in it as you practice it.

But let's consider meditation for a minute, as I suggested, zazen practice. And let's consider mindfulness. These are the two things that you can do to help eliminate stress.

Let's give you a couple of techniques. If you practice these things, they really help. And if you like what you practice, I would suggest that you explore Zen more thoroughly, or any form of metaphysical practice that involves meditation, and learn more about controlling your mind.

As I mentioned before, there are two practices. One is formal meditation, which is zazen, the other is mindfulness.

Formal meditation is what you do when you're just sitting around once or twice a day, meditating. You're taking the time to sit up straight and focus and gain control of your outer mind and make it still so you can go into the inner mind, and the two can join and become one. That's meditation. This is done through the practice of concentration, which is focusing, and meditation, which is letting go. Control and abandon. Focusing and letting go.

Then there's mindfulness, which is what you do the rest of the day and night, when you're not sitting formally and meditating, and this is the practice of learning to be where you are now.

When you are in the supermarket, you should be in the supermarket and only look at what's going on in the supermarket, and not have your mind all over the place. You should shop and put your whole mind on shopping. When you're at work, you should just be working and put your whole mind into work. When your mind drifts, you should bring it back to your work. When you're driving on the freeway to work, you shouldn't be thinking about work and what you're going to be doing in the office, you should be experiencing the freeway and the music or tape you're listening to. When you're in bed with someone, you should be in bed with them. Experiencing them. Not thinking about someone else who you'd rather be in bed with, or thinking about your job and so on. When you're out running, you should be involved with running. When you're dancing, you should be involved with dancing.

This discipline, which is called mindfulness, comes about through practice, and it's lots of fun. It eliminates a tremendous amount of stress. Stress comes because you're putting yourself in too many places at once. You're thinking about too many things. If you didn't think, there wouldn't be any stress. Now, the answer is not necessarily to avoid all thinking. Sometimes that's done in meditation in order to get into the deeper part of mind, which doesn't think, which has more sophisticated ways of processing knowledge than thought-word constructs.

But during the day, sometimes you need to think. Sometimes that analytical form is useful. So the thing to do is to practice mindfulness.

You need to monitor your mind. Whenever you're in a room, you should confine your thoughts to the room, unless for some reason you have to anticipate something coming next.

In other words, you shouldn't have your mind drifting all around.

So begin practicing after this tape, being where you are.

Monitor yourself. Observe when you're in your car, what you're thinking about, and stop thinking and be in your car. When you're in a meeting in your office and someone's speaking, listen to them and don't be thinking five steps ahead. Stay with them and observe. If you need to do some creative planning, which is necessary sometimes, then take your whole mind, sit down, close the door and do your creative planning. Don't drift all over the place.

This ability will be increased and enhanced by the daily practice of meditation, where you are sitting for a specific period of time and doing nothing but focusing.

Naturally, there are times when we need to let go and not just focus, and that's abandonment. That's having fun—dancing, going to the movies and so on. There's a certain amount of discipline in concentration, even in letting go. But letting go is the fun—it's the abandonment.

You need to have both sides to overcome stress.

It's good to focus, but then you've got to be able to let go, to laugh, to go see a silly movie, the kind you'd be almost embarrassed to admit you'd go and see because it makes you laugh.

To be able to jump into the water and swim, to jump in the water of life and swim and let go, to let go of everything.

To lose self-importance and merge with life.

Zen practice will aid you in learning how to let go—because your ability to let go is in complete correlation to your ability to hold on or focus. It's much easier to learn how to focus initially than it is to learn how to let go. To try to let go can be very difficult. But if you learn how to focus, to hold on, then you will find that automatically, you will know how to let go. This is the Zen way.

Learn how to focus. Then, in the practice of meditation, you're going to learn first how to focus before you learn how to let go. When you sit down once or twice a day for 15 minutes, if you're an absolute beginner, or perhaps half an hour or maybe eventually up to an hour, you're going to learn how first to concentrate, to focus. Because when you can focus your mind—and there are exercises and practices to do that—then you will find that you will also have learned how to let go of the mind, that is to say, how to make the mind quiet and still, which will cause you to get in touch with the deeper mind, which will then surface and aid you and show you what it is you should be doing, which you can then, of course, do with great clarity because you've learned how to focus your mind by practicing mindfulness all of the time and practicing focusing techniques when you do zazen.

So the technique then, for all the time, is to be where you are now, to just continually remind yourself, starting now. Now you're listening to my voice and you're listening to this tape, and you should be here now. You shouldn't be worried about what you're going to do or whether it's going to work or not or how you should apply it. You should just listen to my voice and these words. Then, when the tape is over, whatever your next activity is—drinking a glass of water, going someplace else, getting out of the car, whatever it is—you should do that and watch your body and be aware of it.

Be completely one with all of your activities and actions. Then when you sit down to do zazen and meditate formally once or twice a day, you should do that completely.

Again, at this time, I'm not going to teach you zazen—that's a whole subject in itself, meditation.

But I will say that if you'd like a basic concentration exercise, you can simply try sitting down once or twice a day and focusing on something for about 15 minutes. You might focus on a candle flame, a pretty colored rock, whatever it is you like—a flower. Sit up straight when you do it. You can sit in a chair and lean your back against the chair or sit up straight if your back is strong enough or sit in a cross-legged position, but don't lie down because you'll relax too much. Your body will relax and your mind will relax out of habit, and you won't have the proper concentration level.

Concentration is like developing a muscle. The more you practice it, the stronger you get. And you get strong very fast. You will find as your mind is able to focus more, you will let go more.

So if you were to sit down for 15 minutes, what you would do is, for the first ten [minutes], practice focusing. With your eyes open, you can look at an object and just look at it. When thoughts come in and out of your mind, ignore them. Instead, just focus on the object of your concentration.

At first, it may seem an impossible task, and you'll keep getting lost in thought. But as you keep doing it day after day, you'll find that you'll get better at it. You'll find, of course, that you will also, as a corollary, be able to focus on whatever it is you are doing—throwing that football, making that business deal, moving into a higher level of mind, controlling your emotions, or probing within yourself to find out what it is you'd really like to do and be at this time.

So concentration is the most valuable thing there is, the focusing. For the first ten minutes, sit there and focus. Then for the last five minutes of a 15-minute session, let go. Close your eyes and just let go. When thoughts come in and out of your mind, just ignore them. Instead just be still.

- Try to feel that deeper mind of yours.

- Don't try and ask it anything.
- It already knows what you want to know.
- It is all intelligence.
- It is your mind.
- It is the universe.
- Just let it come through you in its own way.

Let go! That's what letting go means. Letting go doesn't mean, "OK now, we're going to try to go in there and get some information out that we want to solve a particular problem."

Your inner being already knows; it's trying to communicate with you.

But it needs to shift you into a different state of mind. And to do that, you need to focus and concentrate so that you can pull your power together and then let go, and the shift will take place by itself. To keep struggling is of no avail. You just waste a lot of energy and a lot of time and get very stressed out. So the answer is to do business and to have a good time. Doing business is focusing and concentrating. And letting go is having a good time. I think having a good time is focusing too, just because it's so much fun, and it feels so good. But do those things, and then leave your life alone.

The answers will come. And when they come, act on them, confident that they're coming from the deeper part of yourself, and if you're not sure, wait. If they're the real answers, they'll stay with you. They won't fade after a day. They'll be deep intuitions and you'll know what it is you should be doing.

If you're experiencing a lot of stress, that means that you're not doing what you really want to be doing, and there are things that you'd like to do that you're not doing. It means that you need more control of your mind and your time and your life to change that.

The practice of mindfulness, of focus throughout the day, and the practice of zazen meditation—I would recommend twice a day, which is composed of concentration most of the time and letting go towards the end of the session and experiencing stillness—these practices will put you in touch with your deeper self over a period of time, and you will be able to figure out what it is you want to do, as opposed to what everybody else has always told you that you want to do. And when you do those things, that's winning—if you succeed at them—and that's your battle and your challenge. And if you develop a Zen mind, you'll be able do these things with no problem.

(Zazen music begins in the background.)

So this is Zen Master Rama, telling you that yes, you can overcome stress. Definitely. But you can't do it by taking a pill, getting laid—oh, that can be an interesting change, maybe, I mean sex is fun, sometimes anyway.

But what you really need to do is to get in touch with your feelings, to find out who and what you are. That's the only way to do it that I know of—to gain a strong and powerful mind, to deal more effectively with your life. The more you do it, the better you'll feel.

So have a good day. And pay attention to what you're doing, keep your mind there and then try practicing zazen as I teach it in my seminars or on tapes or in books, or as other people have taught it—it's all the same. We each have our own special way of transmitting that experience.

(Zazen music ends.)

CHAPTER FIVE

ENLIGHTENMENT

(Zazen music plays in the background, and Rama speaks to the beat of the music.)

Hi there! This is Zen Master Rama. Today our topic is, my favorite, enlightenment! And for the next 45 minutes or so, I'd like you to sit back, relax, clear your mind and consider perfection—in your life, in your mind, in your work, in your play, in life beyond death. Perfection. Enlightenment.

What is enlightenment, anyway? Well, I don't know if you can really put it into words, or perhaps you can, I can't. I'll try.

Enlightenment is having no mind. No human mind. No limitations. Your awareness is eternity—timeless, infinite, beyond boundaries, and yet it exists within all things.

But maybe it would be good to have some background about all this enlightenment stuff. Let's consider it a little bit more closely.

The most noble of all pursuits—to become all that you are, all that you have ever been—is to be enlightened, to know truth, to have knowledge and yet be beyond even truth and knowledge, to be God.

You are God. To be conscious of that, not from just the point of view of the human form. To be endless and beginningless, perfect being. Infinite awareness, beyond pain, beyond frustration, beyond birth and death—that's enlightenment. A part of it, anyway. And we call the study of enlightenment: self-realization or self-discovery.

There are many paths that lead to enlightenment. There are lesser enlightenments along the way to a larger enlightenment, which is referred to sometimes as liberation—the larger enlightenment, that is.

Not just being happy, not just having a peaceful mind or coming to a good understanding, which can change, but being perfect.

Perfect mind, the *diamond mind*.

Radiating all universes through your being. Each pulse beat is the universe. Each breath, eternity.

Enlightenment. Try it. You'll like it.

So let's cruise the galaxies a little bit in the world of Zen, the music of Zazen in the background from their *Samurai* album—the warrior, the samurai.

You have to be a warrior in order to become enlightened. It's not easy. I mean if you think it's tough just paying the bills and driving the car down the freeway and trying to schedule all your appointments, be all the places you've got to be—think about being everywhere all at once and doing everything in all the universes simultaneously, past, present or future.

It doesn't matter. They can't stop you. Nothing can. Because you're eternity.

Obstructions on the way to enlightenment? Are you kidding? Hey, they crucify people here. You think this is an easy place? But what's the alternative? To live in a mundane, boring level of consciousness? Knowing limitation, pain, frustration, skepticism, disbelief, no adventure, no childlike wonder?

Enlightenment, beyond knowledge. Oh heck, it's the best!

(Zazen music ends.)

I'm here today in the city. The sirens are wailing, human beings are moving back and forth. In the hospitals, they're being born and dying. In the universities, they're going to school. Some are getting married, some are getting divorced. Some are unhappy, most—all—are unhappy. Some think they're happy—when the pain that they experience every day stops for a few minutes, they call that happiness. There are billions of people on the earth, and there are billions of earths, billions of universes. It's endless.

What is life? What is death? Why is it that people suffer so much? Well, I'll tell you. It's the way it is. But it's not the way it appears to be. Enlightenment.

There are two universes. Two worlds. Oh, there's more, but for the moment let's just say there are two. There's the world of the *samsara*. Samsara is what you're in now. Everything that you see, feel and experience, your own perception of the world and yourself is samsara. Samsara means illusion. Illusion means things aren't as they appear to be. So right now, you're living in illusion. The things you see are real. Illusions are real, but they're not a complete seeing. Samsara.

The other world is *nirvana*. Nirvana and samsara. They're not opposites. Nirvana is a word that means enlightenment, being beyond illusion—the illusion of birth and death, the illusion of pain, the illusion of love, the illusion of time and life.

You're on a vast wheel of birth and death. You've been through thousands of lifetimes, reincarnation, thousands yet to come. You'll live forever. And forever is a very, very long time. Most people don't know why they are born or why they die. They have no understanding of the forces in life that pull them and push them from one place to another, from one relationship to another, from success to failure and eventually

ENLIGHTENMENT 81

to their death and another rebirth in this or another world.

Human beings find that it's just enough to get through the day, and when there's something they don't understand, they go to church, or they used to, anyway, and the guy in the front of the church dressed up in black is the guy who you defer to when someone dies. He gives you comfort and says there's life after death. He's in charge of the mysteries of the universe, which ordinary human beings don't seem to have the inclination to understand.

Well, beyond the guy at the front of the church, there's somebody else. And that's the enlightened being, or person.

An enlightened person is someone who has gone through what lies ahead of you. They stand both within and outside of the circle of life.

It's not special to be enlightened. It's just different. An enlightened person is someone who has dedicated not just this lifetime but thousands of lifetimes to becoming awareness. They see through the mysteries of life and understand them. They see beyond this life and beyond death. And what the enlightened person sees no one could ever tell or describe. Wonder beyond belief. We live in a universe filled with wonder. It is wonder just to live.

So the enlightened person lives up on the top of the mountain or out in the desert, sometimes in the city—wherever they end up. And those who seek knowledge come to them. Some come because they want their physical lives to improve, and they feel that just being around someone who has the knowledge of life and death—and that which is beyond—is a great blessing. And they go just so their business will improve; the stock market will do better for them. Some come because they're sorry and sad; they want comfort and solace. Some come seeking power. They want to gain the powers that an enlightened person knows about—the power to get anything you want, the power to reincarnate in different worlds, the power over life and death. Many powers can be had—powers to heal, powers to injure. Some come to the enlightened teacher to interfere with his or her work. They take a malicious pleasure in trying to block light and interfere with his actions. Some come seeking knowledge.

It's a great spectacle when there's an enlightened person or several in the world. Many enlightened persons are never very well known. Most aren't. Many are reclusive. They live in little villages in India or up in the high Himalayas in Tibet. Some have no students at all; some have a few. Once in a while, an enlightened teacher goes out into the world and spreads what we call the *dharma*. Dharma is a word that means truth, essentially. They attract some attention, and it's a great spectacle to see who and why and what is drawn.

Nonphysical beings are drawn to enlightened beings. Some come to aid them in their work; some come to interfere. Some just come to watch. Enlightenment is rare in this world. There are worlds where there are many, many enlightened beings. But this particular world, this plane of awareness, is a world in which there are very few at any one time.

Enlightenment is to be outside the circle. What circle? Well, the circle of death and rebirth. There's a circle inside you. Above your physical eyes, above your eyebrows, there's a spot about an inch above your eyebrows. We call it the *third eye*. If you meditate and focus on your third eye, you will see a circle of light. There's a circle of light inside you. If you meditate very intensely on it and concentrate, you may be able to go through that circle of light into another world, another dimension, another existence.

There are circles, and circles within circles. To be enlightened is to have self- knowledge, to have power, to have control. It means that you really don't change, and yet you're nothing but change. Here I get into this kind of oxymoronic explanation of things—apparent contrasts. But let's bring it down to your own individual level. I think that's the best.

OK, you're alive. How aware are you, of anything? Can you see eternity?

ENLIGHTENMENT 83

Do you live in the land of the perpetually happy? When you close your eyes, do you dissolve into that white light of perfection that is God and the universe? No. Of course not. Your mind is filled with thoughts; desires pull you back and forth; your moods shift constantly; you're not sure what it is you want—it changes from moment to moment; there's little or no continuity in your life. That's because you're inside a circle, a circle of birth and death.

Life is a circle. Oh true, you've come forth from infinity. There was a time when you came forth from infinity—your essence that is—or from God or whatever you'd like to call it. Yet that essence has always existed. You've always existed, and you'll always exist. But there are different states of existence, different states of mind in the universe. There are different cosmological theories.

The Tibetans believe there are six worlds. In some Hindu systems, they feel there are 14. We reincarnate in them. The Tibetans imagine it is the wheel of life. There's a big wheel, and the wheel is divided into six portions. These are the six worlds. Some of the worlds are higher and more pleasant, and some are lower hell worlds. Some are heavenly worlds. The earth plane is somewhere in the middle. There are different cosmological systems. But when we look at a picture of the wheel of life and we see the six worlds, we see the beings in the six worlds going through them. They will incarnate in one of the six worlds for a while, and then if their actions have been meritorious, if they've been drawn towards something higher, then eventually they'll switch to one of the higher worlds and incarnate there, until such time that their actions cause them to move to another world above or to a world below.

You reincarnate forever because you exist forever. You can't die. You can't be born, your essence that is. You're on a big wheel, and you go round and round the wheel of birth and death. And when you die, you forget. Death is a sleep, a forgetting. You forget about your previous lifetime. The essence of your being is the same. But at death, the personality dissolves. The you that was in one lifetime will never be again.

But the essence remains. It takes on a new body dependent upon the level of awareness you had in your previous lifetime.

Now, when you look at a picture of the wheel of life, above it there's an enlightened person, a Buddha. And he's pointing, not towards the wheel, but away from it. He's indicating that there's something else besides the wheel of birth and death, and that's nirvana, and that's the path to follow.

In the *Upanishads,* the Indian scriptures, they talk about the path of the sun and the path of the moon. The path of the moon is rebirth. It's the lunar cycle. The path of the sun is the path that leads to self-knowledge, enlightenment, from which there is no return. Right now, you're on a wheel. And you're going around on the wheel again and again and again. You go around and around from lifetime to lifetime. In each lifetime, you never quite wake up. Enlightenment is waking up.

Oh, in some lifetimes you'll wake up more than others. You've had past lives in which you were probably more knowledgeable than you are now. You've had past lives in which you were probably not as aware as you are now. You'll have future lives in which you'll be more aware and less aware. For a while, you'll be more aware. You'll go through a cycle of incarnations, then you'll be less aware. Because the wheel goes round and round and round forever—pleasure, pain, birth and death, lifetime after lifetime. It's endless. All sentient beings, that is, living beings, experience this. It's the endless dance of life, the *lila,* as it's called. Enlightenment is different. Enlightenment is getting off the wheel. Enlightenment is to become pure awareness.

There are ten thousand states of mind, ten thousand planes of awareness within the infinite mind of the diamond mind—not the physical mind that you think with, but your deeper mind. Beyond the ten thousand states of mind, there's something else. I wouldn't even call it knowledge but endless awareness. Imagine for a moment that you were God. Not God as a man or a woman, but God as awareness, the awareness of all of life. Not just the universes that you've seen and experienced, but all endless possibilities and permutations of mind—to be that is enlightenment.

To be that in a physical form is to be an enlightened person. An enlightened person is not someone who is in touch with all of the ten thousand states of mind and all of the infinite permutations of awareness simultaneously always. It would be very hard to go shopping, let alone drive the car. An enlightened person is someone who shifts from one plateau of knowledge to another.

Let's say that you have a car, and in your car you have a fourth gear—it's real strong. You've got three gears that you use most of the time in town, but once in a while, you can really open her up and slap it into fourth gear. Being an enlightened person is something like that. There are normal states of mind that you use for day-to-day activities, and those are the ten thousand states of mind. The average person walks around and goes through five or six states of mind in their whole life. But the enlightened person goes through ten thousand, and that's usually enough. No matter what they're doing, they're in and out of those ten thousand states.

But once in a while, they go into overdrive. Fourth gear. That's when they go into a state of absorption in nirvana. It's not really a state of mind as such. It's hard to talk about these things. It's been referred to as *nirvikalpa samadhi* by the Indians—a state of no mind, beyond the ten thousand states of mind, where there's nothing but perfection, where the self no longer exists, the ego dissolves in immortality. So an enlightened person, after many, many lifetimes of self-search, has developed quite a mind, and that carries over from one lifetime to another. They have a knowledge of the ten thousand states of mind, yet they've got that overdrive gear. They're not exactly like a person is anymore, or any type of being. They're enlightened. And they're not special.

Anybody or anything can become enlightened because enlightenment is the very nature of existence itself.

Enlightenment is in every tree, every brook, every building, every car, every person. It's the substructure of existence.

Enlightenment itself is what everything is made up from.

Everything is made up from everything. Everything is everything. But if your view of life is the view of most people—through the physical universe, through the senses—then you don't see too much, and you don't feel too good most of the time.

Enlightenment is the culmination of self-knowledge. And it doesn't follow any rules, particularly. It isn't religious. It's just knowledge—pure, unadulterated knowledge. Not knowledge you can get from reading any book or attending any lecture. It's a knowledge that comes from meditation, a knowledge that comes from perfecting your awareness, your mind.

A person who is enlightened does not have to reincarnate, or they may. If they choose not to reincarnate, they can just go beyond the circle, the wheel, and just slide into nirvana forever. Or, if they choose to reincarnate—this is all a way of talking, of course, there's no actual choosing as you would think of choosing—but if they choose to reincarnate, they come into the world to aid others. While they're in the world, and they feel pleasure and pain—their bodies do, and their senses feel what your senses feel—inside, they're not bound by any of it. While you in your next lifetime will go off to this world or another world—dependent upon your karmas, the actions you performed and the states of mind you've been in will lead to your next rebirth—the enlightened person isn't bound by anything like that. They are fluid light inside. Oh, you are too, but it's deeper inside you. It hasn't come out yet. A little bit, maybe.

Enlightenment puts an end to suffering.

Enlightenment is self-knowledge. Most enlightened people can do what you would call miracles. They know how to use energy on different levels.

They can heal sometimes—sometimes they do, sometimes they don't. Some have powers, some don't. Some people have developed powers and aren't enlightened.

You might decide that you want to pursue the path to enlightenment.

I used to study Judo, martial arts, when I was in college. I had a great Judo teacher. He was a fifth-degree black belt. Some of the classes had a lot of young kids in them—[ages] seven, eight, nine—and I wondered sometimes what the kids were doing out there because they were just mainly playing around, and they didn't seem to be learning much. He told me that it didn't really matter if they were accomplishing much. Just by being out there on the mat and moving and trying to throw each other and playing, they were learning something. They were gaining something and feeling something from their activities.

So those who follow the path to self-knowledge gain something. Even if they're absolute beginners and they don't even practice a whole lot, they learn something like those kids on the mat. Then, eventually, that will lead them to another step and another step.

No self-effort in the direction of enlightenment is ever wasted. Even if in a given lifetime you don't become fully enlightened, you'll be much happier and more aware. Your mind will work much more efficiently. Your life will be much more together.

There are many little enlightenments that you will experience that will overwhelm you with joy and knowledge. Many powers will come to you long before you become enlightened in the absolute sense.

Enlightenment is a lot like dying. And you might wonder why there aren't more enlightened people. It's because people are afraid to die.

Oh, some people commit suicide. They're not really afraid to die; they're afraid to live. They find that life is so painful, their current life, that they choose to die. But they don't really die. Inside, they know that they go to another life. They may not know that consciously. But enlightenment is like—it is really dying—because in enlightenment, you dissolve the self. All of it—not just the outer self, but the inner self from all those lifetimes—into the white light of eternity. You become that eternity. Now, it sounds attractive on a certain level, and it is, but the mind is afraid of its own dissolution. Life always seeks to be life.

The pathway to enlightenment is beautiful. There are a lot of wonderful things that happen along the way to it. And I can only encourage you—as you listen to me, one who has walked that path for (Rama laughs) a long, long, long time—to follow the path to enlightenment. I wouldn't worry much about becoming enlightened. It's like going to school. When you're in first grade, you don't think too much about graduating from high school. It happens eventually, if you stay in school. Rather, you just learn the lesson each day and live your life each day and have fun each day and go through the battles that you go through. Win or lose, you just keep going, and it happens eventually.

The best thing to do, from my point of view, is to occupy yourself with what's in your life now. Address those situations and subjects as fully as possible with your best efforts.

That's what produces happiness and clarity and knowledge and power.

People who ponder too much about the subject of enlightenment, the absolute enlightenment itself, I find, don't progress very fast. It's like sitting around talking about getting a Ph.D. and thinking about what it would be like, instead of just going to school and doing it. It's interesting to know it's there, but you can't know what it's like until you get there, can you? The closest experience that you can have prior to that is to be with someone who is enlightened, to meditate with them and to feel as best you can with your psychic feelings what it is that they're like.

I can remember when I was in a Ph.D. program at the State University of New York, after I had finished my master's. I think I was in my first year of the doctoral program, and I was very curious. I ran into, in the halls of the English Department on different occasions, some people who were in different stages of their program. I remember meeting a girl who had just finished her oral examinations. I remember meeting another guy who had just defended his dissertation, and so on. And it was interesting to look at them. I had many years to go through before I would be where they were in the program. But I got a kick out of looking at them and trying to figure out what that was like because that's what I was aiming at. Why did I want to get a Ph.D.? Well, I wanted to be a university professor. I liked teaching English, Shakespeare, poetry, things like that, contemporary literature. Turns out I didn't do that for too many years. I went off into another profession or two, but I enjoyed the study very much.

But it was fascinating to see. Of course, the thing that got me to decide to do that was some of the wonderful, wonderful professors I had had as an undergraduate, not as a graduate student. As an undergraduate, I had terrific English professors. I just thought they were so super, and I enjoyed what they were doing so much that I decided that was the profession I wanted to follow. So the way I knew I wanted to get a doctorate and do all that was by being exposed to people who had already done it. I didn't want to replicate them. I wanted to do it my way, naturally. But that's what gave me the sense.

I really think enlightenment is something that you decide to do or strive for, work towards, aim at, whatever you want to call it, after you've met someone who's enlightened because you really don't know what it is [until then]. Oh, you may have a feeling—you want light; you want knowledge; you want to get away from pain. You may have sought for it in past lives, and your own karmas just pick you up and carry you. But I think after you've meditated with someone who's enlightened, that's when you know.

Something touches your heart or your being at a very deep level, and you just look around this world with all its transitory joys and pleasures—nothing lasts here, not even you—and you say to yourself,

"Heck! Everybody here is so caught up, they don't even see life. They don't see beyond their own deaths. They're just all caught up in the game of life. They're on the wheel of birth and death."

Just to see that indicates that a kind of awakening has taken place in your mind, when you can see how caught up everyone is in their jobs, their careers, their families, their problems, their successes, their failures, their wars, their victories, their defeats, their moods.

If you can just see that there's something beyond that, that's great! You're on your way.

When you meditate with someone who's enlightened, if you were to come and meditate with me, for example, or with someone else who's enlightened, you'll have a kind of experience. I can't tell you what it's like. It will be different for you. It depends on how aware you are. But when you meditate with an enlightened teacher, the teacher goes into these different states of mind, those ten thousand states of mind, states of mind that you normally don't reach, and you'll feel something from them, if you're sensitive, and once in a while they go into overdrive. They just dissolve completely. Absorption in nirvana, where they don't even have physical contact with this world anymore. Nirvikalpa samadhi.

And you'll feel something from that, as you sit with them and meditate, as you watch them talk and walk, or whatever they do. Something may touch you, and you might say, "I'd like to be where they are. I'd like to be off the wheel. I'd like to have knowledge. I'd like to have power. I'd like to be beyond the suffering that exists inside…"—your own mind!

All heavens and hells are inside your own mind. It's not what goes on around you; it's within you. And when your mind is lucid and still, and when you can climb into other states of being that are beyond pain and suffering, life is quite wonderful.

Now, the path to knowledge, I should tell you, culminates in everything that's wonderful. Every step along the way, as a matter of fact, leads you to a higher and sharper level of living. It's great. But it's not easy. Let me tell you why. Some people are under the impression that to become enlightened, you meditate 20 minutes a day and chant some mantras, and, I don't know—whatever.

Enlightenment is not like going to church. Enlightenment means that you have to address every part of your life and perfect it. You have to perfect your mind. There can't be any fears that you haven't overcome. There can't be any desires that you haven't conquered. There can't be any sorrows that you have not experienced. There cannot be any joys that you have not experienced.

You're going to merge with life, you're going to mate with the cosmos and dissolve into it and become it. So the ego has to gradually be dissolved. You have to go through permutations and changes that I can't begin to describe.

I'm a teacher of the art of enlightenment. And to try and describe what you must go through on a 45-minute tape is impossible. It's as if someone had tried, in a 45-minute tape, to tell me what it would have been like to go through a Ph.D. program. They could outline the program, but no one could explain what it's like, how you'll change. This is the study of change and that which lies beyond change.

There's only eternity. It's all around us and within us, and it goes on forever. There's only knowledge. And then there's illusion, the way you see things now, thinking that there's a tomorrow and there is a today and that there is time and that there is life and death. Those are just appearances.

Nothing lasts except eternity, and the knowledge of eternity is enlightenment.

So it is difficult, yes. The reason it is difficult is because there is obstruction. As you know, enlightenment is not exactly very popular in this world. History tells us that the enlightened teachers who made themselves largely available to human beings had problems. That's because the level of evolution in this world is not exactly high. As we know, people on the planet are currently preparing to blow themselves up in ultimate thermal nuclear wars. The largest part of our budget here in this country, and in most countries, goes to war, defense, whatever you want to call it, which is not a bad place to put your money. But it simply tells us that we are living among beings whose state of mind is destruction.

Societies in this planet are based upon fear, not upon love. The strong dominate the weak. The most knowledgeable person is not necessarily the person who runs the government, nor the church, nor the business. Usually it's the most powerful or the one who can grab power, the one who can influence. This is a place where the strong often victimize the weak. There is good here, and there is bad because it's a relative world, the world of duality. There is suffering and there is joy. Your life here is very short, and then you're back again for another and another, forever, unless you step off the wheel.

So it's difficult because there are opposing forces. In the universe, there is darkness and light. We call this duality. When you seek knowledge and power, there are forces and people that will oppose you. Otherwise, everybody would do it. It would be very easy. But [there are] people and forces that are not illumined and are afraid of enlightenment.

You've all been to horror movies. I go to them sometimes. I get a kick out of them—things that make you afraid. Do you know what the horror movie is like for someone who is not enlightened? The ultimate horror movie is not *Dawn Of The Dead*. It's not *Frankenstein*.

You know what the ultimate horror movie is for a really un-illumined being? It's an enlightened person. The ultimate horror movie for an entity, an evil force that enjoys destroying others? The ultimate horror for a Hitler or a Mussolini is the enlightened person, because they are scared of knowledge. They are scared of others seeing what they are all about and what they really do. They are scared of truth—the truth of themselves, the truth of the universe.

Enlightenment in all of its varying degrees, whether it's a fully enlightened Christ or Buddha or just people who have had some enlightened experiences and are more aware—a Martin Luther King, a John F. Kennedy, a Gandhi—they're not fully enlightened, but they're knowledgeable, more so than most. What did they do with them here? They shoot them, crucify them, get them out of the way because people are afraid of truth. Well, you may not be that public, but in your quest for enlightenment you must prepare for opposition.

There are powers and forces that will seek to block you, to make your life more difficult. But if you are a professional, if you are up for the study and you take that into account, then you can continue to progress along the path to self-knowledge without getting discouraged. Or if you get discouraged, you brush yourself off, pick yourself up and go forward again and be encouraged. But there is a lot of opposition. I experience it as a teacher. I experience it as a student. You will experience it. But the joys that come from the study, from self-knowledge, just from gaining it, let alone sharing it with others, more than compensate for the opposition, in my opinion. It's a personal choice.

Enlightened teachers have a lot of trouble, and people who help them sometimes have a lot of trouble. People try to interfere with the work and say things about you that aren't true—spread awful rumors about you, misunderstand what you do, expecting that it should fit into their conceptual framework. Very often, people who help teachers have had problems.

We know that many of the apostles of Christ were killed: Eleven out of 12 met violent deaths when they were just talking about God and light. Many people who help me, for example, and other teachers, just by doing simple things—mailing some brochures, whatever it may be—encounter a lot of resistance from other people, from forces and powers that try and make it difficult. But this is part of the game of life, friends.

As you follow the path to self-knowledge, if you learn to lead your life strategically and strongly, you can overcome that opposition. But running away, you never overcome anything. That's why the path of enlightenment is for the warrior, the samurai. You may not think of yourself as a warrior. You may not have big muscles and you may not have a black belt in karate, but you might have a warrior spirit in there somewhere, and it's just waiting for an opportunity to come out. If you do, you might be a candidate for the pathway to enlightenment.

There is no best teacher. Life itself is the teacher. There is no best method. *Zen* is one method, *jnana yoga* is another, *mysticism* another, *bhakti yoga* another. You may have found your own method or path. All that matters is that it works. Then there is deception. People who think they're enlightened and it's just ego.

It is a great study. It has all permutations of every aspect of life and being because it is the study of every aspect of life and being.

But expect resistance and expect joys beyond your imagination. Expect to experience pain. Expect forces to interfere with you and expect to conquer them all, if you're serious about the study. Step by step. Gradually.

Just as there are powers that interfere with those who seek enlightenment or seek to enlighten others, there are forces that aid us, forces in the universe. There are forces that will help you meditate. These are the forces of truth.

How do you become enlightened? Have fun, meditate, don't take yourself too seriously, brush between incarnations and have a good teacher (Rama laughs). Have a sense of humor. It helps a lot. How do you become enlightened? I don't know. Luck, karma, skill, friends in high places, friends in low places. There are certain things that you do need, though. You need a path. If you are trying to make it to the top of the mountain and there is no path, it's pretty difficult.

ENLIGHTENMENT

Once in a while, an individual makes their own path, and you may be one of those, but they are pretty few and far between, let me tell you. Usually you follow a path. A path is there because it's one of the best ways to get up to the top. Somebody figured that out. They saw the easiest way or perhaps the way with the most wonderful views. There are different paths; they afford different views. Some have greater difficulty, some less. Some people like difficulty; some want an easy way. That's why one path is not better than another.

The important thing is to get the path that suits you, to follow that path, and once you've selected it, to stay with it and to not keep changing paths, always thinking that the next one is going to be better. It's not.

Sometimes people like to avoid difficulty by running away, as I mentioned before. Running away solves nothing at all. Sometimes we make a change in life; it's an intelligent selection. Our intuition says it's time to change from one path to another. The one we were on was too slow for us or too fast for us or just didn't have the views we wanted. But to keep changing constantly accomplishes nothing—always thinking the next city you live in is going to be better. There will be more trees, less trees, different people, different buildings, but life is the same wherever you go.

It's good just to pick something that you like and then stick with it for a while and work on it and perfect it. But always thinking that the next relationship is going to be better, the next person—some are just not suitable. There comes a time in life when you just buckle down and have a good time with what you are doing because you realize that it doesn't much matter what you are doing. What matters is how you do it.

Personal power, knowledge and fun come from how you approach something, not what you approach. When you give your best to something, and then you find out how to do better than your best, you feel good. But to run away accomplishes nothing. To take on a challenge and approach it strategically, intelligently and spontaneously—now, that's a good time.

There are different pathways. Some pathways are quicker; some are more time-consuming. Some people aren't in a rush; some are. What's a rush to one person is not a rush to another. Some people run at 15 miles an hour and they find it's comfortable; some find five miles an hour comfortable.

Zen is a very quick path. It's the path of meditation. Some paths stress more working for others—that's *karma yoga*. Some have to do with intellectual knowledge— *jnana yoga*. There are different paths. Some just have to do with just loving completely all the time—that's *bhakti yoga*.

Zen is a path of meditation. The word Zen means emptiness or fullness, meditation. Meditation is the quickest path to enlightenment because when you meditate, you are not dealing with just actions, thoughts, ideas or intentions, which sometimes are good or sometimes not. Sometimes they are ego bound, sometimes they are not.

When you learn to stop your thoughts and become introspective, the universe reveals itself to you, and there is no illusion there.

There are different types of Zen, and there are different teachers of Zen. Some teachers teach more than one subject. In my lifetime, I've taught Zen and other pathways. I've taught some jnana yoga, bhakti yoga, karma yoga and mysticism, which is another path. Those are the principal paths. There are some others.

There are combinations of those, different brand names, generic ones, but those are the primary paths. And all of them involve a certain degree of meditation. Zen is the path that focuses the most upon meditation. It is almost exclusively a path of meditation.

Meditation—zazen, when you're sitting formally—and meditation which is mindfulness when you are active and engaged in activities, talking to people, working on your career, playing tennis, whatever it is, but the mind is set into the meditative state all the time.

ENLIGHTENMENT

Meditation is to be aware of many different levels. It's not just the absence of thought. That is a type of meditation. But it is to be moving through the ten thousand states of mind and eventually beyond them. Anyway, what can I say?

There are different teachers. Most teachers are not enlightened. Very few are. That doesn't mean they are not great teachers. Not everyone is a Jimmy Connors, but they sure can teach you a great game of tennis. Jimmy would only be able to help the game maybe of a few people or maybe beginners, hard to say.

Is it important to have an enlightened teacher? No. Yes. If you are an absolute beginner, it really doesn't matter that much, to tell you the truth. Because what you need to learn are basic types of concentration—things having to do with just bringing more energy into your life, plugging up the holes where you lose energy—just the basics of self-discovery.

If you become serious about enlightenment—yes, it is absolutely necessary because an enlightened teacher doesn't just teach you just through words. When you sit with the teacher physically and meditate with them, the teacher moves in and out of these different states of mind, and that's how you learn to do it yourself.

As you are meditating with them, there is an inner dialogue that goes on, not with words at all. It's an inner dialogue that takes place on a very deep level. That is to say, the teacher will go into a very advanced state of mind, and you'll feel it. That's how they teach you to shoot that tennis shot. As you feel it, you'll find if you meditate deeply, riding the teacher's energy, that you will be able to go into it too. Then when you go home and you meditate on your own, you'll practice it, and gradually you'll be able to get back there on your own. Then the next time you meditate with the teacher, you'll learn another state of mind and so on.

The teacher also makes general recommendations as to ways to improve your efficiency in life, to improve the quality of your mind and your life, to become more knowledgeable, have more fun, to be deeper—all those things.

Every teacher does it differently, but an enlightened teacher, for someone who is very interested about enlightenment, is essential. If you just want to learn how to meditate, lead a better life and get more fun out of what you do, it is not absolutely essential to have an enlightened teacher at all.

The later stages of the enlightenment process are very tricky. They really are. They are not any more difficult than any other part, but in the same sense, there are certain parts of the writing of the Ph.D. dissertation that require specific direction. The later stages of the enlightenment process are trickier, and it is really essential to have a teacher then.

But to be honest, in the beginning, it really doesn't matter. What matters is that there is someone who inspires you to meditate, and you meditate with them once in a while or take a class from them. It is like taking a dance class or a karate class. You'll learn a little bit more, and it keeps you going. On your own, you might not practice every day and meditate, but by plugging into that environment, you sharpen your mind. Remember, all of this has to do with your mind, developing your mind.

The more developed your mind is, the more successful you'll be in everything.

People on the pathway to enlightenment become very successful in whatever they approach because they have learned to discipline the mind. Whether it's your career, your creative pursuits, athletics, whatever it is you pursue, you can bring a tremendous volume of energy, precision and joy into anything because you've learned more about the usage of the mind on which all things depend. As you progress towards enlightenment you'll find you become a winner at anything that you try because you are not so concerned about winning anymore. You are just concerned with excellence, the pursuit of excellence, because excellence gives you power and energy.

I personally only work with people who have excellence, who show excellence, in my business that is. I have a business, the business of enlightenment. I am a teacher. I do seminars—at the moment, Zen seminars. As I mentioned before, some teachers can just teach one way, or they just teach one way. You could go to a martial arts teacher, and the martial arts teacher might be able to teach judo. He might have a fifth-degree black belt in judo. Another has a fifth-degree black belt in karate, another has one in aikido. Then you might need a teacher who has black belts in all three. That teacher can teach many ways. One isn't better than another. The only question is—can the teacher teach you what you want to learn? Do you relate to the teacher? Do you feel simpatico to a certain extent?

Some teachers are very kind. Some are very harsh. Some people like a harsh teacher. They feel that those demands make them learn more quickly. Some like a gentle teacher because they feel that that makes them learn more quickly. There is no right or wrong in any of this.

There are phony teachers who profess all kinds of things, and I think you'll figure out real fast who they are. They just don't feel right.

Sometimes when you're with an enlightened teacher, things feel very intense and it's not going to be what you're used to at all, and you'll feel both pleasant and unpleasant things magnified. That happens when you meditate with someone who goes into very strong states of altered consciousness. Everything is intensified, and you become more aware of all your own imperfections as you simultaneously become more aware of the overall perfection of the universe.

There is a certain degree of pain to be experienced and gone through in the search for self-knowledge. Definitely. Believe it—as there is a certain amount of joy.

But you just do it because you find yourself doing it. There just doesn't seem to be much else that's worthwhile, and it then makes everything else worthwhile because then your career is totally important because you need to bring perfection into it because it reflects on your study of enlightenment and your relationships, and everything counts. So as I said, I only work with professionals. I don't mean at seminars but in my business.

I am a teacher. If you ever come to one of my seminars, you'll notice I have volunteer workers who help you fill out forms and people who run sound systems and all kinds of things—art people, people who work in the office and all kinds of stuff. Naturally, when I work with individuals like that, I expect a level of excellence displayed in both their personal life and in their work, of course. Perfection. That's the standard. What you would call excellence from the enlightened person's point of view is not excellence—that's just ordinary achievement. Everything has to be done perfectly.

Now perfection is a relative idea—true—but yet there's perfection. Why, why, why? Why do everything perfectly? Isn't that just an idea? Isn't perfection just an illusion? Yes and no. Tell me if it's an illusion if they don't fix your car perfectly next time you bring it in, and you get it home and it doesn't work. It stalls on the freeway. And tell me it's not important that things be done right when you're stalled out on the freeway and you have to get the AAA to come tow you and go through the whole hassle again and miss more work.

So in Zen, we do everything perfectly. We feel that our outer actions are a reflection of our inner state, and our inner state is a reflection of our outer action.

We call it mindfulness. Whenever I work with anyone, I only work with individuals who display a level of professionalism, and that's an opportunity, of course, for them to become more professional and to do something for someone else. That's the attitude that one has, not just towards working at a Zen seminar or helping a teacher, but towards everyone and everything in your life.

That's the hallmark of a person who is following the pathway to enlightenment, that they bring excellence into everything, no matter how crappy they feel—whether they are sick, well, upset, down-set —they bring excellence into everything they do. No matter how much opposition there is, no matter how much pain they feel, no matter how excited they get, no matter how much joy there is—it doesn't matter. You are unmoved. You experience all of that, and yet you are beyond it because you are moving in and out of different, advanced states of mind through your practice of daily meditation and mindfulness. And it's that level of excellence that gives you joy in life—not the fact that you won or lost, but that you did a great job. Winning and losing is just someone else's definition. But you know if you did a great job because the car works. It goes down the freeway really well.

Enlightenment is not for people who get thrown by things.

Or it's not for someone who wants to dedicate their life to a teacher. Once in a while, at one of my seminars—or you'll see it with other teachers sometimes even more because they allow it—you'll see someone really drippy. You'll see the person who has to sit in the front row and has to stare at the teacher all the time with that devoted and disgusting and sick look. It's boring, misplaced devotionalism. One should never become devoted to a teacher, any more than one should become devoted to a statue of a god. There is only one thing to be devoted to, and that's your mind.

Unfortunately, in the field of Zen, once in awhile—or in any aspect of self-discovery—you get the culty types who want the father figure or mother figure to tell them everything to do. Somehow just being with that person is going to make it all right. They want a savior; I don't know what they want. I know what they want. They don't want to do any work, is what they want. They want to hang on your energy and try to drain it. I can't help such a person. I don't know anybody who can. That's what they're going through right now. That's the state of mind they're in.

They don't get it.

They don't get that it is only hard work that brings about results, and doing things for others. Forget about your own problems and stop feeling sorry for yourself and assume importance for your activities. Take responsibility for your life and make it into something fine and beautiful in the midst of changing circumstances. That's the challenge. Of course, it's not going to be easy. It's the Earth. But that's what creates power in a person's life is when you perfect your mind, your career, your associations with others. You're not fanatical.

Zen is not a religion. There is no room for a cult. There is no dependence on a teacher. There is only learning how to use your own mind and developing it and making it strong, from someone who knows more about that than you do—the same way that I learned from my professors as an undergraduate and graduate student, and eventually I taught students at the university.

So in Zen, we have no gurus, using the word "guru" as it is used in the contemporary American scene, which is someone who, I don't know, would take all your money and tell you what to do with your life all the time, so you assume no responsibility yourself. A lot of people want that free ride, but it doesn't bring about enlightenment. Just sitting around with someone enlightened doesn't make you enlightened. If you sit with them and you meditate as hard as you can and you go out and direct your attention into your life, something will happen. But this misplaced devotionalism is actually antithetical to the very study itself.

If you are a serious student of self-discovery, then you get your emotions under control and your life under control. You work really hard, and you don't make a big deal out of yourself. You have humility, or you develop it. You believe in yourself, and you don't get a fanatical fixation on a teacher. If it's a good teacher, like a good karate teacher, you go study with him. If you get a kick out of them, you like their jokes and you feel empowered when you are with them, then you go practice the things they teach you about meditation and some advanced thoughts about mind and life. Then that's great.

But never make a teacher into a god. What a mistake!

Oh, you might meet someone who is enlightened, who can do fantastic things—fantastic compared to your average Earth being. Well, you don't have to be too fantastic to do fantastic things compared to your average Earth being (Rama laughs). That's for sure.

They [the enlightened teachers] display miracles. There is no such thing as a miracle. A miracle is just what somebody else doesn't understand. If we went back into the Stone Age and we lit a match, we'd say, "Ahh, miracla, miracla." You know, that would be a miracle because they don't understand how phosphorous and other chemicals combined with friction create fire. So enlightened teachers can do certain miracles, but they are not really miracles. They just know how to use energy on other levels of consciousness. If you understood it, you wouldn't call it a miracle. A miracle is in the eye of the beholder my friend, as is all of life.

So yes, it's important to have a good teacher.

If you don't have one, that's fine too. You are not supposed to. If none feel right to you, then just meditate on your own, read books on the subject that inspire you, to keep you meditating, and have fun with it. Don't become a spiritual bigot. Don't feel that just because you meditate and you're striving for enlightenment that you are in any way superior to any other person, being or thing. Be even. Be easy. You'll last longer on the pathway to self-discovery.

What's important in self-discovery is not a person who does really well for a short time and is just intense, but the person who keeps going, who has a smile, who's kind to others, who works hard at everything, who doesn't take their failings to heart and doesn't let it blow them away—that's just reverse ego—who doesn't criticize others, who keeps their mind on their own business and not everybody else's, and who has a good time with their life. When they suffer, they suffer. They know they'll get through it. They've gotten through it before. But they have a smile, and they're open to new experiences. They're ready for life. They know that tomorrow can be better than any other day that's ever been, or today can because they meditate. They don't just chant a mantra for 20 minutes, but they really meditate. They're learning the arts, and gradually they're moving from level to level and different world and vistas are opening up to them. They are enthusiastic and optimistic but they know that there is difficulty on the pathway to enlightenment. And they're not too concerned about becoming enlightened. They just enjoy the process.

It's like going to school. You get a kick out of it. If you don't get a kick out of it, maybe you shouldn't be in school. Maybe it's better to go do something you like for awhile.

They recognize and value a good teacher, but they don't make a big deal out of the teacher. They make a big deal out of their own life. They realize that sometimes the experiences in self-discovery will be painful. You're learning about your limitations, and they will also be enlightening. You're learning about unlimited sectors of your being. A balanced person will get depressed and discouraged and frustrated and angry sometimes but doesn't direct it towards anybody else, or if they do, they quickly realize they made a mistake. [They] apologize, forget about it and move into the next moment, living in the moment, forgetting the past.

The pathway to enlightenment leads to states of ecstasy I could not begin to describe to you, and knowledge and also a pretty ironic sense of humor sometimes when you've been around for a while.

I personally have fun with enlightenment, the study and the teaching of it. I get a kick out of doing it different ways because I don't think there is any "way." But that's because I don't have to think there is any "way." For you, there is a way. For me there's no way. We are on different sides, at the moment. So I like to play with it. I like to be weird, kinky, straight, in and out, up and down. I like to blow up people's expectations. Create them. Destroy them. Dissolve them. It's fun. This is Zen. It's the quick path. We turn everything inside out and upside down, which is when it gets straightened out very neatly and in an orderly fashion. Professionalism. Higher states of mind.

Fun with life, a life that most people will never even know about out there, can be yours in this study, but only if you approach it with equanimity, poise, grace, balance and professionalism.

This study is not for the amateur. It's not for the dilettante. It's not for the cult follower. It's not for somebody who wants everything done for them. It's not for the one who just wants to stare with that fixed dog-like devotion towards the teacher, or the person who wants to throw bad energy at anybody else, thinking that they were doing a better job than they are. Forget it. Amateurs in self-discovery. No room for them. That's like the guy in the karate class who just wants to beat other people up. They don't last long in the class, as opposed to someone who wants to study the art and realizes that there is a much deeper art to martial arts than simply learning to beat somebody up. It's the study of self-control and discipline and grace. Combat is only one aspect of martial arts.

With Zen, it's the study of the ten thousand states of mind, not just the study of enlightenment. Everything in life is a type of enlightenment. It's the study of grace, control and discipline—bringing that into every aspect and nuance of your life with a goodly sense of humor. Enlightenment happens to some people, but that's not the point. The point is greeting the challenge of each moment with a bright mind, with a warrior spirit, with grace, determination and fun. I've gone a bit over 45 minutes—but that was good!

What more can I tell you? I tell you at seminars how to become enlightened, how to sharpen and develop your mind, how to succeed in anything that you approach.

No one can guarantee your success. I can't. But there are states of mind that you can learn about—unsurpassed beauty as you can see.

You're going to die. And you're going to be reborn and die and be reborn, go through greatness, have people love you and people hate you. You'll love and hate yourself. But there's beauty in everything, my friend—if you have the state of mind to see it.

So Zen, enlightenment, the state of mind to see it—we are so complex, we beings. We house all of eternity. We're everything and nothing. We're nothing. We're a forgotten moment. We don't even exist, which is the real freeing part. We don't even exist. We just think we do. That's the illusion. Enlightened people know this. Enlightened not-people know this (Rama laughs). They know not to know that to know is to—oh, you understand. And if you don't …

So learn to meditate. It's fun. It will give you a strong, wonderful mind. And be even. You don't always have to be the winner, the first, the greatest, have everybody notice you. It's fun to dance by yourself alone sometimes. It's just a kick. That's what enlightenment is—it's dancing alone by yourself.

Once in a while, you'll see someone like me, a Zen master in front of a whole bunch of people, who dances in front of others so they can learn or just be inspired by watching someone else do it in a new way to do it more themselves. But life is just a dance, you know—it's just a dance. Each lifetime, we dance with someone else. But the real dance is within. It's inside your mind. Everything is inside your mind. God is inside your mind—everything.

Have fun with it. Don't be a bigot. Don't be a devotee. Be yourself—unlimited mind. Be a professional. That's right, go to school. Get a job. Get it together. Bring power into your life. Energy. Fwam! As my friends, the Blisses say, "Do something!" Be like the Gwid. Be a great capitalist. Be a great socialist. Be a great whatever you want to be, but do it with style, clarity and precision. That's the hallmark of those who seek higher knowledge and truth. Expect difficulties because they are there. Expect pain. Expect hassle because it's there. But that's no reason not to have a good time. I mean, really, it's only life. What did you expect?

So this is Zen Master Rama—what did you expect?—wishing you well on your journey, and as you go off into that sunset or sunrise, always remember, buy name brand products, take vacations in Hawaii and watch out for dark streets in big cities because there are a lot of strange beings that hang out there late at night, let alone the people. I mean, really, don't you remember anything from any of your other lives?

Life is beautiful all the time; even death is beautiful. When you close your eyes, when you meditate well, you'll understand. You'll just see the light of God, of eternity, of whatever you want to call it. It's perfect and beautiful. That is you.

You are light. You are not a body. You are not a mind. You are infinite light, infinite intelligence, the radiance of all beings, the *dharmakaya,* the endless light of creation.

(Rama playfully imitates the actor Cheech Marin) "That's you. It's not so bad, man, eh? You know, you can kind of get on down with it, eh. Have fun with it. It's all right, it's pretty heavy, but you know, what else could it be? The discotheque of the mind, man, it's OK. Later …" (Back to normal voice.)

So this is Zen Master Rama once again, out the door and into another state of mind, slipping and sliding between realities, stepping through those inner-dimensional vortex points, somehow coming out as somebody else on the other side. Nirvana, Samsara. Juggling one in each hand, winking at a cute girl. It's all in the mind of the Buddha. Miller time, right? Take care. Keep dancing. It's the best, inside your mind, or outside of it. Is there anything outside your mind? That's the Zen koan for the yuga.

CHAPTER SIX

REINCARNATION

(Zazen music plays in the background, and Rama speaks to the beat of the music.)

Reincarnation. Past lives. Future lives. Immortality. Your purpose in this lifetime. Twin souls, soul mates and karmic connections. Past life remembrances in waking states, dreams, during meditation.

Times between lives. Lifetimes. The cosmic journey through time and space. The endless cycle of rebirth, renewal.

Isis, the Egyptian goddess of renewal, symbolized for the Hindus by Brahma, Vishnu and Shiva. Brahma is the creator, Vishnu the sustainer, and Shiva the transformer or destroyer. The cycle of creation.

The circle, the symbol of perfection for the Buddhists. And beyond the circle, within the circle, the ten thousand states of mind that one passes through during the rounds of rebirth.

This is Zen Master Rama. Today we are going to be talking about, guess what?

(Zazen music ends.)

In 1979, I wrote a book about reincarnation. It was written for the popular market, that is to say, not necessarily people who are actively engaged in the study of Zen, but for folks who are out there who'd like to know more about the universe and themselves and the process of lives that they're engaged in. It's called *Lifetimes: True Accounts of Reincarnation*. It was a fun book to do because, while presenting certain cosmological theories in fairly simplified form from the Hindu and Buddhist point of view about reincarnation, I also included a large number of accounts or excerpts from accounts from persons who had had remembrances of their past lives. The book was fairly successful. As a matter of fact, it was just recently reprinted in paperback again. So you might say I've had an interest in reincarnation for a while.

The information I'd like to discuss with you today is a little bit different. It's not so much the startling, exoteric stories of past life remembrance—there will probably be more of those—but the esoteric awareness of being eternal. There are two sides to self-discovery as in most things—an outer, more popular side and an inner side. The popular side presents more of a simplified form. Most teachers of self-discovery, for example, have two types of students. They have students who they deal with in a more exoteric way than the esoteric students. The exoteric students are presented general truths for their daily lives and their absorption, and the esoteric truths are presented to usually a smaller group of students.

So for example, a teacher might have hundreds of students, and he or she would instruct them in methods of prayer, meditation, ways to improve their lives. Then there might be 20 or 30 students or maybe 12, a smaller number, five, whatever, whom the teacher would instruct in the deeper mysteries. Now, it's not that the teacher wishes to exclude anyone. But rather, the teaching, the inner teachings, are presented to people in a form that will best aid or benefit them. That's the purpose of the teaching. So naturally, you don't teach quantum mechanics to someone who is in algebra one. Nor do you teach someone algebra one who's working through quantum mechanics. In the same sense, the deeper inner teachings, the esoteric teachings, are presented to very few because very few would understand them, be able to make use of them, while the exoteric teachings are presented to many.

Today I would like to tell you about the more esoteric aspects of reincarnation. The popular aspects of reincarnation you can read about—you're probably already aware of. But the hidden side of reincarnation is the concern.

Let's talk a little bit about your body. Not so much your physical body but your other bodies. There are different ways to refer to all of this and there are different systems, and you may have been exposed to certain terms and phrases that are used to explain cosmology—nonphysical bodies and all this sort of thing.

The thing that is important to understand in this study of consciousness is that you really can't explain anything verbally. You can only allude to, point in a general direction of. But all the systems that try to present different worlds, planes of being, dimensions, different bodies, chakras, energy centers—all of these systems ultimately fail if you try to make them work or make them all-inclusive—because they're all symbolic representations of something that lies beyond the world of thought and description or analysis. They're meant to point [toward] a direction and they shouldn't be taken literally.

Naturally in the esoteric teachings, it's understood that the only real knowledge comes from personal experience of truth and awareness, not from conversation. If you're with someone who is explaining something to you, a teacher, and that teacher is in a very high level of attention, they're not just in the mind, you might say, but in other levels of mind.

A transference process takes place between teacher and student where knowledge is actually transmitted from one to the other. Naturally, this requires that the student be receptive, that they've gained some mastery of mind. They can stop their thoughts, they've developed their psychic sensibilities so that transference process can take place, and naturally, the teacher has to be able to do that. They have to have the requisite knowledge and experience to be able to do that kind of transmission.

When words are used, it's always good to remember that they're pointing a direction toward something. But it's good not to take them too literally. The words, and particularly the energy behind the words, are to direct your mind or your awareness within yourself, within your mind, to inspire you to explore the parts of your being that a teacher has explored and found and discovered.

Each aspect of the teaching must be individually validated for it to be meaningful, real, and for it to lend a power to your life.

So when I talk about subtle bodies, causal bodies, structures, codings, things like that, it's a good idea not to take it all completely literally. Certainly it's literal. I'm describing something as exactly as I can. But it can't really be put into words. And the purpose of all this is not so you can walk around with new vocabulary words but to cause you to speculate upon the marvel of your own being, and for you in meditation—in zazen—to go within yourself and feel all of this and try to understand what relevance it has for you.

I'm discussing horizons and I'm saying there are many horizons, some of which you have not perhaps conceived of, and by pointing in the direction of those horizons you can walk that way and you will discover them—if you walk that way. If you don't know that they exist, if you don't know where the direction is, then you may just stay where you are and continue to see the horizons you currently see.

The purpose of this dialogue and all of the dialogues, which I certainly feel are interactive even though I'm just talking, [is that] there's definitely an interactive dialogue on an inner level occurring.

The universe is holding congress with itself.

But the purpose of this is to encourage you to explore horizons that you have not yet become consciously aware of, at least in this lifetime. In other words, look at the underlying or feel the underlying meaning and expression in all of the teachings that are espoused by me or anyone else. Not the words. The words don't mean much. They have a power, certainly. They're not meaningless. But they are [meant] to cause you to explore and look and search within yourself. They're supposed to be catalysts for higher stages of attention within yourself, which will only occur when you put the practice of meditation to use in your daily life. That's where the action is.

OK, good, enough of that. Forward.

The bodies. Reincarnation presupposes a few things. One, that there is an eternal ultimate reality, which is always present. You could call it God; you could call it anything you like—nirvana—whatever. There are two primary aspects to that reality.

One aspect is the unmanifest reality, which is usually called *nirvana*. Now again, definitions are going to vary, and one person is going to say, "Well, nirvana doesn't mean that, it means this," and another is going to say, "It means that," and words, words, words. It doesn't mean anything. It's only a word. We're pointing a direction. You'll know it when you arrive.

So, cosmology. Nirvana. The undifferentiated reality. That which is really big. That which is enlightenment. That which cannot be described; it bears no resemblance to anything in your current perceptual field.

Then there is *samsara*, which is the world appearance, the cycle of rebirth. In other words, there are the physically manifest universes and states of mind that you perceive through the medium of ego. There's a sense of "I"-ness. You exist as you listen to me, and that being or sense of perception that is perceiving me, is you. As long as you exist, you are aware of the manifest universes to a greater or lesser degree through the senses, through feeling and through mind. You see the world around you, you feel it, you touch it, you taste it. You think about it, you interact with it.

There's a sense of separativity—you are separate from the universe, therefore you experience it.

Nirvana, or the realization of enlightenment, is a step beyond that. Not simply you experiencing the universes in a nicer, happier, more direct and pure way, but rather the dissolution of the ego and the self. You dissolve into the universe; the universe dissolves into you until there is no longer a difference. There is no sense of individual self as perceiver. In other words, you're not sitting around watching TV. You're gone. You've dissolved. You've become everything. There's no sense of TV, there's no sense of you, there's no sense of anything in particular. There's no sense of time, space or dimensional planes. It's something else that we call enlightenment, nirvana or whatever. No way to put it into words, of course. But a condition beyond mind, as we define mind normally.

Then outside of that or within that, we have the samsara that is the sense of self. I exist; I've had past experiences; I'm currently aware of whatever I'm aware at the moment; I will have future experiences. Continuity in change—that's the idea of self. Everything around us is shifting and changing all the time. Energy is moving in all things. But there is an awareness of that, and what gives energy a continuity, what creates a pattern, is you.

Molecules don't have patterns or atoms. You create a pattern by the perception of something. In other words, we know that an atom has protons, neutrons, electrons, all that stuff.

But the reason it has those things is because of you. If you did not perceive those things, if you did not exist, obviously there would be no patterns. The continuity of awareness is your perceptual field. If there were no one here, no one to perceive any of this, it would not exist.

Existence occurs only through the act of perception. When we become aware of something, it exists. Our awareness creates life. Life does not exist independently of perception. OK, great.

So, reincarnation.

The idea is that everything has always been in one form or another. All of existence exists. Always has, always will—but it takes different forms. There is an overriding unity to existence that cannot be known or understood if you're in the world of perception.

In other words, the highest truths of life cannot be understood as long as you are alive either in this world, or in any other world, or in a passage between, because the truths are so big that the mind can't get them.

In order to understand the truths of the universe—truths meaning not how the universe works per se but just to have a complete knowledge of all, to be that—it's necessary to step outside our human mind form or any mind form whatsoever because any mind form whatsoever is a form.

And form cannot perceive the absolute formless existence. We have to become it.

You have to become that infinite formless creation, which is life, to know it. It can't be known in an intellectual sense.

That's enlightenment, that step outside. In order to do that, we have to, in a sense, reject or leave behind everything we've been, which is perception, a perceiver—I as an individual who was born, who lived, who died, who's reborn. That's enlightenment, to do that. To not be anymore, as we would define being. That doesn't mean it isn't being; the universe obviously is being.

So that's the dividing line. The sense of perception that you exist and going beyond that. Death is not necessarily that.

Death is simply a change in perception. It's not an end to perception as a finite being.

Reincarnation is a process in which a finite being, which is defined by a sense of perception—"I exist, I perceive, I am"—that perceptual field will go through a series of transmutations and it will perceive different things.

But there will be a continuity of perception. That continuity of perception is an individualized being. When that continuity is lost completely, the being no longer exists as they have been. What gives that sense, again, is perception itself—perception of the individual, the body of perception perceiving itself in variant forms.

Everything is God, let's say. Everything is just infinite awareness.

And then, from infinite awareness, something comes forward, and that's a sense of *infinite* awareness and *finite* awareness.

That perception is the birth of a being—as soon as there's somebody around to say, "Wow, look at all this. Far out! Look how big the universe is. Look how small and finite it is. I can see a tree. I can see all universes, all planes of being, all realities and beyond them." While there's a perception of either the very big or the very small, the one who's perceiving is alive. Obviously. You've got to be alive to see and feel.

Now, when you die, while you might not remember this at the moment, the same process continues at death.

You pass into inner worlds and you continue to perceive. That's why I say, death is not the dissolution of the self, or whatever we'd like to call that part of you that is, that perceives.

Death is rather just a change in perception where you'll perceive something else.

Then you will be reborn, meaning that you will come from the inner into the outer again, and you will perceive something else.

This process goes on indefinitely, with the exception of those who dissolve their bodies of perception completely and are absorbed into what we would call nirvana. Again, nirvana isn't a physical place. It's not like going to heaven. It just means no more individualized awareness. No sense of perceiving, therefore no self, therefore no aggregate body of experience, etcetera, etcetera.

It's really hard to talk about reincarnation because you've always been and you'll always be. You just experience different things in different ways.

Some people, however, or beings, get tired of that round of continual perception because they feel it's limited. They feel that the perception of the finite universe over and over in variant forms is kind of an unhappy condition because you never get the whole thing, and it doesn't last.

Whatever you're perceiving in this life at death will end, and then you will perceive something else and so on and so forth. And perception becomes attached. You'll start to like things, you reject other things, and this condition eventually causes pain.

Attachment always causes pain, aversion and suffering to the perceiver. You like this life and you don't want to die, and that's unfortunate. You like pleasure, you don't like pain. When you experience pleasure you're happy; when you experience pain you're unhappy. And so on.

All of this comes about because of individualized perception. Those who seek what we would call liberation or enlightenment want to go beyond individualized perception. The essence of their being wants to dissolve back into the cosmos, into the cosmic hole. They no longer want to go through all of this. Others continue to go through all of this, other bands of perception.

Let's think of a huge ocean. This ocean has always been there, it will always be there, it goes on forever. There are waves of the ocean. These waves move continuously. Some slap against the shore, then they fall back into the ocean and they move someplace else. Others are just continually moving through the ocean, endlessly, forever. As they move through the ocean, they change. The wave is not exactly the same. It picks up some new water, drops some old water, changes shape. But the wave continues on.

The only reason we think of the wave as continuing on is because we think. The wave continues on, but if you weren't around to look at it, and say, "Gee, that's the same wave that existed before," it wouldn't be. If the wave didn't perceive of itself and say, "Gee, I'm the same wave, I may have changed a little bit, I'm a little bigger or a little smaller, but I'm the same guy who was around before. I'm still moving."

There is a sense of time. When there is a sense of time, there is a sense of change. When there is a sense of change, there's life and death and rebirth.

So it is the perception of time and space that creates the illusion of incarnation. That's a level of perception. On the other hand, when that illusion is shattered, that is to say, when you're not looking at the wave, when the wave is no longer conscious of its current, past or future state, then there's no such thing. Everything exists in the mind, in other words. These are all just ideas.

So then, from a structural point of view, the way reincarnation works is as follows.

The universe, which is infinite in nature and mysterious and just plain awesome, created you. OK. Now it didn't really create you. You are the universe; you are an aspect of it. You have several different bodies. You have a physical body at the moment with ears, which is how you're hearing all this. You have a mind that thinks and perceives, senses that apprehend the world, feelings and so on.

But in addition to your physical body, you have two other primary bodies—a *subtle physical body* and a *causal body*. These are non-physical bodies that are composed of energy, that are not visible to the senses. But anyone who has developed their psychic facility can see these bodies as clearly as you can see a physical body with sense perception.

The subtle physical body is the body made up of energy and it has about the same shape and size as the physical body. The subtle physical body is made up of luminous fibers, and when people talk about the aura—seeing someone's aura—the aura is the outer surface of the subtle physical body. It's made up of energy. It's not solid as the physical body is. It changes its shape more than the physical body does. Now, we know the physical body, of course, is energy, atoms, protons, neutrons, energy moving around. But it seems to hold a pattern, more or less.

It changes from time to time. The cells renew themselves and change every seven years, and all that sort of stuff. Well, it's born and it dies.

The body of perception, which is the subtle physical body, does the same thing, and it's made up of energy, fibers; the *chakras* —the energy centers that we meditate upon—are in the subtle physical body.

The subtle physical body protects the body's physical health and it protects the mind. It's the radiant energy or life force that is you.

When you get sick, when something happens to you, it's because there's a problem with your subtle physical body. When something goes wrong with the body of energy that surrounds and protects your physical body, it will later show up in your physical body. But the problem always starts in the subtle physical, and then it manifests in the physical.

Beyond the subtle physical body, which is more our interest when it comes to reincarnation, there is something called the causal body.

The causal body, which is just a word to express something that is hard to define, is the part of your being that lives from one lifetime to another.

Again, it isn't really the causal body, it's the awareness of incarnation that exists from one lifetime to another. But let's just say for the moment, the causal body sort of sticks around. The causal body is like the DNA or RNA in that it is the coding that determines your level of evolution.

Right now, you are in a certain level or state of mind. You are also in a certain type of body. You are in a human body as opposed to a cat's body. You are on the planet Earth as opposed to Mars. You are in a certain dimension as opposed to other dimensions. Within this dimension, within this structure of the universe, on this planet, in this body, in this current lifetime, you are at a certain state of perception. All of this is determined in a very orderly way. There is a coding, just in the same way that the DNA and RNA have caused your physical body to grow in a uniform way. You developed feet, arms, head, and so on; you just didn't grow into an amorphous blob.

There is something that controls perception, or your inner evolution—which is the causal structure. The causal structure determines the rate and method of evolution, the level of intelligence, your awareness of the universe.

Reincarnation can be compared to a process of going to school. We go up to first grade, second grade, maybe stop at the end of high school, maybe go to college, maybe go to graduate school, but there's a sense of progression. So there is a type of progression that occurs through the cycle of incarnations. We evolve, in other words.

And there are different cycles of incarnation. There's not just one, there are different levels of mind. All inner structures are not the same. The cosmos is a very big place—with lots of different types of beings—and they follow different evolutionary patterns.

Now, the essence of your being is everything.

In other words, the part of you that exists from one lifetime to another is composed of all things. You are the energy of the universe. We call it the *dharmakaya* or the clear light of reality.

The ultimate intelligence of all things is your essence. Your mind is the universe; your body is all things.

But yet, the cool thing about the universe is that it can format itself into tiny little manifestations that are not entirely aware of all aspects, or sometimes hardly any aspects of life.

And those are individualized—what we call sentient—beings, things that take incarnation, as opposed to nirvana—that dissolute infinite intelligence in reality that does not have a sense of separativity.

The ocean without waves, just existing forever, unchanging so to speak—that's nirvana.

On the other hand, there are these little waves that are whipping around and changing and growing and going through different formations forever.

These are sentient beings. You. People you see and perceive. These are all waves—that go on forever. You go on forever, but just as the wave whips across the ocean and changes shape a little bit from time to time, so do you.

There are laws or forces that govern those changes, and those are manifested by the causal body, just in the same way that your body grows in an orderly fashion, matures in an orderly fashion and decays in an orderly fashion. So the causal body is the determining factor in the changes that occur within your structure or growth rate.

Now the important thing at this point is not to understand how the whole universe works and all the different cycles of evolution—that's interesting information, but it's not necessarily relevant to you. If you've got a Chevrolet and you want to get it working better, what you need to know is about Chevrolets. The knowledge of the Ferrari or the knowledge of the Harley-Davidson motorcycle might be interesting intellectually, but it won't really help you with your own car.

It's best then to confine this discussion to the evolution of the human form, unless you happen to be a cat or dog that's listening, or a bird—or a spirit or a force.

But for now, we're talking about people on the planet Earth because that's where it is. And we're considering what all this reincarnation stuff means to you.

Well, what it means is that you are experiencing right now—I mean right now—your past.

Everything that you have done has led up to what you are now. That's the theory of reincarnation. Everything you do now will lead up to what you will be. That's the theory of reincarnation.

The wave that's moving along the top of the ocean has a certain formation. The reason it has that formation is because of what it has been through up until this moment. What it will go through will cause it to change form. So you are a wave of awareness and you are in this world and you are aware of a certain amount of stuff (Rama laughs), of consciousness.

If you wish to become more aware, then it's necessary to do something that you haven't done. Because everything that you've done, if you just continue to do it, will only make you as aware as you are now. If you don't do as much as you have been doing, you will become less aware. Eventually, you will die.

When you die, you'll become aware of other things.

Your next incarnation, the level of awareness that you have in it, is dependent upon what you do in this incarnation.

Your awareness in this incarnation is dependent upon what you did in your last incarnation, and so on and so forth.

But things change. If you change your focus in this lifetime, it will affect your next lifetime. Naturally, it also affects this lifetime. If you eat too much today, tomorrow you'll weigh more on the scale. If you eat less today, you'll weigh less tomorrow. There are immediate changes that occur, but those changes are more subtle. If today you eat a lot, tomorrow you'll weigh a little more. But if you eat a lot every day for the next six months, you'll weigh a lot more six months from now. So six months from now, we could say, "Gosh, look at the tremendous change that occurred." But the day-to-day changes that are occurring don't show as much, so we tend to miss them sometimes.

At the time of death, whatever you have focused on the most will determine your next life.

By next life, we're not simply talking about location, which is more having to do with karma, which we're not really discussing today—not what planet, not what kind of family you'll be born into. Today we're discussing the exoteric, excuse me, the esoteric aspects of reincarnation. And that would mean, therefore, evolution of awareness. The exoteric aspects of reincarnation are the karmic effects. How come you have the job you have now? Because of what happened before. How you can change that? All that sort of thing. But today we're just looking at pure awareness and its evolution.

The evolution of your awareness is something that's taking place moment by moment. In other words, the esoteric understanding of reincarnation is, reincarnation is not something that occurs at death, it's something that takes place at every moment.

The exoteric explanation is death and physical rebirth.

The esoteric explanation is that death and rebirth are occurring at every second, but sometimes we notice those changes more than others.

Whatever you dwell on, you will become in your next life—but not really in your next life. You'll become it in this life. It isn't that suddenly, at death, magically you will die and then you will be reborn in a different form. You pick up exactly where you left off.

Let's say, for example, in the early part of your life you were not really aware. Then you started to meditate and you started to become more aware. You started to use more of your mind. In the early part of your life, you watched a lot of television and the level of intelligence that was projected into your mind and your general state of awareness was not real evolved. If that's all you did all your life, then your next life will be at the same level. But if, instead, you started to develop your mind through the practice of Zen, and you became aware of more of the states of mind, the ten thousand states of mind, levels of mind, then at the end of this life, you will be a lot more aware. You'll be in higher stages of attention. You won't be so limited.

Then, in your next life, that awareness will come back to you. You don't lose it. You may lose it temporarily, in the sense that for a while, when you're born into a new lifetime, that evolution doesn't come out. But it does come out.

Even as a child you will be drawn to certain things. If you develop more of a refined sensibility you'll be drawn towards more refined things, even as a child. Naturally you'll be influenced by environment, by mental conditioning, by the people around you. You could have had a very evolved awareness field in your last life, and then if in this lifetime you surround yourself with unevolved people, it could make it more difficult for that evolution to come out. But eventually it will.

The same thing can happen in this lifetime. You could have lived in a very refined state of mind, and suddenly you surround yourself with a lot of unrefined people. By that I mean people who aren't as aware; they're aware just of mainly the physical world. They're not in all those hundreds and thousands of states of mind. If you interact with those individuals, then you will lose some of your evolution, if you interact with them exclusively.

The tennis pro. The tennis pro is a hot tennis player—plays competitive tennis. Suddenly the tennis pro becomes a teacher, and all he does is teach fairly basic students. After a while, his tennis game will diminish because he is not doing anything to continue maintaining it on a high level. If he continues to compete and also teaches tennis, then he may advance. If you want to advance, you play with someone who plays a better game of tennis than you do, and that's how you learn. You have to stretch yourself. Whereas if you play with people who don't play as well as you do, it's unlikely that your game will improve.

What you focus on determines what you become.

If you spend an hour or two a day meditating and focusing on light, then you will eventually become light.

If you work on developing your mind, then you will gain a strong mind. If you work on developing your body, then you'll gain a strong body. It isn't that it will happen at some later date. Every time you do a push up or a sit up, your body gets a little stronger. You may not see the muscles bulging yet—that may happen over a period of time—but it does not happen all at once. A little at a time, the wave changes. If we look at it an hour from now, we'll see that it may have grown into a tsunami, a tidal wave, but the effects are happening all along. We just don't see them until they become more apparent to the eye.

The esoteric teaching of reincarnation then, is—that it's happening all the time.

At every moment we're going through a change. Our being isn't solid. It has a certain codified form that is held in structure by the causal body, which I'll talk about in a minute. But it changes all the time, not just at death. In other words, reincarnation is now. It's happening now, your awareness is changing now, and we'll see the larger effect perhaps at the time of death or in the next life. But not really.

Your next life won't be different than the end of this life. The end of this life will be a summation of whatever you've done in this life, and this life, of course, depends upon the prior life, and so on and so forth. Every moment gives birth to the next moment and influences it—that's the chain of perpetual being.

Getting out of that chain of perpetual being, where one moment leads to another, is getting off the wheel of birth and death. That's enlightenment—stepping outside of that pattern because that pattern is endless. The wave can never get away from itself. It changes. But it always has that continuity of change.

Every moment leads to another moment. How can you get out of that?

Naturally, you might ask, "Why would I want to get out of that? I exist; I'll always exist. Isn't that pretty neat?"

Well, yes it is.

You will always exist and you now exist, and you're a changing wave. You'll never be as you've ever been before, probably. It's possible. But at every moment, you're changing. Yet within an individual incarnation it doesn't seem that you change that much. For example, at about five or six, the personality forms, and you will develop certain character traits and those traits will probably stay in place. Some of those traits are carryovers from previous states of awareness, from your last life and preceding times. Some of them might have been developed in this lifetime.

The reason they stay in place is because you have a certain idea of yourself that develops as the ego becomes aware of its surroundings in the world. And through the experience of memory, you recall what you've done, and you therefore attach yourself to it and perceive yourself through prior experience. So for example—this is how come you get stuck—you fell down a lot when you used to run. Now you don't run because you think of yourself as a person who falls down a lot when they run. You see? In other words, you are new at every moment. You are an extension of the previous moment of your awareness, yes, but you can completely and radically change if you can unhook yourself from what you've been. Granted, you will still be in a perception, a body of perception that you can't get out of, unless you can move beyond the level of perception.

The ten thousand states of mind that we talk about in Zen are all levels of perception. Right now you are in one of those ten thousand states of mind. That means that you're perceiving life in the world, in the universe, in a certain way.

You can think of each of the ten thousand states of mind as a different dimensional plane, and right now you're in a certain dimension. If you had Excedrin headache number 99, the whole world would look different to you. You'd be in a different dimensional plane, a different state of mind.

Love is a state of mind, you see. Fear is a state of mind, and so on. There are lots of them. You may not have experienced all that many in your life, but there are ten thousand. Who's counting anyway, right? Each is completely different—a completely different state of mind—and bears no resemblance to the others.

The wave of your awareness – OK, what you are is awareness; you're a little band of awareness.

You're like an M&M, a peanut M&M, green, red, whatever, and you are aware. But what are you really aware of? I mean just who are you anyway?

You are aware of a state of mind. And your awareness—that which you are—moves from one state of mind to another. There are ten thousand of them.

Reincarnation is a process of your awareness, the person or being or whatever it is inside you that is aware of all this.

- Not the memories, not the feelings, because ...

- The being that's ultimately inside you—the awareness factor—is what perceives or feels the feelings or has the memories or anticipates the future.

- But that which feels the feelings is what you are.

- That which I'll call perception—because it perceives, that's what it does—that's you.

- You are perception.

- You are that which perceives.

- The rest changes all the time, but the perception remains.

- It continues.

- You, "the perception factor," (Rama laughs) perceive the ten thousand states of mind.

- Each state of mind has lots of permutations, and it goes on forever, not dimensionally in any particular direction; it just always is.

- Perception is the wave, the fact that it is a wave. But the wave changes.

- Well, you change as your perception of something changes because you define yourself as merely a reflection of whatever you happen to perceive.

- And all perception is merely the perception of a state of mind.

If you're in a fun house and there's a mirror that makes you look fat, if you look in it, you'll look fat. Another mirror makes you look skinny. When you look in it, you look skinny. Well, let's say that each state of mind is a mirror.

And there are ten thousand different mirrors, and in each mirror you have a different shape, and your entire life, all of your lives,

is simply a process of standing in front of a mirror looking at yourself.

Your "self" is the universe, and you are perceiving the universe through a state of mind, and one state of mind leads to another.

You can stay in one state of mind for a long time. In other words, your mind is a mirror, and it reflects life. But it reflects life according to the curvature of the mirror. You are perceiving life in the universe in a state of mind. When you change from one level of mind to another, the world appears to be totally different and in fact, it is—because what creates difference is perception.

Therefore there's no continuity at all—it's enough to drive you nuts—in the universe. Because every time you change states of mind, it's all different—which means that the universe isn't any particular way. It strictly depends upon perception.

There's no ultimate objective reality within the ten thousand states of mind, and most people don't like to hear this. They can't handle it. Freaks them out! Because it means that there's no objective reality. Yaagh! (Rama laughs.) There is none! But there are objective realities.

In other words, there's no single unifying reality—that's nonsense. There are ten thousand realities though, and each is definitely unifying. Maybe that makes you feel better. They move in and out of each other constantly. Your lifetimes are spent as perception in one state of being or another, perceiving the universe in those states of mind. That's all there is, and it goes on forever.

There are some beings who reach a point where they no longer want to move continually, aimlessly, through the ten thousand states of mind because, of course, there is something else, and naturally there is an objective reality. It just doesn't happen to be objective in the sense that you would think of it as objective. It's neither objective nor subjective, it's beyond subject and object. That's what I was talking about before, and that's nirvana.

Nirvana or enlightenment, or whatever we'll call it, is outside of the fun house. You're walking around in the fun house forever. Is it fun? I don't know. That's for you to decide. Some of the things in the fun house certainly aren't fun. It's no fun to look in the mirror that makes you look real fat and makes everything look terrible. It might be more fun to look in a mirror that makes you look thin and bouncy and perky and beautiful. All of them are illusory, in that none of them give you an absolute clear view of what is. They all distort life slightly. All states of mind do. Therefore, everything is considered to be unreal.

That's how it's discussed in the esoteric philosophy—meaning that, when you look at a couch, you don't really see the couch. You see the couch as perceived by a state of mind, and you can see the couch in any of ten thousand states of mind, and you'll see ten thousand different couches. Which couch is the real couch? Do you want to walk through Door Number One, Door Number Two or Door Number Three? Should you take the box - the mystery box—or the money? It's hard to say. So [the question] therefore, is—which is the real couch, in which ten thousand states of mind is the real couch?

They are all the real couch. They're all different perceptions of the real couch. Wrong. They're different perceptions of your, our mind. Your mind is made up of the ten thousand states of mind.

The couch doesn't even exist outside of you. There's no wave, remember, unless you perceive it. Yet there is something beyond the ten thousand states of mind because obviously, no one state of mind is better than another. There just happen to be ten thousand.

You get stuck in them, sometimes for a long time. You can get stuck in one state of mind for a thousand lifetimes or in a general area of mind.

Some states of mind afford better views than others, but they're still states of mind. Outside of the state of mind that you're in or all states of mind, there's something that cannot be described, and it cannot be perceived by any of the states of mind. Some states of mind are more open to it, and others are less open to it. The more evolved states of mind are more open to enlightenment. The less evolved states of mind are less open to it—they're afraid of it, and some of the most simplistic of the ten thousand states of mind don't even know it exists and would deny it. That's just the level they function on. They can't perceive that there could be anything—some of the most simplistic states of mind can't even perceive that there are other states of mind other than the individual state of mind that is having the perception.

You see this with people. For example, a person could be in a state of mind where they feel that their religion is the only religion, there aren't even any others, anything else is just crazy. Another person—"Well, see, there are lots of other religions and I wouldn't want to practice them, and they're probably not very good, but there are others." Another person in another state of mind—"Well, see, yes, there are as many religions as there are people, and each one is as good as any other."

But none of those states of mind could see, perhaps, that there's something beyond religion. In other words, they see religion as a way of looking at God and truth. But none of them actually take their minds and merge it with God's and see what God sees. They can't handle it because then, even their ideas of religion would fade away because religion is just a perception of the human mind. It's an orderly way of trying to understand spirit and matter.

But maybe, from God's point of view, or the infinite's point of view, there aren't even religions, there aren't even worlds, there aren't even people.

What does God see, in other words? God is the Universe. That's just too much. They can't deal with it. Some are more liberal than others; some have better views. There are big houses and there are small houses. There are rich neighborhoods and there are poor neighborhoods. There's variation in the universe. There's variation within the ten thousand states of mind. There are different states of mind, and at any given moment you are in one of them and you are perceiving life, the couch, the wave, your existence, pleasure, pain, loss and gain, past, present and future.

Reincarnation is the movement from one state of mind to another.

Ultimately, that will culminate in a physical change. Because you are in one type of state of mind, you are incarnating in a certain universe, in a certain body, in a certain world, with a certain level of perception. Those are the outer reflections that have to do with what we call *karma,* which is the law of cause and effect. But ultimately, all karmas are dependent upon state of mind.

You can get into a state of mind in which you no longer want to be in the ten thousand states of mind. That's the joker in the deck, and that's when you look for enlightenment.

Enlightenment means not that you don't necessarily like the ten thousand states of mind—it's not a question of liking or disliking; they exist as they are—but something in you wants to go beyond all that, to not just be looking through mirrors all the time, but wants to perceive the reality, wants to be free from this endless round of perception.

Enlightenment is that.

If you were enlightened now, what you could do is sit down and meditate and go beyond the ten thousand states of mind—that is enlightenment. You may exist within the ten thousand states of mind; the enlightened being can look through those states of mind, but they are also outside of them.

You visit a country and everybody in that country is bound by certain laws. But let's just say that you have diplomatic immunity. You can go in and you can obey the laws or break the laws; it doesn't matter. You can visit the country. Someone visiting the country who doesn't know that you have diplomatic immunity will assume that you're bound by the same laws as they are, and if you commit a crime like they do, they go to jail, but you don't. But they don't know that. You look, to the person who doesn't know that you have a different status, like everyone else.

So an enlightened person lives in the world, passes through the ten thousand states of mind, but they're not bound by those states of mind. They can step outside of them. They can go beyond perception.

Again, here the words break down. How can I possibly describe it? I can't. I don't know anyone who can.

Enlightenment does not put an end to awareness. It puts an end to limited awareness. It doesn't necessarily put an end to incarnation. It puts an end to reincarnation in that once you attain that status, once you break through the ten thousand states of mind, you will never again be limited by the ten thousand states of mind. If you're born into another lifetime, you remain enlightened; that which is your essence is beyond the ten thousand states of mind. It may take a while for that to surface again, from one lifetime to another, but it's there anyway, even if your individualized mind doesn't perceive it, the outer mind. The enlightenment is there.

All beings exist ultimately in a condition of inner enlightenment. Enlightenment is in all things.

The path of reincarnation, then, is simply the path of changing awareness. What you are reincarnating into are different states of mind.

That which reincarnates is the awareness that perceives each state of mind. That's reincarnation.

The whole show is on the inside. And it really doesn't matter that you change bodies from one lifetime to another. That doesn't really change anything. That's just a change in location, not in you. Oh, the memories will fall away from your last lifetime; they're not really necessary in this lifetime. You might remember past lives. For example, let's say that you remember meditating in another lifetime. That's interesting information, and if you're meditating in this lifetime it's probably true. Because that's what you were doing before, and it carried over into this lifetime. In other words, you're no different in this lifetime than you were in your last lifetime. This lifetime is simply a continuation of your last lifetime, as your last lifetime was a continuation of the prior lifetime.

Death doesn't change anything. It just gives you a new location, some new clothes, but you wash out the memories. The physical mind dissolves and doesn't return. But the overriding state of mind that you die in is the state of mind that you are born into. There are other things that we call karmas. They will determine the location, the type of body, how much money, birth into a wealthy family, a poor family, opportunities that will be presented to you throughout life. I have another tape on karma where we discuss more of the exoteric aspects of reincarnation.

But the inner aspect of reincarnation, which is the important part, has to do with where you put your mind, and the more expansive the state of mind you enter into, the less suffering there is. Because the more expansive states of mind of the ten thousand states of mind are less attached states of mind—they perceive more light. They know more about the universe and the way it works. Ultimately they're still bound states. They don't reflect life perfectly, but some mirrors reflect the way things look more accurately, some less accurately.

If you see a couch and then you have a mirror on the other side of the room and it's completely bent, and you look at it and the couch doesn't at all look like the couch that you just saw when you looked directly at the couch, the mirror is not a good reflector.

Some states of mind really bend life out of shape. Some of the ten thousand states of mind do the opposite. They're pretty good reflectors. But none of them show you what really is. Yet all of these things are. Each is a part of life; each state of mind is. Each reflection is an element of existence. That's why when we say that they're unreal, when I say that the ten thousand states of mind are unreal or hallucinatory—hallucinations are real, dreams are real, but there are some things that are more real.

I say that they're unreal in the sense that they are not as real as some things are. But that doesn't mean they're completely unreal and that they don't exist. Everything is perception. A hallucination is a perception of a certain reality. It's a perception of a certain state of mind.

So then, reincarnation is a process of moving from one state of mind to another.

Whether you're in a body or out of a body is immaterial, to tell you the truth.

Disembodied beings are in a certain state of mind. Embodied beings are in certain states of mind. The disembodied being stays in the same state of mind that it was in when it was embodied, unless it does something to change that while it's out of the body. So you move in a cycle—this is inner reincarnation—from one level of awareness to another, from mirrors that reflect life more accurately to mirrors that reflect life less accurately.

We talk about spiritual evolution in a sense that spiritual evolution is a movement from the mirrors or states of mind that reflect life less accurately to the mirrors that reflect life more accurately. But even if you hit the ten thousandth state of mind that reflects life most accurately, that is not the same as enlightenment. It's a more enlightened condition, but enlightenment is when you smash all the mirrors, and whatever is left is reality. When there are no more mirrors, you break perception itself—the prism of perception breaks. That's enlightenment.

Then the light just floods through and you realize, well, I mean you just can't say what it is or what it's like because it's beyond discussion. That's enlightenment, that's liberation, that's freedom, that's perfection. Yet each of the states of mind is a kind of perfection, has its own beauty, has its own horror. All are reflections of your mind.

Your mind is the ten thousand states. These are ten thousand aspects of your mind, not your physical brain cells and so on, but your mind, your awareness, your perception has ten thousand forms. Beyond your perception, there's something else—beyond those ten thousand forms. But those forms can only think about or ponder what it is. They can't know that. You have to step outside of perception itself.

When a person is evolving, they're moving, as I said, to clearer reflections. The reflections get more and more clear, and as a person is devolving—if you're going down cycle—things are getting fuzzier and fuzzier. Drinking alcohol, for example, takes you into a lower state of mind. If you drink a lot of it, things get very fuzzy and they're not very sharp or defined. That brings you into a lower state of attention. Some things—meditating and some other things—bring you into higher states of mind, [as does] the way you lead your life, your purposes, your goals and so on.

Zen is the study of the ten thousand states of mind and that which lies beyond the ten thousand. You are the sum total of your perception, and if you want to move into better perceptual fields, you need to awaken your mind. As you awaken your mind, you become free, happy, powerful.

Anything that you might want to be is around somewhere, and you can become it, if you'd like to. But you just have to get into the state of mind that allows that to occur. In order to do that, then, you need to learn the ways of mind. There are specific ways to do that.

The *casual body* holds the structure. The casual body is the coding. So you're not just scattered all over through ten thousand states of mind. The casual body is the linkage that holds together the different states of mind. Just as the subtle physical body holds together the physical body, the casual body holds together the awareness. It is the body of awareness. Normally, that body of awareness changes in a linear progression.

In other words, let's say we're looking at 50 states of mind in a row. And of those 50 states, there's one at the bottom of this circuit that least accurately reflects life. Then there's one that most accurately reflects life, and then there are 48 in between. Normally you move from one state of mind to another at a kind of slow progression, but it is possible to move through those states of mind very quickly, and that's Zen. Zen is a very quick movement.

In other words, let's say that you are incarnating and you are in a very low state of mind, and it might take you ten thousand, a hundred thousand million lives to move from lower states of mind to some of the real higher stages of attention. And it's only from the higher stages of attention that you can eventually move beyond the ten thousand states of mind. In other words, you have to hit the highest—you've got to get up to that ten thousandth state of mind. If you get to that one, then you can jump, potentially, beyond the ten thousand states of mind to enlightenment. Remember, this is all a way of talking. It's not really like this. I'm just trying to describe something that's beyond words. So don't get too stuck in the images here, OK?

The problem is that it's a long climb up to ten thousand, and it's not necessarily so orderly. It's possible to go up and then go down because there's a certain force of gravity that pulls you back.

That's why a lot of beings never become enlightened—it's not an automatic process. If someone tells you in reincarnation everyone eventually becomes enlightened, it just takes a certain amount of lives, that's not true. Not at all. Certain beings, certain waves will always be waves. They will never go beyond that condition. They'll be different kinds of waves. They'll whip in and out of those ten thousand states of mind forever, forever!

But in order to reach enlightenment, you have to be able to get to the ten thousandth state, and even that is not a guarantee. From there, then you have to make the big jump, but it can be done.

It can be done.

Others have done it.

You can do it, if that's what you choose.

Every state of mind that you climb up, you will be happier and more complete. Again, you don't have to get to the ten thousandth; each one can totally, radically shift and improve your awareness. So it's a little game you play. How high up can you get? And the way you shift states of mind, well, that's the study of Zen or different forms of self-discovery in which you are taught how to do that. How to balance your life, meditation, ways of using energy—you know, there are just a million factors that go into moving from one state of mind to another. That's the study of self-discovery, where you're discovering the different states of mind. Each is God; each is perfect in its own way. None of them are bad. Some are happier, some are unhappier. Some are very painful, some are very pleasurable. But you go round and round in them forever.

What gets frustrating for some people is the fact that you might get very high up there, but then you kind of get pulled back again. In other words, you moved into very high and pleasurable states of mind for a while, but then the wheel turns around and you find yourself pulled down again because there are certain forces—we call the force illusion or *maya* —that cause us to make mistakes sometimes. And suddenly we find ourselves back in.

So an enlightened being comes into a world because they help, you see. In other words, they've done it or whatever you want to call it. They're off the wheel. They have the diplomatic immunity. They walk around in the world like everyone else, but there's something—if you could really see—that's strikingly different about them. They're not bound by anything that happens here. When they die, their next incarnation, where they end up, will not be determined by this one. They are not bound by the laws of experience here because they're liberated. They will experience different states of mind and in those states of mind, they will suffer, they will know joy and so on. But ultimately, they're free of all of that. In other words, that doesn't stay with them like it stays with you.

So the best way out, is to find someone who's out and listen to them because they've obviously figured it out, and they know and can explain to you or show you how to go through the ten thousand states of mind to get to the one whereby you can make the big jump.

Or maybe even you don't want to do that. You just want to get into some nicer ones than you're in now and know how to do that—you've probably had past lives, since you've existed for a long time, forever, where you were in better stages of mind than you're in now.

But even though you've existed all this time, you still haven't become enlightened.

Enlightened beings are rare in the universe. They're the joker in the deck. They're outside of the circle. They can't be born and they can't die, even though they can take a physical incarnation and their bodies will be born and die, meaning death and birth don't affect their stateless minds. Yet they will go through, in any incarnation, something similar to everyone else. The person who has diplomatic immunity still eats and sleeps. They can still stub their toe, but yet there is something different about an Aqua Velva Man, right? Does she or doesn't she? Right? Only the Zen Master knows for sure, and he's not telling. Naturally, of course, etcetera, etcetera. You get the idea. Yeah.

So the universe is pretty cool. You'll always exist in one form or another. You're a wave and you're changing and moving from one level of attention to another.

But if you're not completely crazy about where you are now, the state of mind that you're currently perceiving as perception, then you should do something to change it. That change will come about gradually, yet all at once. Each aspect of it happens all at once as you do it. Each time you do a push up you're stronger. "Gradually" implies that you won't necessarily see the changes unless you see very carefully—if you see details for a while.

When you really start to meditate, when you start to take the Zen program on, or whatever form of self-discovery you use, if you really stick with it and progress with it, then you will see, over a period of time, tremendous changes in your life and state of mind. Those changes came about, though, because each time, at each moment, you did something that caused you to move in a certain direction. That's reincarnation. The wave is choosing its own direction. Whereas most people don't do that. Most people are just—they don't understand how any of this works. They're just scattered around through life by desires. They chase their desires, they run away from their fears. They have no idea how they get from one state of mind to another or that even other states of mind exist, other than the one that they're in right now, since they tend to forget everything all the time.

I've seen a lot of my students—I've moved them into a high state of mind and they're much more aware for awhile, but then they don't do the things that I've shown them how to do. So then they drop down into a lower stage of attention. Or they do the opposite of what I told them to do. That will then, of course, simply cause them to move into a lower state of attention because I explained what would give them energy; they did things that would drain their energy, so they go down. It's the darndest thing because I stand outside of all this—I get a kick out of it—and I can, of course, recall where they were before. I can see where they are now. But they don't. They honestly don't remember the higher stages of attention they were in, even though they were there maybe six months ago, in which they were completely different beings and the couch didn't look like it looks now.

The same happens the other way. You forget where you've been. You will forget the stage of attention you were in that was lower, which is just as well. It's like not remembering one lifetime because you are in a different lifetime. You really don't need to remember the other lifetime, what you did in it, per se. It won't make any difference. That's last week's TV show. Watch this week's.

But if you can summon up power from past lives and bring them into this life, and that can give you a boost into the next state of mind up or further, well that's a good thing. That's worth doing.

But just remembering what you did in previous lives doesn't mean a thing. It's nice to remember that you had higher states of mind, but that won't necessarily get you there. It might even make things painful.

Once you were rich, and now you are poor, and if that's going to make you feel very unhappy about your current state, what good is it going to do you? If, on the other hand, it reminds you that you were rich before, and you can become rich again because you know how in there somewhere, and if that inspires you to try and it causes it to happen, then that remembrance is worthwhile.

Again, this is all a certain perspective in which the most important thing is raising your level of attention. There are other perspectives and other states of mind in which it doesn't matter. I could enter into those and we'd have different discussions because there are ten thousand ways of looking at things. And I don't exactly have a point of view per se.

If you are interested in the other stuff about reincarnation, pick up the "Karma" tape – which is exoteric jazz about physical happenings that are of great concern. That's the other side.

This [the "Reincarnation" tape] is what goes on within—these are the secret teachings which most people forget as soon as they've heard them (Rama laughs) because they move to a different state of mind. But the mere hearing of these teachings, so they say—not because I said them, the teachings are independent of the teachers—the mere hearing of these teachings can bring one into a very high state of mind if you meditate upon them.

Ultimately, from my point of view you've got to be practical, and you need to go do something and that's—you need to do whatever will bring you into the next higher state of mind and get some evolution going. Then life can be pretty wonderful. When you don't do that and you allow yourself to get dragged down to the lower states of mind, life can be very uncomfortable and very painful.

But there's something beyond all states of mind, my friend, and it's the best. It's better than the best! Better than Dutch apple pie, right? And that's enlightenment. It's worth striving for. It's worth doing something about it. It's worth becoming. Again, that's the perspective of the enlightened.

(Zazen music begins in the background.)

So, is there life after death? Is the moon made out of green cheese? What's really happening anyway? Where are these states of mind? Who am I? What's going on? How'd I get here? What world is this? They gave me a travel brochure. They said: "Earth, right? Enjoy it." I'll never use that travel agent again. Clearly it was a dated brochure. What a place! What an incarnation! I don't know about you, but I'm getting out of here soon. (Rama laughs.)

Oh, diplomatic immunity is great, right? But you still have feet. In this place you have feet. You know, there are worlds where you don't have feet. There are worlds where you don't have bodies. There are states of mind where you don't have a mind. I mean there's a lot of stuff. The universe is very big. (Rama laughs.)

So this is Zen Master Rama, cruising the ten thousand states of mind, stepping in and out of realities, wondering why the whole thing is and knowing simultaneously that—what the heck, right?

Keep meditating—you'll get it. Just keep meditating.

(Zazen music ends.)

CHAPTER SEVEN

KARMA

(Zazen music plays in the background, and Rama speaks to the beat of the music.)

Hi there. Zen Master Rama here, talking with you about karma and reincarnation today. The poignancy of life. Incarnation. The intersection of different spheres of existence in time and space, matter and energy—life.

We are alive, for a brief moment. And there are many, many wonders to see. And sometimes we think that life is random. We just go through life without a plan, without a direction. Things seem chaotic.

Chance. Is there chance? No. There's karma. Karma causes all things to happen. It makes the sun come up every day; the moon go through its 28 phases; it causes your birth, your death. It's what makes your days and nights, days and nights.

Karma. Why do you meet someone? Karma. Why don't you meet someone else? Karma. Why do you love one person more than another? Karma. Why are you in the career you're now in? Karma.

There is only one thing that karma can't decide, and that's how far you will evolve in this lifetime. How much you'll wake up. How much you'll come to see and know before you leave this place again. That is up to you. The rest is karma.

(Zazen music ends.)

It's good not to think of karma as an alien force that's outside of yourself, because you are the generator of karma. Karma is your own energy—the energy patterns that emanate from your life, from your actions, from your thoughts, feelings and desires, your attractions and aversions, hopes, dreams, plans and schemes—karma.

The idea is simple. For every action there's a reaction, for every cause there's an effect, for every effect there's a result, and a new situation is created. Karma can be examined within the structure of an hour, a year, a lifetime, thousands of lifetimes. But the active principle is the same—you, your choices, your decisions, your awareness. How aware are you? What determines how aware you can become?

Karma, as I said, indicates action, but not necessarily physical action; nor is karma a result in the sense of a reward. Some people say when something happens to them, "Oh, it's my karma," as if there was someone out there giving rewards or punishments. Something good happens to you and you say, "Oh, it's my karma," meaning you have good karma. You've done something good in the past and it comes back to you. Something bad happens to you, whatever you construe that to be, and you say, "Oh, it's my karma," meaning that something unpleasant has occurred because you've done something that you would consider to be inappropriate, bad, whatever, in a prior time. Karma is really much more complicated than that. That's a very simplistic view of it.

Karma, first of all, comes from the mind. Karma is engendered by states of mind. For example, if you're in a happy state of mind, that will engender one kind of karma. If you're in an unhappy state of mind, that will engender another kind of karma. It's best to think of karma, not so much in terms of physical action, but as waveforms of vibratory energy.

Example—if you and I were to go today to a nice still pond, one of those lovely still ponds that dot the New England landscape, and there was no wind at all and the pond was mirror smooth, and we were to take a small hippopotamus and drop him from a height of about 50 feet into the water, OK, the hippo would crash into the water and waves would be generated throughout the pond—also, probably a lot of scandal and controversy because in small New England towns, they're not used to the hippopotamus descending from the sky, as we are out here in California. These things happen all [the] time; it is no big deal at all. But be that as it may, the hippo drops, hits the water and ripples occur, OK?

Two kinds of ripples will occur from the dropping hippo. One kind will be ripples on the lake, and as the hippo crashes into the water, the ripples will go out in a circular direction and they will cause an effect. Perhaps there was someone in a very small boat, and as the hippo comes down and crashes into the water, the ripples or waves will overturn the boat causing one of the two passengers of the boat, Sally, to drown. Bob will now inherit Sally's estate since he had recently married her, and he saw in a psychic vision that a hippo was going to be falling from the sky in Massachusetts and hitting this particular lake on that particular day. Knowing that Sally couldn't swim and he could, he thought it was a hot opportunity to take her out on a boat trip. So, the karma of the hippo falling, the result, is Bob's inheritance of a large amount of money that previously belonged to Sally.

Now, other aspects of this—well, Bob would therefore engender another kind of karma because he caused Sally's death. Causing Sally's death—the courts can't get him, obviously, because they don't believe that you could psychically see that a hippo was going to be striking the water in a small New England town just outside of Boston. So it would be ruled an accident, act of God or whatever. However, if you had dropped the hippo, if you had arranged for it, naturally, you could be sued for involuntary woman-slaughter or something like that. Because what business do you have dropping hippos from way up in the sky onto small lakes? Also, a great amount of controversy would be generated probably, if you left the scene and you didn't identify yourself as the dropper of the hippo, as to what to do with the hippo.

Now we've got a hippo in a small town, OK. We've got a dead woman floating around. We've got Bob going out and buying his new Volvo, or whatever else, with the money that he inherited from Sally. Now we have a slew of headlines in local papers and maybe even a few television crews going down to the lake, OK? "Hippo Strikes Lake!" You know, that sort of thing, and I don't know what could happen.

Whole careers could change—somebody did a good story on the news, might be able to leave Boston and get a job in New York at a larger station—move their family. The hippo-landing site could become a new place of worship for people who believe in extraterrestrial hippopotami. People would start to tell stories and gossip about the meaning of it. At Harvard they'd immediately dispatch a research team, and MIT would probably dispatch another competitive research team, to try and understand exactly where this hippo came from, calculate the angle of impact, so on and so forth. Do studies. Graduate students would do dissertations on the subject because hippos just don't normally strike small ponds in New England. Meanwhile, Bob is now vacationing in the Bahamas, with his latest prospect, Mary.

Karma. Karma comes about from actions. The karma that is most interesting is the mental karma because ultimately it generates physical action. Let me explain what I mean. Most people think of karma in terms of doing something. OK, Bob drops the hippo, hippo wipes out small town, whatever it may be. So—this is a ridiculous tape I realize, but bear with me, it will make sense eventually—so you could say Bob's action caused a reaction and that's karma. OK, now does this mean that in some future life that a hippo will be dropped on Bob? No, not at all. See, that's where the most common misunderstanding of karma comes in. Just because you do something or create an action of some type, it does not mean that an action of the same type or nature will be returned to you. That is absolutely not the case.

What karma means is that a mental state will shift. Let me explain. Bob has been a nice guy, OK? He never really liked hippopotami anyway. But he conceived of this wonderful plan when he had the psychic vision of seeing the hippo strike the small New England pond—maybe Lake Waban, let's say, which is a ridiculous name, which is by Wellesley. Now, the hippo strikes Lake Waban in Wellesley and Bob, who was prior to this a pretty nice guy, wipes out his wife and inherits the money. Bob will now change because Bob wantonly took her life. Because the hippo was just innocently falling from the sky; the hippo did not intend to wipe out Sally. Bob's intent was to wipe out Sally, and he succeeded. Bob will now change.

When you cause something to happen, whether it's physically or you simply think a thought or feel an emotion, it causes a shift in your attention field, in your awareness. Shifts in your awareness ultimately will result in a pattern shift in your life. So Bob, who previously was your easy-going guy, will now be in a very different mental state because he just killed somebody for profit. This will cause Bob's attention field to drop. When Bob's attention field drops, he will now be on a new pattern in life. Certain things that might have come to him, won't come to him. Certain things that wouldn't, would.

Bob, for example, now will become a different kind of person as his mental state shifts, because we only are our mental state. And as he becomes that different kind of person or personality, he will make choices that he wouldn't have made. He will associate with people he wouldn't have associated with. In other words, a new future will open up to Bob, and in Bob's case, the future will not be as bright. Because whenever we wantonly destroy, injure, harm or take life, unless it's a case of self-defense, we are employing an aggressive, primal energy that puts us in an aggressive primal awareness field, which limits the structure of awareness, which causes an end to happiness, which requires an unimpeded state of awareness.

Let me get even more graphic here. Let's say that you are sitting around at home and you feel perfectly good and you're having a nice time. Really nothing has to be added—you feel really good today or this evening and you're just sitting at home and having a nice time. Suddenly, as you're sitting there, and you're completely peaceful and you just feel good to be alive—this is one of those rare moments when you feel good—your body feels good, your mind feels good and you're just happy, you don't have to do anything—suddenly, you start to think about someone you know, who you think is very, very attractive sexually. Now prior to this, you hadn't been thinking about them. They didn't exist for you. Suddenly they pop into your mind, and as you begin to think about them and turn them over in your mind, you begin to fantasize a little bit. And you begin to think of them without their clothes on. You begin to think of them cavorting with the hippopotamus. You begin to think of them doing weird and kinky things with you, whatever it would be.

As you start to think about this, of course, your blood pressure rises a little bit, you start to get a little bit jazzed and excited, the kundalini starts to move around and you begin to have a good time—so it appears. You begin to fixate, or think more about this person and you begin to desire them. You begin to become a little bit sexually aroused. Now what will happen is now you're jazzed, and this person will be someone who is perhaps available to you or perhaps is not. If they are available to you, now that you're excited, you might call them up on the phone, get together with them, go to bed with them, whatever, which would create an interaction between the two of you, an energy transfer between the two of you. Maybe it would produce an offspring; maybe it would produce an argument. Maybe it would change your life.

On the other hand, they may not be available to you, in which case, suddenly, you're going to find yourself in a state of desire—meaning your awareness field has moved into the desire plane. When your awareness field has moved into the desire plane, you're not going to be happy. You can't have them. That is what you want. Suddenly you were sitting around at home having a good time and now you're not having such a good time because your mind, which was in a state of equilibrium and tranquil composure, has moved to the desire plane—which is not necessarily a bad place to be. But the desire plane brings about results.

The result of the desire plane is desire and either fulfillment or frustration.

Fulfillment in the desire plane normally leads to another desire. It does not put an end to desire per se, but it causes a brief hesitation. So you have sexual desire, you have sex, you fulfill the desire. There's no desire for a while, but then later on, the desire will come around again. It's just a brief hesitation—it's a hyphen between desire.

Before, you were not in the desire plane at all. You were satisfied and content. This was not a big issue in your life. But by focusing on something that stimulated your senses, i.e., the naked body of the individual whom you would like to enjoy, you aroused your senses. You stimulated something in yourself that led you into the world of desire. Once you are in the world of desire, it's a real bitch to get out of it. That is why almost everybody is unhappy all the time—because everybody is in the desire world.

There are two worlds—count them, two—the world of desire and the world of enlightenment and they are definitely not the same thing. It pays not to get them confused. The world of desire leads to more desire. The world of enlightenment doesn't go anywhere. It just is in itself what it is—endless, luminous perfection, happiness and freedom. The world of desire leads to more desire.

The world of desire is the world of karma. All action is generated by desire. It is the desire to move that causes us to stand up. It is the desire to live that keeps us here or that causes us to reincarnate. It is the desire for a sentient experience that causes someone to come back. Aversion is another type of desire—not wanting something. It is just reverse desire. It's as strong and powerful a karmically binding force as desire is, because it engenders action.

In the *Bhagavad-Gita*, the famous Indian spiritual book, they discuss karma and reincarnation and enlightenment and other things. Krishna, in conversation with Arjuna, says, "Arjuna, you cannot avoid action."

Everyone acts. Even if you keep your body from moving, that does not stop action. Your cells are moving, your thoughts are moving, your moods are shifting. Everyone acts; everyone is stuck in the world of action—the world of action is forever. Your awareness field, that which you consider yourself to be, is in bodily form at the moment. At the end of a lifetime you'll leave this world, and then you will go beyond the body. But your awareness field will stay together in a certain sense and then it will seek, after a while—because it's in the desire plane—to return to things that are familiar. It will seek a new body in a new lifetime, and you will reincarnate. Then you will go through more desires, more fulfillments and more frustrations. This goes on forever.

Life is forever. Death is only a temporary abridgement, a short pirouette through time and space, where you don't really die. We talk about death as if it is an ending. It is just a state of transition where you will move from one world into another. You will move from the *physical planes* into the *causal planes* and from the *world of matter* into the *world of pure energy*. Then the essence of your being reincarnates.

Your next incarnation is largely determined by this incarnation. As I mention in my other tape on reincarnation, which discusses the more esoteric aspects of reincarnation, whereas this tape is more concerned with the exoteric or physical effects of reincarnation, your next incarnation is based upon your awareness at the time of death. When you die in this life, whatever your awareness is—awareness meaning not just the mood at the moment but the total overall awareness that you have, i.e., not just at the very moment that you die, meaning your mood—you might be experiencing pain and confusion—but your overall perceptual field, the structure of your overall perceptual field, will determine your next lifetime. That structure has been determined by the way you've led this life. If you've been very aware, if you've meditated, if you learned to still your thoughts, if you've become more aware of the inner dimensional planes, then that awareness is yours.

You are your awareness. And that awareness, at the time of death, moves forward. The personality structure at the time of death dissolves. You will never be exactly the you you are again. But the essence of your awareness field definitely goes on after death. It goes through death, it goes into *non-physical states* for a time, and then eventually it's pulled back and it reincarnates. The level of incarnation that occurs will be largely dependent upon the state of awareness that you had at death. In other words, that's karma.

There are also physical karmas that carry through. So for example, in a prior lifetime you've set in motion certain vibratory currents, and those currents will continue to work their effect in the world. Jesus Christ may no longer be with us, or John Kennedy or Adolph Hitler or Marx or Lenin or John Adams, but their effects continue on in the world, just like the hippo that fell from the sky and created waves—waves in a pond, waves in the world, changes in people's lives. Those waves will be passed on from one person to another to another.

Each of us is endlessly generating waves with our physical actions. When you say something to someone, it has an effect on them. That effect will be passed on by them to someone else because you'll change the way that person thought or felt, causing them to react differently. That reaction will be passed on to everybody they encounter. In turn that subtle change will be passed on, and so on and so forth.

If you could see the earth from a vibratory point of view and not be distracted by the physical, you would see something like radio waves, billions of them, cascading constantly in very complex patterns all over the earth. These waves are emitted from the thoughts, feelings and actions of each individual life form here. That's what karma is. So you do have an effect on the universe around you. If you think positive thoughts, if you're happy and progressive, then that energy goes out and affects everyone on the whole planet, in subtle ways, perhaps, but it does.

If, on the other hand, you are filled with hate and you're morose and you're depressed, that energy will live on also—if you're cruel to others and so on. Never feel that you don't have an effect. You do have an effect. No action is wasted. That's karma.

Now, karma doesn't always mean that everything works out justly. For example, you're walking down the street, you're in a nice state of mind and someone mugs you. They attack you. They hold you up. They steal your wallet, maybe they hit you over the head, maybe they shoot you. Is that your karma? Have you done something in a prior lifetime that wasn't so good? Did you do that to someone else in this lifetime? Not necessarily. That may just be what's happening. In other words, you are not always receiving things that you have done. There's just some off-the-wall sucker out there who decided to do that. Now they are generating karma for themselves of a negative type. But you were innocent.

Innocence does not protect you from the evil designs of others. Just because you're innocent that does not mean that others cannot harm you. History teaches this lesson. Some people are under the assumption that because all of their lives something like that has never happened to them, that nothing ever will. They think that they're "protected." There are certain protective forces in the universe that do watch over us, but the innocent die, too.

Karma, then, is a very sophisticated and very complicated thing, but what it really has to do with are mental states. The state of mind you're in causes you to act in a certain way. Your actions will bear results. The things you do will come back to you, not always physically though. Let's say for 20 years you gave lots of money to spiritual causes because it really turned you on to do it. Now, does that mean that in your golden years, suddenly people are going to start showing up at your door with checks for you because you gave $100,000 over a number of years to spiritual causes that aided the enlightenment of others? Not necessarily. But what will happen is, you will be in a better state of mind—that will be the karmic effect.

The purpose of life is life, and the ultimate result of all karmas and actions is state of mind. You are your state of mind—happiness, completion, awareness, enlightenment and so on. These things do not occur to us randomly. They occur because of vibratory and karmic patterns. There are certain things that you can do that will have a karmic effect, which is happiness, illumination, fulfillment. There are others things you can do that will have a karmic effect, which is unhappiness, misery and so on.

You hear the preacher on the radio say, "For every dollar you send in, God is going to send you back five." Not necessarily, unless you've gotten the five recently. That's not karma—that's a quick way to hustle up some money. What will happen is, whenever you engage in a selfless action that contributes to the welfare of others, this will create a vibratory pattern that will lead you into a higher state of mind, and the result will be that you will be much more happy, fulfilled and aware. What more could one ask? Whereas, when you do things in a selfish way, let alone in a destructive way to others, then you are bound by that karma. Your state of mind will go down. You will find yourself becoming depressed, nervous, anxious and upset.

There are selfish actions and there are selfless actions. Selfless actions create a higher karma, which brings you into higher states of mind. When you're in a higher state of mind, you will see things that you never saw before. So for example, you gave money to the United Fund or to your local spiritual cause or whatever it is that turns you on. When you did this—and you could have just kept that money for yourself, or maybe you put in a few extra hours at work so you could do that—when you did this, you did something noble. This will cause a release of energy. It causes a vibratory shift. It means you're moving into a different plateau of consciousness. Just like there are different roads that lead different places, so there are different levels of awareness that lead different places and we shift in and out of them. These are the ten thousand states of mind that we study in Zen.

KARMA 153

When you give—let's say you gave to United Fund or your local spiritual cause—when you give, what happens is you go onto a certain highway. That action of giving is in a certain vibratory level, meaning "giving" exists in a certain plane of consciousness. It's a highway we call "giving." To give means you got on that highway. That highway will have a certain view. Let's say that highway runs way up to the top of the mountain. From the top of the mountain, you can see things that you couldn't see on another highway, which was called selfishness.

Selfishness is a state of mind. It is a plateau of attention, and it has a certain view. All states of mind have certain views. So in the case of selfishness, now you're on a lower highway and the view is obstructed—you can't see very well, so you might have an accident. On the higher plateau, on the higher highway, you'll suddenly see a career opportunity. You will meet somebody you wouldn't have met. You will attract people who are more selfless. Opportunities will open to you because you can see them. That's what karma really is. Do you follow?

Karma means that through your thoughts and feelings and actions, you are generating a state of mind. That state of mind has a view. That view will cause things to happen to you or not happen to you. So the real active force behind action and interaction is state of mind. There is a point, in other words, to noble thoughts and noble actions. It's not simply a moral fantasy. You can experiment with this—like dropping the hippo into the water, ripples are created.

When you meditate and practice Zazen, when you stop your thought, when you focus, you're creating karmas. You're shifting your state of mind to a higher vibratory level that will give you a much more expansive view. When you allow desire, anger and frustration to dominate you, you're losing power, your airplane is falling to a lower altitude. If it falls too low, it will crash.

Everyone experiences desire. Desire is not bad. It's not bad to desire someone. It's not bad to have sex with someone. It's not bad to do whatever. There is no good or bad from the point of view of karma. There is only reaction, structured reaction. Love leads to one state of mind, hate leads to another, indifference to another. All states of mind continually revolve in the cosmos.

There are ten thousand states of mind. Each has a different view. Each brings about different results. And as I indicated, at the end of this lifetime, the culmination of the states of mind you have gone through will create your next lifetime. So there is good karma and bad karma, which means, in other words, karma will lead you to a state of mind that has a larger more expansive, happier view, or a dingy, darker view that's much more limited. That is all karma really is, and that view will enable you to make choices and have experiences.

Now, there are physical karmas. Physical karmas are a little bit different. Again, those are the reactions of the ripples. OK, the boat is in the water, the hippo hits the water and the boat turns over. Those are physical karmas. Those are on a physical level. They are reactions and results from action. But those are bound to a particular lifetime. The only thing you take with you when you die is your state of mind.

It is your state of mind that affords everything that happens to you. For example, you could be a real nice person. By that we mean that you have created a lot of good karma, which has led you into higher levels of mind. You die and you're reborn into this current incarnation. You could have had a really tough life. That doesn't mean that you had a lot of bad karma. That's just how it was. You were born into a country, let's say, that went through an economic depression. Everybody experienced that to one degree or another. That doesn't mean that your karma led you to that state. Your karma is the state of mind that you're in, and that state of mind will cause you to deal with every moment in your life in a certain way.

If you had good karma, meaning you're in a really good state of mind, when the depression comes to the land, it won't throw you. You will keep a positive and optimistic attitude, you'll generate energy, you'll go through it happily because you're in a good state of mind, and also you will see opportunities that others wouldn't. Whereas, if you had bad karma, meaning you were in lower states of mind from the actions, thoughts, feelings and impressions from your previous life, then when the depression comes, you'll be overwhelmed by it and you won't see opportunities and you'll suffer more.

We can't help what happens to us physically all the time. You are going to die. Your physical body will disintegrate. You can't help that. You can prolong your life, make it a little longer. You can make it a little shorter depending upon how you eat, whether you exercise or not, what you expose yourself to. But sooner or later the cells will give out. They transmute. What you can do is determine the state of mind you are in, and the state of mind you are in, is heaven or hell. All heavens and hells are within the mind, within your mind. Heaven is a state of awareness. Hell is a state of awareness. There are lots of states in between that are mixtures of both—ten thousand of them, ten thousand states of mind.

So then, let's think of karma this way—there are several different types of karma.

- ॐ There is a karma—a *physical karma* —that occurs within a given lifetime. That karma does not carry over after death.
- ॐ There is a *mental karma* —that occurs within a given lifetime—and it does carry over after death into the next incarnation.
- ॐ There is a *physical karma* that an individual generates in a given lifetime—that may continue on or will continue on in one form or another after their lifetime, after they have ceased to exist in a particular incarnation.

All karmas, however, originate in the mind because of mental activity.

The types of thoughts that you think create a state of mind. The reason you think the thoughts that you do, results from your level of energy or power. The level of energy or power that you have is caused by various forces that you expose yourself to in the universe, and the way you lead your life, the way you structure your intelligence. While this is a result from a previous mental condition, it's a carryover, yet you have the ability to modify—to a certain extent—the characteristics of your current state of mind. That modification will be somewhat restricted to the state of mind that you were in previously.

In other words, you can only conceive of what lies beyond the state of mind you're in from the point of view of the state of mind you're in. However, within any state of mind there is a gradation, since all states of mind are basically structurally the same. That gradation will run, we could say, from darkness to light. So, for example, [suppose] you're in a really confused state of mind. But even in that confusion, there will be a higher and lower end to it. And in the higher end of the confused state of mind—meaning there's more light or there's more view—you would be able to conceive of something that is beyond the confusion that you're in. Whereas, in the lowest end of it, you might be able to conceive of something even more confusing; and then there'd be a central point.

Anyone has the ability, if they choose to—and this is the freedom of perception—to move to the higher end of the state of mind that they're in. From that higher end of the state of mind, they can generate another state of mind, which is successively higher. So by generating good karma, even within the limited state of mind, you can move to the next state of mind, and so on and so forth, up the ascending ladder to the higher states of mind. Or you can move downward by dwelling in the lower states of mind.

There is no "specific gravity." In other words, some people believe that they are drawn to lower states of mind and that enlightenment is really hard because you're working against gravity. Not really. Not really. All that exists is the state of mind that you're in. That state of mind has been generated by *causal* activities, by previous states of mind that go all the way back forever. Yes. But it really doesn't matter what happened in the past. All the past has done is generated the you that you are now. Dwelling on the past isn't going to change anything. You are whatever you are at the moment.

That is to say, you are your state of mind. But you can choose to move to the higher end of the state of mind that you're now in, in a way of speaking, and from that point of view you will be able to glimpse the next state of mind. If you dwell on that highest aspect of the state of mind you are currently in long enough, eventually you will tip the scales and move to another state of mind that's more luminous. And you'll start in the bottom of that state of mind and you can work higher, or you can go in the other direction. States of mind change continuously. We don't always walk from one state of mind into another. We might just oscillate back and forth for a whole lifetime within one, within the polarities of a certain state of mind.

Now, as I mentioned, there are different types of karmas. Let's reexamine, just for a moment, all those different ones, just so they're nice and clear for you because this is what makes up your lifetime and your world.

To begin with, there is the type of karma that you experience within a given lifetime. That is a physical and a mental karma. There are two kinds. But let's talk about the physical karma for a moment. The physical karma you experience within a given lifetime comes back to you. But it can't come back to you after you're dead. It will reflect in a mental karma after death and into the next life, but it will not recapitulate again, although it will continue on and affect others. Let me give you a for instance.

Let's say that you go to school and you do really well in your classes—you get very good marks. That will create a karma, an effect that will allow you to get into a good college. Let's say you do well there and you get a degree and that degree enables you to get a certain type of job. That job provides a certain level of income, which will allow you to live in a certain way. Now, at the end of this lifetime, when you die, you won't carry any of that with you.

In other words, the karma will continue throughout the life, that degree will always be there, your career knowledge will always be there. That will carry with you. But in your next lifetime, when you're born again, of course, the fact that you had a degree in your previous lifetime won't impress an employer. You've got to get another one.

If you committed a crime and went to jail, and let's say you got a life sentence, you would spend all your life in jail. When you die, that's not going to have any effect on your next life. The karma is complete within a lifetime. They are not going to lock you up as soon as you are born again because you didn't finish all 150 years of a sentence; you only did 70 of them. But the karmic patterns that you set into motion will continue.

So Gandhi and his passive resistance or the words of John Adams or John Kennedy or Martin Luther King, or the effects of a [dictator such as] Idi Amin, or whatever, will continue. Their words will live on, their actions will live on, the effects that they have had on others—or the effects that you have on others—will continue on and be passed on. That continues, naturally. But the karmas that you physically create in a given lifetime, that you create this lifetime, will end with your death, and they don't carry to your next life. But they do, in a certain way.

The mental karma, which is our second kind of karma, will continue. Because what you do in this lifetime will generate a certain state of mind, and as I indicated before, at the time of your death, that state of mind will stay with you. You may not remember the particulars—what you did, what you thought, what you felt—but the sum total of that awareness will generate a state of mind, which is the state of mind that you will be born into. It will come back to you after a while.

Let's say that you committed a crime and you went to jail. Let's say that while you were in jail, all you did was dwell on more crimes, and you beat people up, and you just did a lot of horrible stuff and you were filled with hate and anger. While in your next lifetime they won't lock you up at the time of birth, the physical karma will continue. If that's what you were all your life, then in your next lifetime, you will be born into the same state of hateful mind with all its limitations. So what you do does go with you. It does follow you, and because you're born into a life with that state of mind, it will provide you with a certain window or view on existence, which will then cause you, perhaps, to steal things, to commit crimes, to get locked up again, or just to be unhappy and miserable. You will start out unhappy and depressed because that's the state of mind you left off in. In other words, it does matter what you do and think. It does affect your next life, not as some people tell us. It doesn't have a direct physical effect, but it does, through the state of mind that you carry with you.

Then there's the "ripple effect karma," which is just something that you set in motion by your actions, which affect others. It doesn't affect you after you leave this world, after your body dies. You might incarnate in another world, not necessarily on the planet Earth. Obviously, things that you set in motion will not necessarily affect you. But you do bring the cumulative state of mind with you. If you went to jail and you were put in jail—let's say you committed a crime, and your crime was the result of a crummy state of mind. Let's say you murdered someone, you're in a horrible state of mind. If, however, when you got to jail, you thought about it and you realized that you were in a screwed-up state of mind to do something like that, and you started to live a different type of life there, and you started to think better thoughts, you started to control those desires, you started to clear yourself up and you went into better states of mind—at the time of your death, you would be in a better state of mind. In your next life you'd be born into the world with that state of mind, and that state of mind would provide more opportunities for you.

The person who gives selflessly in this lifetime immediately goes into a better state of mind. That is "instant karma." You could be in a good mood and you start to get upset or angry or worried. Immediately that will cause your energy level to drop, and your state of mind will drop, and suddenly you'll be unhappy. You could be unhappy or even happy, and decide to do something for someone else that was not ego-oriented—some kind of pure giving. And if you did that immediately, your state of mind will brighten. Again, that doesn't mean that because you contributed $1,000 to the United Fund that someone's going to rush up to you now, or in your next life, with a check for $1,000. What it means is that you'll be happy and aware in all circumstances in this life and in your next life. It will carry over in your state of mind. Your state of mind, again, will, in a certain way, influence your destiny. It will cause you to see opportunities that you would not have seen otherwise, or perhaps to avoid problems that you would not have been able to avoid, had you not been in as clear a state of mind.

Now, enlightenment is a little different. Good karma leads to good karma, and bad karma leads to bad karma; that's true. If you create nothing but good karma, you will only experience lovely states of mind. Again, what we would call painful experiences can occur to you, and you didn't have to generate them. There are wars in the world. There are wars in the mind. But your good karma will protect you, meaning it won't necessarily stop you from experiencing a war, but it will stop you from experiencing an inner war. You will be in a higher state of mind regardless of the physical activities that are taking place around you, which will guarantee your happiness and peace of mind.

Good karma leads to good karma, and it leads to rebirth. Now this is—we're getting a little bit technical here, and this part might not be of interest to you or it might. Good karma leads to rebirth also. In other words, the urge to do things that are positive and selfless is a desire. The desire for higher states of mind is a desire. That desire, while a nice desire that leads to more pleasant experiences, is still a desire and it still causes you to reincarnate. It causes you to seek nobility and higher plateaus of awareness. And that causes you to fixate on higher states of mind, and when you're fixated on higher states of mind, you don't really become what we would call enlightened.

Enlightenment doesn't simply mean being in heavenly states of mind. It doesn't mean being a saint. A saint is someone who has been very selfless and, over a period of lifetimes, generated a tremendous amount of good karma, which has caused them to enter into very lovely states of mind which they experience, and for them, the world is beautiful all the time. They are at peace with themselves. They're happy, they're bright, they're aware. On the other hand, the insane fiend, the crazy person, the psycho killer, is on the opposite side of the spectrum. They are tormented beings who are confused, frustrated, filled with anger and hate. These individuals have created a lot of bad karma, and now they are reaping the reward of their bad karma, which is that state of mind that is total misery, no matter what they do. While they may injure others, they can only injure their bodies, not their minds.

Your state of mind can't be affected by another, really. Someone can temporarily cause you pain, or even mental pain, but your overall state of mind is impassive to outer suggestion, unless you personally make a modification. True, you can alter your state of mind by associating with others closely who are in a different state of mind. That can happen. And sometimes it doesn't happen. It depends. If you're hanging around with a lot of people who are doing drugs, that doesn't mean you're necessarily going to use drugs also. It might. But, then again, it might not.

Enlightenment, then, does not come about from creating good karma. Nor does it come about from creating bad karma. Certainly, good karma leads you to a closer window to the enlightenment experience. Because it's very, very difficult to make the jump beyond finite states of awareness to infinite awareness when you're in confused and lower states of mind. If you could get into the highest state of mind that you could—if there are ten thousand states of mind, let us say, and the ten thousandth state of mind is the highest state of mind—from that state of mind you would have a window whereby you could perhaps move beyond all states of mind, metaphorically speaking, to enlightenment, which doesn't preclude the ten thousand states of mind—it's just an endless condition of infinite, perfect awareness.

Simply by performing good actions and thinking goods thoughts and doing good deeds you will not attain enlightenment. That is the point here. It takes something more. But in order to get to that place where you can add something more, you need to first purify your thoughts, have happy emotions, give as much as you can, be charitable, kind, honest, strong. By doing all those things and moving to higher states of mind, the window will open whereby the possibility of enlightenment will come about. That is why it's necessary to gain control of your time and your life and your awareness and to have some understanding of the workings of karma and reincarnation, if you're interested in enlightenment or success. Success will come about because you are in higher states of mind—whether it's business success, personal success—any kind of success will be determined by your state of mind.

If you create good karma, then you'll go into a higher state of mind and in that higher state of mind, you might be more apt to meet someone. Let's say you wanted a romantic partner who is in a higher state of mind, a nicer person. The reason you will meet that person is because you are in a state of mind that will cause that meeting to occur. On the physical level, it will look like chance, but there's no chance in the universe. Because you are in a certain vibratory pattern, you will know on that certain day, without knowing necessarily how or why, to drive down a certain street, to go to a certain store where you might meet someone. If you're not in that state of mind, it won't happen. You'll meet somebody else.

The same is true of business opportunities, personal growth opportunities—the higher your state of mind, the more in touch you are with the psychic aspect of yourself, the more success you will have. The more control of your mind, the ability to concentrate, and so on, will create success. And naturally, if you explore the higher states of mind as far as you can, you will create that window to enlightenment.

Enlightenment is different. And on this tape, I'm not going to discuss how that happens. But let's say that it's only by creating as much good karma as possible that you generate the possibility of enlightenment. Without that, there is really no possibility of enlightenment. It could happen. Yes. It is possible to move to an enlightened state of mind from a lower bardo or level of awareness. It can happen, but it's extremely unlikely. Extremely.

So now you know lots and lots about karma—good for you. The point of all this is that it is always possible to get into a higher state of mind. The way you get into a higher state of mind is by generating good karma. Good karma is generated by lots of things—anything that will bring you into a higher state of mind. But if you allow yourself to be depressed, to think negative thoughts, to get angry, to be jealous, if you allow yourself to dwell on those things, you'll pull your state of mind lower. You will pull it down, and then that will cause you to make mistakes, do things you wouldn't do if you were in higher states of mind, which will generate more karmic patterns. You will get momentum going, you'll go further and further down and become depressed and discouraged and miserable. At any point, you can turn it around and go up. At any point, you can turn it around and go down. That's up to you.

You need to realize that no matter what your state of mind, you can always go up or down. That's what's fun about the process. What's fun about the process is that no matter how low your state of mind is, you can always go up instantly by doing something selfless, by sitting and meditating, by reading a book or listening to a tape that discourses on higher states of mind where there's higher vibratory energy present, by doing something for someone else, by giving selflessly of your time, energy, money—whatever it is—by stepping outside of yourself. There is an art to generating higher states of mind. There is an art to generating lower states of mind, degenerating, and you have practiced both in your life and in other lives. That's the science of mind.

(Zazen music begins in the background.)

So this is Zen Master Rama, in one state of mind or another. Looking at limitless horizons of mind. Always looking at limitless horizons of mind. Watching the procession of infinite and eternal being playing itself out in countless, myriad forms and formations. In essence and in substance, in sickness and in health, and there's no real parting in death. There is only eternal awareness. So be cool.

CHAPTER EIGHT

PSYCHIC DEVELOPMENT

(Zazen music plays in the background, and Rama speaks to the beat of the music.)

Psychic development. What lies on the other side of seeing? How can you know what someone thinks of you, when they're not there? How can you avoid the traps and pitfalls that others may set up for you, or see opportunities that might not present themselves to your physical mind and body? How do you develop your intuition, so that you can just know what's true and what isn't?

What is the border between the mental and the psychic? When are psychic impressions just imagination and not accurate information? Why are some people more psychic than others?

Psychic development—with Zen Master Rama.

We live in a world filled with automobiles, highways of the mind, urban disasters, billions of people living on a tiny planet, sharing the diminishing natural resources of the earth. Pollution—air pollution, noise pollution, psychic pollution—it's getting dark out there.

But it's always light in the inner worlds. In the inner-dimensional psychic planes, there is no pollution. There's endless, infinite, awareness.

Beyond mind, beyond time, beyond space, there's immortal awareness.

The universe is a giant mind. Some people have the ability to tap into that mind. We call them psychic. Others don't. We call them dull. But they have potential.

The unlimited mind, the *diamond mind* of the Buddha, is your mind, if you can get in touch with it, if you can figure out where it is and what to do with it, and stop thinking so much and tap into that psychic part of your being.

So sit back and relax for the next 45 minutes or so, and let's talk about psychic development. How you can escalate your level of awareness with patience, practice and a good sense of humor. What to expect, what to avoid. How to know what you don't know. Psychic development.

(Zazen music ends.)

There are two ways to come by money in this world. One is to inherit money. The other is to make it, to acquire it. If you inherit money, you can squander it and lose it. You can use it, or you can make more money. You can also start with no money and acquire money and get richer and richer, or you can acquire it and lose it. Once you know how to make money, even if you lose it, it's easy to do it again.

So in a world of psychic development, some people come by their psychic development through a kind of inheritance. It has to do with reincarnation, of course. In a prior lifetime, they developed their awareness field by the practice of psychic development exercises, meditation, zazen, things like that. And that state of mind, of course, stayed with them. They are that state of mind. They were born with these psychic sensitivities.

Everyone is psychic. You are psychic. Psychic is not a particular talent; it is an ability that we all have. Everybody has a left foot. Some people may just walk with that foot, some people may drag it, some may learn to dance with it. Everyone is innately psychic. It's a part of your mind.

What does it mean to be psychic? Essentially it means to feel, rather than to think all the time.

There are two general modes of perception. There are many, but there are two that we see most frequently in this world, and that's thinking and feeling.

Feeling, not in the sense of the senses—hot, cold, pleasant, unpleasant, pain, pleasure—but feeling in a more intuitive sense. Feeling love from someone, feeling anger from someone, that kind of feeling—a non-sensorial feeling having to do with the emotional body and the psychic body.

Thinking is analysis, perception, measurement, random association. It's a way of figuring something out. But to be honest, most decisions are not made through analysis.

As you well know, you may think and think and think about buying that new car, asking someone out on a date, trying a new career, working out and using that new play in a football game—but will you really do it? The ultimate point of decision is usually not rational analysis. To be honest, most people make their choices predicated upon a feeling because analysis really isn't that good a tool. Ultimately, we can do analysis of the stock market, but it's not going to tell us what the market's going to do tomorrow.

A lot of people make fine livings by forecasting through analysis, but unless it's a simple forecast based on logical deduction or induction upon, let's say, a company's performance, their net worth, likelihood of the current market—those things you can kind of analyze and make a projection for, or you can make an overall projection of the market due to consumer spending, certain signs and indicators—ultimately, [that] really doesn't mean a whole lot. Otherwise, everybody could simply figure out what the stock market is going to do and everybody would become wealthy. And that isn't the way the stock market or anything works.

Then there are those people who get a feeling and if they follow the feeling, they will usually succeed.

Now, there are all kinds of feelings, of course. You can get the wrong feeling. You go to Las Vegas and you get a feeling that number 21 black is going to come up on the roulette table, and it doesn't. In some cases, the odds are not with you and in some cases they are. Naturally, when you're playing at Vegas, the odds are heavily against you and you have to be pretty psychic or intuitive to win consistently. But in an even situation, a person who has developed a psychic sensibility will usually come out ahead, depending upon how sensitive they really are, how psychic they are.

The psychic perception, then, is a feeling, as opposed to a thinking. Not a feeling that's engendered through emotion necessarily. Emotion may accompany the feeling or may be associated with it. But it isn't really that kind of a feeling. It is not, let's say, feeling that we're lucky or feeling that we're happy because emotion will color psychic perception. It will interfere with it.

Psychic perception does not come through the thinking mind, nor does it come through the emotional body or emotional feelings.

It comes from the psychic plane of intuition, which is another stage of our mind. It's another avenue within mind and to reach into that avenue, a stillness has to be developed and cultivated because the impressions from the psychic plane, which is a plane of direct and immediate seeing or intuitive perception, are clouded over by emotions and thoughts and the general dullness and malaise that develops in our contemporary world through the lifestyle, population density, pollution and cultural and social conditioning that most individuals experience in the modern era.

It is very, very difficult to hear a radio station that might have wonderful music if there are two larger stations next to it on either side of it on the dial. They are blaring out music that you don't like. The signal can be lost in the disturbance.

So within you there is a continuous signal. A continuous perception is taking place deep within the mind. But it's hard to hear that signal because it is blurred over by your own thoughts, your desires, your fears. It is blurred over by your emotional swings. And as you live in this world, unless you live a very different type of life, you lose your sensitivity. You become dull.

Sensitivity can be regained by leading your life differently. People who are involved in psychic development, in Zen, in what I loosely call self-discovery, lead different types of lives. The lives they lead are not necessarily the lives of renunciation. You are not living up in the hills and trying to get away from everybody. It could be in the urban metro plane, with active careers and families and all that sort of stuff. Rather, it's a structuring of the elements of your life in a particular way, for a particular purpose—a structuring or restructuring, a continual restructuring of your mind that enables you to develop and cultivate the feelings that come from the psyche, hear them, act upon them, benefit from them.

Psychic perception is a much more efficient and accurate method of seeing and knowing reality.

You may suppose that there's someone outside your door. They haven't knocked. You could think, "Gee, there's somebody outside my door," but you don't know. You can't tell from within the house, unless you go over to the door and open it and see who's there. You can analyze and think, "Well gee, logically maybe someone will be arriving, maybe someone won't be arriving," but your analysis won't tell you anything until you have the observable fact. You may go and open the door, and there's somebody there whom you don't want to see, and by opening the door you now have to deal with them. If you are psychic, you can tell that they're coming. You'll know. You don't need physical information. And you can avoid that individual if you choose to.

If you're psychic, you can see into the minds of others, and you can use that opening to aid somebody. Sometimes someone's trying to tell you something and they don't even know what it is. If you're psychic you can perceive that, and know. Someone may love you and they can't show it. Someone may seek to harm you and they mask it.

If you are dependent upon your ability to deduce information logically through direct observation, through the senses, you can be fooled.

The car looks like a good car when you buy it. But then, after driving it from the dealers, it breaks down—nothing but problems. If you had been psychic, you would have been able to touch the car, look at it, feel it and know that it was a lemon, it was a turkey. You would know that the job that you're applying for is not the right job for you. It might look good, the offer might sound great, but in some way it's going to cause more problems. It's going to drop your energy level. It's not going to work out—the company is going to fold, the pressure on the job will cause you to be too stressful, whatever it is.

Being psychic does not necessarily mean seeing the future. Some people have visions of the future. They apprehend that something is going to take place. Great. But that really is not the larger part of being psychic. Being psychic doesn't necessarily mean seeing an event that has not yet occurred, per se.

It's rather seeing the inner nature of something. In other words, I don't want you to get involved with the world of psychic development so you can be another Nostradamus and forecast the future. You may have that ability. Great. But what good is that ability ultimately going to do you? It's not going to change anything.

You see that there's going to be an atomic war in 1999. Fantastic. Now that's not going to change anything. You might be able to move out of the path of the missiles. That might be of some use, yes. But it's not going to stop the war because if you see it and that's the future, then what can you do about it? It might be helpful a little bit, but by and large, you know and I know, if there's a massive atomic war, it's not going to matter where you are. Also, it's hard to do that, by the way.

Just read the predictions of psychics in your local, national, whatever it is, newspaper, and you'll realize that most of them don't do too well. They did an interesting study at a university. They had the freshmen class make the same number of predictions that some of the well-known psychics do every year, and they found that the freshmen class did better.

If you figure out all the predictions that most psychics make, you know once in a while they will hit one and you will hear about it, but they probably miss nine out of ten. That doesn't mean that it was random chance that they saw the one that came true. They really did see it. But what I'm saying is—it's very hard to perceive the future on a regular basis simply because the future changes.

There are probabilities and a person who is psychic is following a line of probability to see a probable future, and that probable future occasionally becomes the actual future. But it can change. They can see something that was a probable future, but another causal fact will interfere and that future won't happen. In other words, it's risky business.

Being psychic, then, does not really involve, by and large, seeing the future. In the popular mind, that's what the psychic is all about, but being psychic means rather simply seeing and perceiving things as they are. The car is a lemon, it's a dud, OK, and it's going to have all kinds of problems. You don't have to see the future to see those events occurring. The car is already a lemon, meaning it wasn't constructed properly. When you use your physical eyes and you look at the car, you can't see that because you are just seeing the shiny polished exterior. If you're psychic it means you're using another part of your mind to look at the car. You are not seeing its future. You are seeing right now. Right now, you can see that the welds weren't done properly. You can see that the valves aren't running well. You can see and therefore forecast that information, based upon the way things really are, that the car is definitely going to have problems. Therefore, you don't buy it.

So the psychic ability is really not so much to do with forecasting futures, but seeing things as they are now. Seeing beyond the surface—that's psychic.

There are all kinds of psychic arts. Healing, OK, and da-da-da-da-da-da. You know, it goes on and on.

But today we're looking specifically at how to develop the ability to see things as they really are. This is a very handy ability to have. There are plateaus of awareness, planes of consciousness, worlds. There is the physical world that we live in, which we perceive through the senses, but there are other worlds.

Right in front of you there are other worlds right now. Most people can't see them. Those worlds are as real, if you will, as the physical world that you normally perceive with your day-to-day awareness.

There are occult worlds, psychic worlds. All kinds. We have different names for them.

The psychic world, or psychic plane, is a dimension. It is a dimensional plane that you can gain access to, and it's a dimension of feeling and clear seeing. As I indicated before, the hindrances to being psychic are a general dullness that develops from living in the material world—and being a material girl—or one's own thoughts and emotions that are uncontrolled.

The way to change that—and develop your psychic ability—is by learning to create a shield between yourself and the sensorial and vibratory bombardment that we experience in our modern world, and also to be able to create a sense of discipline, togetherness, energy and power—a precision within the mind; control of the emotions.

By control of the emotions, I simply mean not letting your moods take you wherever they will, but rather a sense of being the helmsman. You are directing your ship. The winds may be blowing south, east, north, or west. But you are directing the ship. You are not just letting those winds blow you wherever they will. You are directing your sails and your rudder so that you don't capsize; you don't just get blown all over. You get where you're going. Most people don't do this. The winds of life blow them where they will.

Psychic development, in other words, is not a fanatical, freaky study which has to do with just predicting the future and talking to UFOs and being able to find out curious facts that are basically irrelevant to one's time in life. That may be the popular view of psychic development. I'm suggesting this certainly isn't the Zen view. It is not the view of advanced self-discovery.

Psychic development is a very important and necessary skill in leading a successful and happy life because your intellectual processes, inductive and deductive logic and other forms of logical analysis, and your senses—seeing, feeling, tasting, touching and smelling—don't give you enough information to be able to tell the real from the unreal—the "what's going on?" with your day-to-day life.

If you knew that a friend of yours had cancer, you can advise them to go to the doctor. There may not yet be a visible sign. Maybe they'll have a check-up, the doctor will find it. If you waited for a visible sign, it might be too late.

If you knew that there are those around you who are engaged in psychic manipulation, using the power of mind to invade your mental privacy, to drain your energy, to interfere with your life, to cause you not to succeed—if you're psychic, you can perceive that, and you see that the smiling faces aren't smiling at all, inside. And you can eliminate those individuals from your life and cancel their effect.

If you're psychic, you'll know that there's a certain area that you can move to, in a city, in a country, on the earth, that will empower you, and there are certain areas that can drain. You can see those differences. You can feel them.

If you are psychic, you will know the proper career to follow that will empower you. You will know, or be drawn to, people whom you will benefit from and whom you will benefit.

If you're psychic, you will become much more aware of the beauty of life.

Psychic perception doesn't simply mean seeing something always in a de facto, this-is-how-it-is sense. If you're psychic, when you look at a rose, you will see and feel the essence of the rose in a way that a person who simply looks at it with their eyes and touches it with their fingers will never know.

Most people are blind. Just as the blind person can't see a rose, they can only touch it, and you can see all its wondrous colors and formations—so the psychic person lives in a world of blind people.

That is really how it appears.

There are all these people running all over the planet, totally deluded beings, who don't "see" what life is for, what their own lives are about, because they don't see psychically. Therefore, they miss most of the beauty of life.

The psychic awareness lends a true perception not only of events—whether the car is a good one or not, whether the job is good or not, what the person thinks of you—but just of life itself. It is its own raison d'etre.

In other words, you can just see the beauty of everything, which is really there, but most people miss it because they're so clouded by their thoughts and emotions and their conditioning.

They get you when you're young. It's true. When you're young, when you're a kid, you are conditioned. You are taught language, customs, right and wrong. You are filled with fears. You are taught to appreciate certain things, to avoid other things. And this conditioning, this mental conditioning, interferes with your psychic perception. If, instead, you were taught how to develop your psyche, you would come to know the things you should avoid by feeling them, and the things that you should be drawn to.

The teaching that we receive is not necessarily very accurate. By that I mean the value systems that our cultures have developed are not very open. They are very restrictive. We live in an age that is not enlightened. Crime rate, wars and so on, indicate that this species on this planet is not very enlightened. So there are all kinds of practical advantages to developing your psychic perceptions. And then there are some that aren't practical, in the sense of day-to-day success, but rather they're more personal.

When you live in the psychic state of mind, you're happy. You don't have to do anything. Think of it this way. Right now, you're on the earth. Let's say there's a lot of cloud cover, it's not sunny, it's gray, you're depressed. The clouds may come in for a long time. But if you get in an airplane and you zip above the clouds, everything is sunny and wonderful. Unrestricted visibility. The clouds are the desires and thought forms and conditioning, the dullness that develops by leading the type of life that most people here lead. They live in these clouds all the time. Beyond the clouds, there is a psychic dimension, and when you go beyond the clouds it's always sunny. It is always beautiful.

Life is always beautiful, but we don't see it when we enter into lower states of mind that are, in effect, cloudy. Our perceptions aren't clear, or let us say, not accurate.

How do you develop your psychic abilities? Well, to begin with, naturally, you have to want to and believe that it's possible. Now, I assume that you want to and believe it's possible, otherwise you would not have acquired this tape. So you fulfilled the first two requirements.

As I suggested, there are really just two steps, or perhaps three, in psychic development.

- One is building a shield between yourself and the descriptions of the world that everyone else has.
- Second is a continual reordering of the mind and the mental structures along with the ability to think in prescribed ways, to analyze in prescribed ways and to stop thought for periods of time.
- The third really has to do with gaining control of the emotions. Again, being the helmsperson and not being blown all around by the winds of emotion. While there will be the winds of emotion—they won't go away—you can navigate or even use them to expedite your journey to get you where you want to go.

So let's consider these three conditions, and they're all obviously completely interrelated.

First and foremost, it's important to build a shield between yourself and the world. The way you do this is by allowing yourself a kind of a buffer or cushion in which to grow. If we have a little tiny plant and we want it to develop, we put it in a greenhouse. There the little plant will perk along and grow and be real happy. If we were to put it outside in a windy world with harsh elements, the little plant might not develop. It might croak. It might die. Eventually the plant will become really strong, and then maybe we can transplant it outdoors.

There's something very fragile about the beginning stages of psychic development. Eventually, one becomes very strong, and the cushioning isn't as necessary. It is still logical because we live in an abrasive world. We don't live forever. We have limited personal power. We have limited energy. We have a limited life.

And you can't use your energy for all things. You have to determine those things that you direct your energy towards, otherwise you get yourself in too many places and nothing succeeds.

Life wears us down. We all die here.

Depending upon the way you expose yourself to energies and powers and forces, both physical and non-physical in this world, you will determine whether you have a lot of energy or you lose energy. Some places drain you. Some people drain you. Some enhance you. Some situations will empower you. Some will take your power away.

It is necessary, rather than just kind of arbitrarily bouncing around in the world and letting whatever happen may, to start to pick and choose among the numerous opportunities that life affords you.

The overall purpose, which is kind of understood, is that you wish to develop your psychic ability. With that as a forethought it will now be easier for you to make choices because that will be the point of decision. Will this job hinder my psychic development or help it? Not simply, is it a pleasant job? Does it give me immediate satisfaction? Will this relationship hinder or help my psychic development? Will this practice? Will this pleasure? Whatever it is. That is the cutting edge that you use in psychic development.

Naturally, you practice psychic development when you make that analysis because you have to feel, since things are not always apparent, whether it will or not.

Just that is the practice, you see?

Doing that every day, with every situation, not in a real intellectual way, not sweating over it, worrying—that will only drain your power and energy—but just feeling from moment to moment what you should do, and doing it.

Again, this feeling is the sensitivity that you will develop in time, and I think it's always wise, particularly in the beginning, to balance your new intuitive and psychic understandings with good old common sense. The two should not be different. A good psychic perception follows your common sense. So I wouldn't launch on your career of psychic perception and start to make a lot of random choices based upon your new-found psychic abilities, without first subjecting them to the analysis of common sense. Some day you might become very, very psychic and very sensitive, and you don't have to bother. But in the beginning, common sense should, in a very premeditated way, arbitrate your psychic perceptions.

Suddenly you have a psychic perception to quit your job and move to India. That might not be a psychic perception. You might be getting carried away. It might be a faulty perception. Then common sense says, you don't have enough money, you need the job, you don't know what India is like, and so you decide not to do it. This might be smart. If your psychic seeing was very developed and you practiced it for years and found that, through a trial and error process, you could now determine what is a psychic intuition and what is psychic garbage, then sure, if you get the feeling, do it. But I suggest caution, because you can't tell.

Don't listen to voices, don't listen to voices!

If you hear voices talking to you, forget it. Disregard the information, even if it's right occasionally. You are dealing with non-physical forces that are trying to influence you, that come from outside of yourself, and who knows what they will have to say and why.

For the same reason, I suggest that you do not get involved in what I would call *channeling*, tapping into spirits that are not physically present and all this stuff. Your own psyche, your own mind, has the ability to properly reflect and determine through feeling what is correct and what is not.

You don't need anybody to tell you what's right or wrong. What you do need, perhaps, is someone to show you how to come to those understandings, which come from meditating, learning to be more aware, overcoming mental conditioning and cultural conditioning, learning how to do systems analysis of your energy and these sorts of things—the arts of Zen and self-discovery —which will enable you to unfold that psychic ability.

Again, from my point of view, the psychic does not have much to do with channeling, spirits and things like this. All you're doing is getting information from a source which may or may not be accurate and which may or may not have underlying motives for your harm or perhaps for your good will. But it seems to me, when you can do something yourself, it's better to do it yourself.

In the psychic process, we're not trying to bring others through our minds.

We are trying to eliminate everyone else from our minds—their effects, their energies and their influences. We are going to do a house cleaning and get everybody out of the house, so we're there by ourselves, so we can see what's what and feel what's what, without influence of others. "To thine own self be true and it must follow, as the night the day, thou canst be false to any man." Shakespeare—he knew.

It is necessary to come to a sense of inner truth, and no one can do this for you. I can't do it for you, your friends, your family, spirits, forces. We like to pass the buck and have somebody else take responsibility, but that doesn't solve the problem.

You need to develop your psychic ability so that you can tell what's what, what's real, what's not, what's helpful and what's harmful. It is a fun process, actually.

Going to a psychic isn't necessarily going to help you. It might. Again, there are people with psychic abilities, and you might be in a jam and your mind is very confused and you can't see what's what. That person might give you a helpful insight, but then again, they might not. If you get a good psychic, you'll get a good insight. Still, that will only help you for the moment. Tomorrow you will need another insight, and you don't want to become addicted to using a psychic. You want to become a psychic yourself.

That is why I suggest that you take the time and devote the energy to developing your own mind, and then you will be able to do whatever you need to do. That's the way of Zen. The way of Zen is to become independent and strong, and not to rely on others for our own perceptions of our life or truth, but to do it individually. And to go to a teacher of Zen to learn how to do that, not to get answers for individual life situations, but rather to learn how we do that. Then, once you can do it, you're all set. You are on your own and you go lead your life, whereas, in some traditions, there seems to be a sense of reliance on someone else.

Zen is very closely allied with Emersonian self-reliance in that sense. Anyone who practices Zen for some time, if they practice it properly, will gradually develop their psychic sensibilities. Some people may develop those sensibilities more, some less—it depends on many different factors. But anyone who meditates for a period of time will gradually become more sensitized to all of life.

It is important, then, to build that buffer around yourself. You need to start to think about your life and the way you lead it. Ask yourself, "Does your household create a feeling of beauty and sensitivity?" [Does it give you] what you need? You are trying to become sensitive. If it doesn't, redecorate it, move to another location.

Do the people you associate with engender that sensitivity? Are they harsh and abrasive and generally unaware? Start to associate with people who are more aware. Meet them. Take a yoga class, study different forms of self-discovery, whatever. You will meet people who are drawn to those things. Some people are crazy and fanatical—avoid them. They won't help. But people who are more balanced and calm and introspective, associating with them will raise your energy level.

Physical disciplines are very helpful—studying martial arts, dance, running and things like that. As you gain more discipline over your body, you will find that a corollary discipline will develop in the mind because the two really go together. Those of you who are already adept at some disciplines of the body will find that the study of Zen and meditation will give you much more control than you now have. You will be able to take your art to higher levels.

Naturally, the practice of zazen meditation is paramount to this development of the psyche and the restructuring of one's energy [as well as] doing an energy analysis—topics which are endlessly involved in fun, and which I certainly can't go through entirely here. I've developed tapes on those subjects.

Meditating everyday is essential. If you meditate every day and learn to control and stop your thoughts, you'll become psychic. It's that simple.

If you start to give more thought to the world around you and stop exposing yourself to situations which drain your energy, and instead do things for yourself that make you feel better—make your body feel better and your mind feel better—you will discover through a trial and error process that you will have more energy.

Then you need to begin the third part. You are meditating every day now. You are looking at things and not just doing them, but you're asking yourself, "Is this beneficial? Is this helpful to my sensitivity and my awareness, or am I just wearing myself out?" Great.

Then you have to learn to control your emotions, to be able to glide through them. Again, meditation will help you here and particularly concentration exercises. By practicing concentration exercises and meditation, zazen, you will find that you will gain the ability, when strong emotions strike, to not be swayed by them.

If suddenly you get depressed, it doesn't have to throw you or change your course of action. You won't necessarily give up. You can push those emotions aside eventually, or you can cultivate happy emotions or become emotionless at times when you need to be very, very sensitive. You need to develop a quiet mind and a happy life. You need to shield yourself from the bombardment of the world at some times. And then, at other times, you go right out in the middle of it and have a great time with it and be unaffected by it, in the same way that you learned to be unaffected by emotions.

You don't want to become so sensitive that you can't interact with people in the world. If you get to that point, you are not practicing psychic development. You are running away from the world, and you've made yourself weak.

Psychic development makes you strong.

It develops a common sense attitude in which you don't expose yourself to forces and people and situations that would drain you, not because you're afraid, but because you're smart. Why waste your time being around people who drag you down? You don't live forever, at least in this life.

So practice meditation, concentration exercises, and begin to think more about regaining your sensitivity by avoiding draining situations. Not because of fear but because of intelligence.

Try to be still inside. Learn to quiet and stop thought, and you will find that you will be able to develop your mind. Your psychic intuition will start to come about, and [you should] practice it. In every situation, feel before acting, just for a second.

Look for a feeling, and you'll learn through a trial and error process when it worked and when it didn't.

You will feel it's a good car and you'll buy it, and it won't be. Then you know that that wasn't the right feeling. You will feel that this could be a good person to know and it will work out well, and that was the right feeling. Eventually you'll learn to isolate that feeling, through practice. That is how you become psychic—through practice.

(Zazen music begins.)

Music is largely psychic. It's a feeling. It is not logical. It's a feeling. Art, life, why we live—feelings.

As you evolve and develop your psychic abilities, you will enter into perceptions of life, truth, beauty, and you will gain a power—a power to live your life in an intelligent, perceptive and strong way.

You will gain the competitive edge in daily life.

So this is Zen Master Rama, encouraging you to develop your psyche, to become more aware, to become more sensitive to life, to become strong. And to figure out whether that's a good car to buy or not, whether that's a good gal or guy to be with or not, and to open up the higher dimensional planes so you can penetrate the mysteries of existence and enjoy the wonder of being—the wonder of being—you!

The wonder of being you. Have fun with it.

CHAPTER NINE

ZEN: CONCENTRATION AND MEDITATION

Hi there! This is Zen Master Rama. (Zazen music plays in the background.) For the next 45 minutes, I'll be talking with you about concentration and meditation—zazen.

There is a wonderful continuity to life, isn't there? Continuity comes in different forms. There is the continuity of being—a sense of self, awareness of this world, of your life, the elements in your life, things that you think and feel, things that you desire and want to have or to experience, things that you'd like to avoid, unpleasant things—pain, frustration, depression. The continuous awareness of self, a sense of yourself continuing in time and space, is continuity—continuity of awareness.

One of the funny things about awareness, within that framework, is that it never assumes it will end. And in a way it does, and in a way it doesn't. When we're alive, we never picture ourselves dying, yet someday each of us dies. Someday in a room somewhere, perhaps a hospital room, in an automobile, perhaps outdoors, you will leave this world. You won't be here anymore and everything that you've known will fade from your view, and it will happen at the darndest time. You will be quite convinced that it couldn't be happening then, and yet you'll be powerless to stop it. Then another kind of continuity occurs, and that's the continuity that is beyond death.

Death is a doorway, but it's a very small, thin doorway, and only a portion of our being can walk through that doorway. The rest stays behind and is lost or transformed into something else. At the time of death, we walk through a doorway and our spirit, which is very thin, slides through into another world, another existence, another experience.

But for now, we are here. We are in this world. And in this world, there are limitations—and no one likes to be limited. We all want freedom. We all want to be limitless. Limitations exist in the mind. Freedom exists in the mind. Heaven exists in the mind. Hell exists in the mind. There are objective circumstances and situations. You can be in jail. You can be free. You can live in a country with restrictions on travel. You can live in a country where they don't restrict your travel.

But happiness, awareness, consciousness has little or nothing to do with physical restrictions.

There are ten thousand states of mind, ten thousand planes of awareness. Most people spend their entire lives confined to a few of these states of mind. Let's imagine them in a scale going from the left to the right. Let's say that number one is all the way over on the left, and let's say that number ten thousand is way over on the right. Number one is very dark; it has almost no light in it at all; it's hard to distinguish it from complete darkness. Number ten thousand is bright light. It is hard to distinguish it from light, yet there's a subtle difference. And there are gradations in between—9,999 to be exact.

Now naturally, since there are ten thousand, there's something more, beyond ten thousand. But the ten thousand states of mind are the place, the arena of experience, where you spend your time and your life.

Most human beings only experience a few of these states, and most of them are fairly far down in ranking, down around 100.

Each state of mind is not simply a mood—moods will exist within the state of mind. But it's a way of seeing life and experiencing it, a way of knowing.

And you are your state of mind. Your state of mind creates your view, or your window, on life.

You may live in Beverly Hills, in a beautiful house with a beautiful car, with a beautiful wife. You may live in a tenement in East Harlem, alone, in poverty. But your house has a window, and it looks out on something. It may look out on your swimming pool with the kids playing in it. It may look out [on] a gang down the street who are selling drugs to passersby.

You have a window, and that window, which is your state of mind, will determine everything that happens to you—because it affords you a view on life.

Opportunities, creative ideas or the lack of them—happiness, frustration, brilliance, talent, success and failure—all of these things are determined by the state of mind that you're in.

You are the experiencer of states of mind. Yet your state of mind dominates your awareness to such an extent that you can't conceive of any other state of mind other than the state of mind that you're in. They're just mere words.

Concentration and meditation are practices that enable you to alter your state of mind.

Within a state of mind, the state of mind you're in now, there are different possibilities. There's a higher end to the state of mind and a lower end. The higher end—let's call it the right side of that state of mind, which leads or borders the next state of mind that has a better view—has more light in it. The lower end has less light.

If you spend enough time at the lower end of a state of mind and if you lose enough energy, you can drop to the next state of mind down. You might drop from 100 down to 99. If you spend enough time on the right hand side and you accumulate power and energy, you can kick

ZEN: CONCENTRATION AND MEDITATION

up—maybe to 101.

When you change a state of mind, your whole life changes. Nothing remains the same. Nothing looks the same because you have changed.

You yourself are a continuous awareness, but you don't really have a formation.

In other words, we grow accustomed to thinking of ourselves as a personality with a history—I've been here and there, I've done this, I like this, I don't like that. All of these ideas that we have about self are an accumulation or an aggregate within a state of mind, and they chain us to a state of mind, to these ideas.

Zen is about breaking out of your ideas and experiencing life and not ideas.

For example, when most people see a tree, they don't see a tree at all. What they see is an idea that they have developed throughout the course of their life of what a tree is. Only when they were very, very young did they see a tree. Only at that time were they at all aware of what a tree looked like, or perhaps it would be more precise to say what the tree felt like. Other than that, they have no idea of what a tree is. As they grow older and they accumulate more ideas and experiences around "tree" through associations with trees, experiences with trees, they no longer see what a tree is, or feel it. Instead, they have a much more limited view of what a tree is. They have an idea. This is true not just of trees, but of squirrels (Rama laughs) that live in trees, people, dogs, cats, jobs, the world, philosophies, everything.

The more ideas you have, the less you feel and see life directly.

Zen—which means meditation, stopping thought—is about going beyond ideas to direct and immediate experiences. Inherent in this is a sense that there's much more to life. There is much more than the state of mind you're in. There are 9,999 other states of mind. And beyond that, there's something entirely different that is impossible to put in words, which we call *nirvana* —which is just a word to suggest that there's something else that's wonderful and amazing and fantastic that lies beyond the ten thousand states of mind.

A person who undertakes the study of Zen and learns concentration and meditation is like a gymnast. Most people can do limited things with their bodies. The gymnast can do a lot more. You become a gymnast of the mind.

Very few people have any idea of what life is about, of what their minds can do, of the forces that affect them throughout the course of their life that cause success, failure, pleasure, pain, and awareness.

In the study of Zen, through the practice of concentration and meditation, you will expand your awareness to gain knowledge and power and illumination.

You may just gain a little more knowledge, power, and illumination if you only practice Zen a little bit.

If you practice Zen deeply, in a very, very in-depth way, then you will discover that you are limitless being, and you may attain what we call enlightenment, which means moving beyond but not excluding the ten thousand states of mind.

Enlightenment is the ability to freely transact within the ten thousand states of mind without a continuous self or awareness, without the limitations that are normally imposed by conceptual mind.

There is no way to explain enlightenment. It's just a word to indicate something beyond, not just a little bit beyond, but something very, very far beyond the normal human condition—a state of knowledge, quiescent beingness.

Meditation, then, and concentration are practices that enable you to become more conscious and to utilize the moments in your life completely. Concentration and meditation are also taught in other forms of self-discovery, in yoga and in other practices.

Zen differs from many other practices in that its emphasis is almost exclusively on concentration and meditation in two forms.

One is zazen, which is the practice of direct concentration and meditation, where for a period of time you are not active physically, and you sit down to practice concentration and meditation exercises.

[Two is] mindfulness, which is a practice that an individual engages in at all other times, which is an advanced usage of the mind in a variety of different ways—to increase the power of the mind, to develop it fully, and to employ that development in direct physical, mental and psychic ways.

In other words, when you practice mindfulness, you're able to accomplish basically anything you might like to within the parameters of your capabilities. But you realize those capabilities.

Most people are unhappy—let's face it.

The reason they're not happy is not because they're good or bad, but they're in states of mind that are limited. In those states of mind, happiness is fleeting. Let's say there's a country that's filled with volcanoes and doesn't have any grass or pastures. If you're in that country, all you're going to experience are the volcanoes. There is just not going to be any grass or pastures. It is not that the country is good or bad—that's just how it is.

Most human beings are in very limited states of mind. The states of mind they're in are not good or bad, but they have volcanoes. They are filled with unhappiness, desires, frustrations, jealousies, angers, lack of clarity, lack of awareness overall.

Some people climb a little bit higher up on the scale of consciousness and they seem to know more, feel more and experience more, and perhaps they are more successful. We say that such a person is deeper or more aware, more dynamic, charismatic. There are different formations of this. Sometimes it takes an intellectual tack, sometimes a spiritual tack, sometimes an artistic tack, maybe a physical tack. It depends. It varies. There is no way it has to be.

These individuals have learned something. They may have just stumbled upon it, or they may have studied a type of self-discovery that gave them the knowledge to be more successful and more profoundly aware, to be happier.

Whatever they did, whether it was accidental or intentional, allowed them to stumble upon some higher states of mind. Yet very few of those persons could teach you how to do what they've done. They could give you a general prescription, "Well, I bought stock at this price and it rose suddenly to that price, and then I sold it and then I leveraged some real estate." Or they might say, "Well gosh, I sat down and I meditated for two hours a day every day, and after a while my awareness field changed."

In other words, they could explain what they did in physical terms, but you have to be in the state of mind that they were in to experience what they experienced. You might employ the same prescription, and it might not generate the same results because you're not in the same state of mind that they were in.

A Zen master is an individual who is an instructor, specifically of the subject of awareness.

And if the Zen master is enlightened, that means that they have the power and the knowledge to teach an individual who wishes it and who's serious about the study how to range through the ten thousand states of mind. Their ability is not simply to share their own experiences or to give a general prescription, but rather they are experts, not only at experiencing the ten thousand states of mind but also, since they are teachers, they are aware of how to express, or bring about, or transmit, that information to others.

I used to be a university professor. Before that, I was a graduate student and a college student. Naturally, after many years in academia, you learn that a lot of the professors in universities are wonderful scholars. The reason they are professors is because they have Ph.D.'s, and they've written great papers and books. But they are terrible teachers. Their talent is scholarship.

Teaching, on the other hand, does not involve necessarily writing papers. It involves transmitting information and sometimes enthusiasm, methods of analysis and so on to another individual. It is a particular talent that an individual has. Such a person should be a teacher. They are good at transmitting something. Then there are people who can learn something and experience it. You might be a great real estate developer, but maybe you couldn't teach anybody else how to do it. It comes naturally to you.

There is a difference between knowing something and being able to teach it. Of course, there are people who are great teachers. They have that ability to communicate and transmit something. They can understand it and then look into another person's mind and see what that person needs to do to come to an understanding of the material. But a teacher may not be conversant in very many subjects. In other words, the combination of the ability to teach and scholarship is rare. That's why great teachers are always few and far between.

On the subject of Zen and meditation, a particular demand is placed upon the teacher. The teacher has to be first and foremost a scholar, in that it's really impossible to teach Zen, to teach about mind and the ten thousand states of mind and what lies beyond them unless one has directly experienced these things. Naturally, the laboratory is one's own life and one's own mind.

An individual who teaches Zen, if they teach the advanced formations as well as the introductory formations of Zen, is someone who must have personally experienced—through years and years of meditation, concentration, practice and engaging in dialectical situations of mind—varying states of awareness. And not just a few—if they've experienced a few, they can teach a few, and that may be more than someone they're teaching knows or has.

But someone we call a Zen master is someone who is conversant, not just with a little bit of mind, a little bit more than most of humanity, but someone who is an expert in mind.

Also, in the study of the ways of mind, powers develop. A true master, a Zen master, a Tibetan lama, an Indian sadhu—if they're a real teacher and not just someone who's looking for a following—has developed, in their intensive inner practices and studies, certain powers. These powers, which are sometimes of the miraculous nature [and] sometimes of the nature of transmission of attention, are used strictly to enable the student to progress.

We hear wonderful stories about some masters who can walk on water and do all kinds of great things—do healings, things like that. These are true powers that can come from a person who engages in the study of mind. But the major power that a real teacher has is not the ability to do things like walk on water or heal. Those are interesting talents, and they're useful sometimes.

But the real power that a teacher of mind develops is the ability to transmit power and knowledge directly to an individual. Because in the teaching of the ten thousand states of mind, particularly as one advances further—not so much in just learning basic concentration and meditation, basic zazen, but after a person has done that and they progress further—the teaching is done through transmission. This is where we differ from teaching algebra or calculus or English. Those things are taught through verbal instruction.

The majority of the ten thousand states of mind cannot be discussed.

It is rather a question of teaching a person to step outside of the conceptual framework they have, showing them how to do a systems analysis continually of more progressive ways of their energy balance, so that more energy is coming into their lives than out of it, and transmitting directly blocks of attention or awareness to an individual psychically. In other words, once you've gotten your first-degree black belt as a student, which is just a beginning from the point of view of the master, or maybe the seventh-degree black belt, then at that point the instruction changes. Now it's not so much basic moves but advanced fighting.

Initially, when I teach a person to concentrate and meditate, I focus upon basic exercises that will cause a person to strengthen their mind terrifically, develop new talents and abilities, become much more successful and independent, overcome a lot of their fears and frustrations and gain control of their time, mind and life. But once a person has done that, if they do that, if they work on it—and it happens if you work on it–it will take varying lengths of time for an individual to accomplish this, according to the intensity of their practice and their own natural inclinations and abilities, the level of mind they start in.

Once a person has reached a certain level of proficiency, then the teaching changes. In the teaching of concentration and meditation, the focus is more upon a transfer of awareness, where you will now give advanced lessons. Those lessons don't take place here. They take place in advanced states of mind.

So a teacher will alter the balance of power by actually lifting a person into other states of mind, and then, in those states of mind, the teaching will take place in non-verbal ways through direct experience. Again, these are the mysterious ways of knowledge and power and enlightenment that I can only allude to in words. I can't possibly explain what this process is like. The only way to find out what this process is like is to advance to the stage of mental control that a person obtains after a number of years of practicing the basic disciplines.

The basic disciplines of concentration and meditation bring about immediate and wonderful results. But what I'm suggesting is that there's something beyond that. And that's when a person really begins to explore altered attention and awareness. That is when the most profound experiences of mind start.

That teaching process is lengthy because there are many, many states of mind to go through. And in each state of mind, there is a different aggregate of self to explore.

Eventually, after you've led a student through all of the ten thousand states of mind, then the trickiest part of the study comes along, and that's moving from that knowledge and that level of fluidity and awareness to enlightenment itself—which is something very different than the knowledge of the ten thousand states of mind.

That's an overall glimpse of the study. In other words, we have our elementary school, our high school, our master's program and our doctoral program. Some people just go on through the college program. They don't go into the graduate school program, but they become teachers of Zen. And they are able to teach quite a bit. They are not enlightened themselves, but compared to your average human being, they have a tremendous, tremendous degree of knowledge. It is like learning to fight and you've been in a couple of fights, but suddenly you're studying with a third-degree black belt who, with one movement, can have you on your back. But the third-degree black belt is in no way near the level of knowledge of the seventh-degree black belt.

There is a certain point that you reach where the distance between the belts is much further. Some go through graduate school and they become teachers of very advanced states of mind. Some become enlightened. Those are the individuals who can teach individuals how to be enlightened.

Concentration and meditation is a practice in which you learn how to use your mind in ways that are foreign to most human beings.

Most human beings have almost no mental control at all. Concentration and meditation are not taught in schools. In schools, we're taught subjects—how to read, how to write, things like that. But we're not taught about mind, states of mind, and how to use mind in a variety of different ways.

The study of mind is the study of life because all of life obviously interacts with mind. We can't dismiss aspects of our life, our careers, our relationships, our loves, our hates—all of these things are bound into the study of mind. The study of mind is the study of life itself. The study of concentration and meditation is not simply the study of exercises and focusing. It is that, but to truly engage in the study, you engage actively in every aspect of your life. And, of course, a revolution occurs in your being.

The average person who studies martial arts, even after a year or two, becomes amazingly proficient in self-defense. Were they to run into the common neighborhood bully who is capable of beating up most people on the block, they could drop him with one kick—because the bully's knowledge is simplistic. It may seem impressive, if you're just a kid on the block, because he's been in 50 fights, and you've only been in one or two. But after a couple years of martial arts, where you have studied the discipline of fighting and learned from an advanced master who learned from an advanced master and so on, you're studying such a high-tech form of self-defense that the bully, with all of his knowledge and all of his battle experience, will have no idea what you're doing when suddenly, that foot connects with his head and he's on the ground—and it's all over.

In the study of mind, you are engaging in a very high-tech study, the ultimate high-tech study, and that's the study of being. Even after a year or two of intensive study—let alone five or six years, or a lifetime, many lifetimes—you will possess a knowledge and power of mind that far dwarfs most human beings. Your ability to use mind in whatever way you choose is outrageous. Again, a lot will depend upon how intensely you approach the study and the state of mind in which you begin, and so on.

There are factors that influence progress. There are no guarantees, except that if you do it, your mind gets stronger. The high range powers and high range experiences come later.

Oh, if you study with an enlightened Zen master, then it is possible to have high range experiences from the beginning, not because of your ability or your state of mind, but because the master is capable of generating, even in the novice, very powerful experiences through the transmission of awareness and mind. In other words, his power is sufficient to boost you up and give you experiences that you would not have yet on your own. The purpose of these experiences is to rapidly progress you through the states of mind and encourage you to work harder. It is another window. You are afforded a window.

You visit a wealthy person's home and look out the window and you see what it's like there, and that might inspire you to work harder—if you want a window like that of your own. Whereas if you've never seen such a thing, you don't know it exists, you might not try.

That is why some teachers perform miracles. "Unless they've seen, they will not believe," they say in one book. The idea is that some people need proof.

I once went to a demonstration. This guy was opening a karate school. He had all kinds of medals and pictures of himself fighting and things like that. He was trying to get some students because he wanted to teach them the art. What he did, the way he was trying to get the point across was, he simply took a few concrete blocks and split them with his hand. Everybody quickly got the idea that there was something to all this karate stuff. In the same sense, sometimes the Zen master, or a teacher from another tradition, will perform miracles. Not just to delight and amuse people, but specifically to raise their awareness as a way of grabbing their attention and showing them that this miraculous occurrence—which is not the point—indicates that there is something more.

The study of mind generates a variety of different experiences, most of which are beyond the perceptual range of the average human being. Things that are impossible, that skeptics say are impossible, are everyday experiences when you live in advanced states of mind. You live in a world of constant miraculous awareness, only because you've learned to use your mind. The skeptics who say it can't be done are simply in extremely limited states of mind, in which they can't even perceive the possibility of anybody doing anything that they can't do.

The real miracle is mind itself. Your mind. And your mind is capable of incredible things. But it is through the practice of concentration and meditation-zazen—and mindfulness, that you are able to accomplish so much, to succeed at what you would choose to succeed at, to be what you would like to be—to become aware that there are things that you can be that you're not even conscious of yet.

In short, the practice of Zen enables you to use your mind in an extremely effective and precise way. It allows you to succeed at whatever you would like to—within the parameters of possible success, owing to circumstance, and whether it's material success or psychic or spiritual success, or whatever. You can do it when you have mind at your disposal.

So, how do you meditate?

Well, the best way to really learn how to meditate is to go and study with a teacher. If you see a teacher on a regular basis, the same way you would see a martial arts teacher on a regular basis or a teacher of computer science or philosophy or English, or whatever it is—if you attend class on a regular basis and you practice what the teacher shows you, you'll learn, naturally.

But for starting on your own, I have a simple program that I would suggest you follow. I would like to outline it for you in the next five or so minutes, maybe ten minutes. If you practice this program, if you don't have a teacher, it will enable you to make very steady progress in meditation and concentration.

Then, someday, perhaps you'll meet a teacher for more advanced instruction—not simply someone who can repeat the things that I'm telling you, but someone who has the ability to transmit experiences and awareness, a master of mind.

The following are my suggestions for the practice. These are not to be taken in an absolute form as the only way to concentrate and meditate. This is just a simple approach. It will produce powerful results when properly employed. But this is not to be construed as a complete course in how to meditate. I can't teach that over a tape. That is something that I do in person, which is why I do seminars.

There are other methods of meditation, and you shouldn't be afraid to try them. In this business, it's not that there is a best way—it's whatever way works best for you. This is a simple program, but you should feel free to alter it in any way that you choose that you find beneficial. You don't have to be stuck with it, but it works very well.

If you are new to meditation, I would suggest that you meditate, to begin with, once a day for 15 minutes, then, eventually twice a day for 15 minutes. Once you're comfortable with that, I would increase your time to half an hour twice a day, then 45 minutes twice a day, then an hour twice a day. Once you have reached an hour twice a day, it's not really necessary at that point to add more time to the practice of concentration and meditation. Rather, at that point, you should increase the proficiency of the two hours a day. You should spend your two hours a day, an hour in the morning and an hour in the evening, with less and less thought. Don't increase the time at that point—increase the power of the two hours.

If you're a beginner, perhaps for the first few weeks or a month or two, practice 15 minutes once a day. After a month or two, add a second session. After another month or two, maybe after around four months or six months—or you may just find that you want to do it sooner—increase your time to half an hour twice a day. Then, after perhaps nine months or a year, increase the time to 45 minutes twice a day, and after about two years, increase the time to an hour twice a day. The time is not the key element. The key element is what you do during the time.

I wouldn't jump to an hour twice a day to start with, because you'll be wasting your time—because you will not be able to sustain high levels of awareness for that period of time.

It is better to meditate for a short period of time intensely and go do something else with that extra time, than to sit there and space out and just think you're meditating and concentrating. Very few people are capable of an intensive level of concentration and meditation for very long periods of time. You develop that ability the same way that you develop muscles, by working out. In the beginning, you can only do a few push-ups, maybe one or two, then five, then ten, then 50, then 100. So your mental agility and power will develop through practice. That's a simple training schedule for you.

Of course, the next question is what to do when you're sitting there practicing concentration and meditation.

A few general suggestions—wear comfortable clothing, nothing that restricts you or makes you feel uncomfortable. Try to always be physically clean. If you can, take a shower beforehand—it helps—or wash your hands and face. If that's not possible, you can still do a fine meditation, but these things are helpful.

Most people find it helpful, if they meditate at home, to find an area of the house where they meditate on a regular basis—maybe a room, an area of the bedroom, perhaps outside on a porch on a nice day or on the lawn. You find a few areas that just feel right—they have a good energy. You sit there and meditate, and you build up a vibration and a force there that makes it easier to meditate. Sometimes it's fun just to meditate in a different place to break up your routine. Don't feel limited.

There are two practices—concentration and meditation.

For the first year or two, you probably will be almost exclusively practicing concentration. You will try meditating, but it won't come until later. So I'll address mostly the practice of concentration.

When you concentrate, you're focusing on something.

When you meditate, you're letting go and dissolving. You're losing awareness of anything in particular at all, even the awareness of awareness. In meditation, you are seeking to stop all thought. It is very hard just to stop your thoughts. Try it. Not to have one thought, image, idea, or associative feeling in the mind is difficult for most people.

Rather than just trying to stop your thoughts, which is hard and frustrating, it's easier to concentrate and focus on something. As you focus completely on something, all other thoughts will be forced out of the mind because your attention will be dominated by the object of concentration. This develops your mental power exquisitely.

Let's take a simple session as an example. You're going to sit down. You're an absolute beginner, and you're going to meditate, let us say, for 15 minutes. If you're an absolute beginner, I suggest that you meditate with a watch or a clock, and what you're going to do is make sure that you sit there for a full 15 minutes.

In the beginning, it's good to spend most of your time concentrating with your eyes open.

You need to sit up straight. If you want to sit in a chair, that's fine, or in a cross-legged position on the floor—whatever suits you, but the back should be straight. You may be bothered by this initially. It may not be comfortable for you; that's because the muscles in your back are weak.

It is desirable to sit in a cross-legged position, but it's possible that's uncomfortable for you. If you'd like to be able to do this, I would suggest that you take some yoga lessons, where you will learn stretching exercises that will loosen up the leg muscles so that you can sit in a comfortable, cross-legged position. This is a well-balanced position whereby you can sit for protracted periods of time with ease and with balance.

The main thing is to sit down, keep your back straight, relax and have an object on which to concentrate.

You might use a candle flame; a brightly colored rock; a yantra, which is a geometrical design specifically for the practice of concentration and meditation; or something else.

Place an object within your view, hopefully at about eye level. You might have to look down a little bit.

Some people have a meditation table on which they put an object of concentration—a candle, yantra, something like that—so they don't have to stare down at the ground where they have an object, which might be uncomfortable and would put your head in too much of a downward position.

Now you're going to concentrate. It's a good idea, in my opinion, to use a mantra before you begin a session. It's not necessary, but I think it helps.

A mantra is a powerful sound which, when focused upon, clears the mind and helps bring you into a higher level of awareness. The most powerful of all mantras is "Aum" spelled A U M. You have probably heard it. If you repeat that sound several times with your eyes closed before you start the session, while you're sitting there, it will help clear your mind. It has a vibratory energy that helps eliminate thought. But you don't simply repeat the sound. You focus on it.

You chant the word, "Aum". (Rama demonstrates) A U M. When you chant that sound three or four times, or you could even do it silently within the mind—but it's easier for most people to focus when it's done out loud—that's a good beginning.

Then, open your eyes and focus on the object of concentration. Now, for the next ten or 15 minutes if you're a beginner, let's say for two-thirds of the time you've allowed for the practice of zazen, you are going to simply look at the object, blink whenever your eyes become uncomfortable, and focus on it.

As thoughts come in and out of your mind, ignore them. Simply continue to concentrate. Then, about two-thirds of the way through, close your eyes.

I would like you to spend the remainder of the time focusing your attention on a *chakra*.

A chakra is an energy center that exists within the *subtle physical body*. Our physical bodies are surrounded by a body of energy, which is not perceptible for most individuals. But as you develop your psychic facilities through the practice of zazen, you will be able to see and feel this body of energy around you.

The subtle body has certain junctures or points of intersection that we call chakras. They are like windows that look into other dimensions. There are three that are useful for concentration practice.

- ॐ Around the navel area, there's a chakra.
- ॐ In the middle of the chest, there's a chakra.
- ॐ And between the eyebrows and a little bit above, there is a chakra.
- ॐ There are more, but these are the most useful for the practice of zazen.

Choose one of these three points and hold your attention there, just as you held your attention on the object. Let's say you were looking at a candle flame. You focused on a candle flame for ten minutes. Thoughts come in and out of your mind, but you just focus more and more intensely.

Then, after about ten minutes, if you are a beginner, close your eyes and focus on your navel center. The first time you do it, or the first few times, you might even want to touch that spot for a minute or two.

Hold your fingers very lightly against your navel, or in the center of your chest around the area of the heart, or between the eyebrows and a little bit above. As you press very gently there, it will be easier for you to focus. These are not random spots. There are windows here, windows that lead into other levels of mind. Each will generate a different type of experience.

The chakra around the navel area is the power chakra, and as you focus on this center you will develop tremendous will power.

The heart center—which is in the center of the chest—develops the psychic centers, the psychic abilities, sensitivities, and also brings about a tremendous stillness within the mind and extraordinarily develops one's ability to experience love and beauty. It also develops your ESP and many other things.

The third eye, which is between the eyebrows and slightly above—focusing in this area develops your intuitive wisdom, your knowledge, your higher mind, and gives you visions into other planes of reality.

Let's say that the bottom center is connected with power, the middle center is connected with feeling—feeling love, feeling awareness—and the top center has to do with knowledge. The combination of knowledge, power, and feeling creates a balanced individual. That is why I suggest that at different times you focus on each of these chakras.

Initially, it may not seem like you're doing anything and you are just thinking a lot. But you are doing something, as long as you're trying. It is like doing push-ups. You can be doing push-ups and all the time thinking it's not doing anything, but obviously, as long as you're trying and doing them, you're getting stronger. After you've practiced doing your push-ups for a while, after two or three sessions, you won't necessarily see huge muscles like Arnold Schwarzenegger has, but you will begin to see and feel a difference. It is the same with the practice of concentration.

Initially, it won't seem like anything is happening, but something is. Inwardly, your mind is becoming stronger and you're gaining personal power. After a while, that power will begin to manifest in your life. You will find it's easier to study. It's easier to do your job. Your mind is sharp, clear and defined. You are more aware.

And a feeling will come after a while. You will just feel better. You are more in touch with everything in your life. Then knowledge and power will come to you, later, through these practices.

So for five minutes or so, focus on one of those three areas. Hold your attention there, and after your 15 minutes are up, chant the mantra again. Chant "Aum," or another favorite mantra, several times.

Then, at the end of a session, we always bow down to the ground. That is our way of giving the meditation to eternity, of letting go of it, of letting go of our self.

If you practice this way, you will develop your mind. Practice 15 minutes once, twice a day, then a half-an-hour, then 45 minutes, then an hour. After you've practiced for a while, you might want to try meditating. This is all concentration, which is the most important to start with.

But let's say you've been doing this for a year or so, or six months, or whatever—then you might want to begin to try something a little bit different. Perhaps you should spend half the time initially, instead of two-thirds, focusing on something outside—a candle flame, yantra, colored rock, whatever it is. Then take a little more time, maybe 25 percent of the time, and focus on one of the three chakras. Then take the last 25 percent of your time and don't focus at all, simply let go.

Now, this is not something that I recommend you do too much of because most people will sit there and space out. Their letting go won't have power. This is meditation. In other words, during the letting go phase, you want to strive to have no thought whatsoever in the mind. If you're just sitting there and zillions of thoughts are whipping around, it's not accomplishing anything. It is better, if that's the case, to focus. You will gain more from that than sitting there in a quasi-meditation, in which there are just a lot of thoughts kicking around.

I would suggest that you only do it for a limited period of time, after you've become fairly accomplished at concentrating. Once you've become accomplished at concentrating, you will discover that you can sit there for those periods of time without thought or with reduced thought. Eventually, after some years, you may find that you'll sit for half the period of time without any particular focus at all, and you're able to stop thought.

Eventually, you may be able to sit for two hours without one thought. At that point, it's no longer necessary to practice concentration. When you can stop all thought, it is no longer necessary to concentrate, although it's still kind of fun, to tell you the truth.

If you follow this program, you will find a tremendous increase in your mental awareness—if you practice it faithfully. Again, it's a personal matter. There is no way to measure it. All I can tell you is that most people who do this see dramatic increases in their level of personal power and success. Of course, you will accrue more power, and higher levels of mind will start to open for you. Once you're doing this on a regular basis and you're seeing progress in your life, then it's time to seek out a teacher, someone who can show you the next steps. Also, there are many other matters that enable you to meditate better. These are matters that I discuss on other tapes and in books, and that other teachers talk about. This is just the hard-core practice.

It is necessary to learn how to do a systems analysis of your life, to learn about the effects of places, people, jobs. There are millions of things that go into the study of meditation. This is the daily practice. Mindfulness and what you do with your attention the rest of the time, what you do when you're dreaming at night and so on, in order to enlarge the awareness field that you have, is a very vast subject. And that's not our discussion at this point.

So that's how to concentrate and how to meditate. If you practice these things—simplistic though they may seem—they will enable you to develop a great power in your life. Again, it doesn't seem very complicated when the guy just lifts weights all the time. There is not much to it—a bar, some weights, and he lifts them. But if he keeps doing it, he can quadruple his strength. It is the same [with concentration and meditation].

This is like working out. It is working out—working out with your mind. Most people don't do it at all. The only concentration they have is on the television set. That isn't very powerful or profound. If you do these exercises on a regular basis and you become consistent, then you will become a gymnast of the mind. And once you learn to concentrate and focus for extended periods of time, and then to stop thought, you'll be ready for more advanced lessons.

(Zazen music begins.) So I would encourage you to concentrate and meditate.

There are thousands of worlds, thousands of dimensions. The beauty of life is incredible beyond belief. A clear and solid mind—let alone enlightenment, enlightened awareness—is the best thing. Life can be extremely wonderful. It is—when you're in a state of mind to see it.

Practice, and new worlds and new vistas and new horizons will open to you.

So this is Zen Master Rama, wishing you well in your practice.

CHAPTER TEN

TANTRIC ZEN

(Zazen music plays in the background, and Rama speaks to the beat of the music.)

What is Tantric Zen? For the next 45 minutes or so, you and I are going to take a journey through eternity.

Somewhere in the middle of the L.A. trendiness, Boston conservatism, New York chic and San Francisco intellectual mellow, somewhere in the desert or on the top of a mountain or on a subway, somewhere in Berlin or in outer space or at Disneyland, in the embrace of someone you love or someone you can't stand (Rama chuckles), somewhere in meditation, somewhere in Japan or India or in your own mind, there's a place where everything meets.

There's a place where everything comes together and where it's all the same. It's a state of mind, that is, where it's all the same, in which it's the same. That state of mind, in which all things are the same, is the state of mind of Tantric Zen.

And it's inside your mind. Everything is inside your mind. Even you are inside your own mind.

The future, the past, the present, photographs from your childhood, your funeral, the stars, the distant stars, the core of the sun—everything is made of energy, and life pulses through all things.

Success, failure, pleasure, pain, small furry animals, household products, freeways, Star Wars systems, profound states of enlightenment, purity, nobility, cowardice, treachery and betrayal—all are states of mind, and all are interlinked in the dance of *tantra*, the dance of awareness, the disco of the mind, the ballroom of cosmic consciousness.

Life is poetry, you know?

So what is Tantric Zen? Well, I don't think I can give you a straight answer, since I don't happen to be a very straight Zen master. I think I'm on an angle. I'm on an oblique angle through all of existence.

But it sure is nice music in the background, the music of Zazen from their *Samurai* album. And the music is part of the tantra, the dance of life. Before your eyes, before your awareness, is the procession of eternity, and it's all joined together somewhere—it is one.

Tantra is the perception of the oneness and the perfection of all things. Not just the perfection of light, but [also] the perfection of darkness—seeing God in both beauty and horror.

In other words, all things are spiritual. It doesn't matter what you do or who you are or what kind of blue jeans you wear, or whether you wear an ochre robe or whether you're sober or asleep or dreaming. It is all the same—in the mind of the Buddha.

(Zazen music ends.)

So then, what is this tantra stuff? What I term Tantric Zen, I could also refer to as old Zen, the original face of Zen, or new Zen, contemporary Zen practice—no mind, the mirror of existence. Tantric Zen is Zen in its essence.

Bodhidharma, who brought Zen from India to the Orient, taught a very pure type of Zen, in that it was—pure Zen.

Zen is meditation, the actual experience of life—directly, immediately, with no buffers.

Over the course of time, different schools of Zen have evolved, principally the Rinzai and Soto orders of Zen. There have been lots of Zen teachers, Zen masters. Books have been written about Zen, commentaries on sutras. A whole hierarchy has developed for the teaching and practice of Zen. And Zen has become, to a certain degree, institutionalized.

Tantric Zen is the original Zen—Zen without rules, Zen without form. Zen can certainly take rules and form. So Tantric Zen might have some rules and form, but it would also remain formless, even though it has rules and form.

Tantric Zen is the awareness of the infinitude of all things. To gain that awareness, to be it, is enlightenment. Enlightenment frees you from the pain and suffering of limited states of mind.

Tantric Zen, at first, does not appear to have a method. It seems to be kind of random. In Tantric Zen, you could meditate on a Brillo box or you could meditate on the clear light of reality. In Tantric Zen, you can be humorous and make fun of anything, or you can be very serious. In Tantric Zen, you can break the rules—you're encouraged to do so and discouraged from doing that simultaneously—because Tantric Zen doesn't have much to do with ideas, although these are ideas about Tantric Zen. And with these ideas, I hope to paint you a picture of something.

Tantric Zen is a state of mind. Now let me give you a little classical background here. In most forms of self-discovery—different pathways that lead to knowledge, empowerment, enlightenment and a generally good time—there are lots of do's and don'ts, thou shalt's and thou shalt not's. Those do's and don'ts are there to help persons who want to expand their mind and learn more about the nature of being and be freed from the limitations, the limited states of mind, that most persons experience. These prohibitions and these doctrines of encouragement telling you to do this—these are good things; these will help you, make you feel better; these are the things that will interfere—are practical, realistic and in most cases, true and helpful. They have been set forth by teachers who have walked the path that leads nowhere for a long time.

So this is great. I like it. I like the whole thing. I like all parts of it.

In Tantric Zen, there is no rule. There is only your own immediate experience. Now you might say, "Well, right now I'm having my immediate experience. Am I practicing Tantric Zen?"

And I would say, "Yes, you just don't realize it."

Then you might say, "Well, if that's all there is to it, why bother to study it? I'm already doing it."

No, that's not it at all. Yes, your immediate experience is Tantric Zen, but how aware are you of your immediate experience? Probably not that aware.

Tantric Zen is the exploration of everything, since everything is a part of enlightenment. Yet the state of mind of Tantric Zen, if I can refer to it as that, is not at all limited.

For instance, let's say that you were following a path of self-discovery that indicates that you shouldn't eat meat, that you shouldn't have sex and that you should avoid hanging around in lingerie shops (Rama chuckles). You should avoid worldly pursuits and activities. You should be a renunciate and leave all this urban pollution behind and go off to the pristine slopes of the mountains and meditate and become enlightened.

Now, the things they're encouraging you to do are sensible, in that they're saying that when you eat meat, it has a certain energy or vibration that stimulates thought, to a certain extent, and makes it more difficult to meditate. Sexual practice is usually very confusing for people, whether they meditate or not. It uses up a lot of energy, but the main problem with it, of course, is that it causes you to intertwine yourself with another person's being—to pull their energy into your body, so to speak. It brings about attachment, and with attachment comes jealousy, frustration, anger, depression—all states of mind that are not helpful if your goal is to stop thought and enter into luminous states of awareness. And I don't think I have to explain why they wouldn't want you to hang around in lingerie shops. But I'm willing to, if you're not sure.

In Tantric Zen, the thought is that it doesn't matter, but it does.

> It doesn't really matter what you do.
>
> It is your state of mind that matters.

If you're in a state of mind in which all things are one, then you can spend your time in lingerie shops. You can have sex whenever you're in the mood, or maybe if you're not. You can eat meat or fish or vegetables.

It really doesn't matter what you do. But, you might ask, "Won't I be affected by all these things?" Yes, chances are, you'll be affected by them, and they'll pull you right down into lower states of attention.

For most people then, the prohibitions and the encouragements are a good thing.

But if you are able to maintain very powerful states of mind, then you'll find yourself in everything that you see. And sex won't be sex, and meat won't be meat, and lingerie shops won't be lingerie shops. Nor will fasting be fasting.

Everything is dependent upon your state of mind.

> That is all there are, states of mind, ten thousand of them in all;
>
> beyond all states of mind—nirvana.

If you're in a very tantric state of mind, then your experiences will be quite different. Example, example, example—let's say someone has a sexual encounter and while they're having that sexual encounter, they hook up to a primarily sensorial display board—feeling, touching, tasting, smelling—all that sort of stuff—sensation, pleasure, pain. Now, normally, that will take your awareness and your attention and bring it again into the sense plane.

Once you're in the sense plane after having sex, you don't necessarily leave the sense plane. It has brought your attention into a certain place.

Imagine there's a building and there are hundreds of floors, 10,000 in all in the building. Now, if you go down to spend time with someone—to floor number 45—after you say farewell, you're still on floor number 45. From the point of view of tantra, it doesn't matter—if you are able to go to floor 45 and still be on floor 10,000.

That is to say, if you're in the tantric state of mind, what someone else experiences when they have sex is not what you'll experience at all. They will experience the physical display board.

You may experience a little of that, but what you will be experiencing will be meditation.

You won't even notice what your body is doing, particularly. Very few people can do this, admittedly, but that doesn't mean it can't be done. It can be done by a real practitioner of tantra.

The same is true of eating meat. One person will eat meat and it will lower their attention field. Another person won't even be affected by it because they're not in the state of mind whereby they'll be affected by it.

They are in a state of mind in which all things are reflections of eternity, and any avenue that you follow leads to light. All roads lead to Rome. If you follow anything far enough in the universe, it will eventually lead to light.

There are all kinds of wonderful stories, of course, about practitioners of tantra who seemingly break all the rules and yet are enlightened. But they don't try to break the rules. In other words, the thought isn't, "Well good, let's find out everything we're not supposed to do and go do it." Or the thought isn't, "Oh boy, I can just enjoy absolutely everything and become enlightened." Neither of these are real case scenarios.

Let us just say that life draws us in different directions, sometimes simultaneously. And when you follow the direction that life draws you in, if you stay in a very powerful state of mind, then you'll see eternity.

So the practitioners of tantra don't decide to break the rules. They are not particularly hung up on having sex or eating meat or drinking alcohol—or anything. It's just that one thing is the same as another for them. They don't strive to do these things, nor do they strive to avoid them.

Some people, of course, say they're practicing tantra. There are a lot of books on tantric sexual practice in local bookstores. These are usually pretty silly books. They are telling you how you can magnify your sexual experiences or things like that by doing certain kundalini exercises while you're having sex, and how it will keep you in a high state of attention. Now, there's nothing wrong with trying. It might work for you, and there's only one way to find out, right? But in most cases, it's just silly.

In other words, people who are capable of practicing tantra are individuals who have meditated for many, many years and developed very strong and powerful states of attention—real strong minds. It's like being, I suppose, immune to a disease. Let's say that you can easily catch a communicable disease and someone else is immune. If you walk into a room in a hospital where someone has a communicable disease, you'll pick it up and be sick. Whereas someone else has an immunity, so they can walk in and walk around the room, and it's no big deal. They might pass through the room on the way to another room, not because they think that they should hang out in the room with the sick person or they want to show that they're disease-resistant or they're trying to prove anything. They just were walking in that direction, and they happened to pass through that room.

Naturally, they didn't think much about it. It wasn't a big issue for them because for them, there was no disease of that type. They just won't pick it up. They're just walking through another room.

But for you, it's a very big deal. That room is charged because you know if you go into that room, you're going to get really sick, maybe die.

So from the point of view of a person who's seeking enlightenment, knowledge, empowerment, to do better with their life, to be more successful with their career, to find out what it's all about—it's very important to find out where the rooms are that you should avoid and the rooms that you should go to.

Tantra is a practice that's not for everyone.

It takes a really broad state of mind to practice tantra.

And in my opinion, Zen is tantric.

Zen is a very fast path to enlightenment—fast in comparison to some other paths, not fast for the person who practices it. There is no sense of speed. There is no sense of rush. When you go out jogging and you jog at your natural pace, you don't feel that you're hurrying. Someone who jogs about a third of the speed that you do when you zip by them will think, "Boy, they're really going fast. They're rushing." If someone runs by you, and they run twice as fast as you do, you might think they're rushing. But not really. If you're moving at your natural pace, there's no sense of rush.

Zen is a very quick path to empowerment and enlightenment and knowledge and development of the mind and all of its faculties—creative, analytic and other. But it's not fast for the person who's comfortable with it. It is just fast in comparison to other paths. The mind develops very quickly with the practice of Zen.

Zen is for the tantric individual. By that I mean, if you're a real stickler for the rules, I don't think that you'll have much fun with Zen, at least not original Zen.

There are monasteries in Japan where they teach Zen with rules, more rules than you can imagine, and you might feel comfortable with that. I don't teach that type of Zen.

It is necessary to have a very liberal and simultaneously very conservative mentality to practice Tantric Zen. If your mentality is just liberal, then Tantric Zen won't work because all you'll want to do is play around and be broad-minded. If you're completely conservative, then Tantric Zen won't work for you because you'll reject all liberal attitudes and ideas and just be stuck in being conservative. Whereas, if you fluctuate between liberal and conservative, Tantric Zen will work for you.

In other words, Tantric Zen is not being kinky, nor is it libertinism. Nor is it being conservative and austere. It is eclectic. It is a real mixture of all things. And it's for a broad-minded person who can one day go up to the top of the mountain and leave everybody behind and meditate in solitude and have a great time, and the next day they can be down in the shopping mall walking around and enjoying looking at everything. At one time in their life, they can give up eating meat and feel inspired by that, and then suddenly, at another time in their life, they can be eating meat and have fun with that, and they don't see a contradiction.

They could be celibate for a while, then they could go through a sexual phase, or maybe always be celibate or always have sex.

There would not be a sense of discord in that person's mind because they see that all things contain life and light. And there doesn't have to be a reason for doing something. You can become celibate and not have relationships because that's what you find yourself doing. You can have relationships because that's what you find yourself doing, not because it's right or wrong.

The emphasis in tantra is not on what you find yourself doing—it's on meditation.

Tantric Zen is all about the practice of zazen meditation, and the theme is—or the thought—that if you meditate well, you'll be in very powerful states of mind and then it really doesn't matter much what you do. So rather than minding your p's and q's, you meditate instead. You can gain power by avoidance. You can gain power by doing certain things. You can gain much more power by meditating.

If you spend your time meditating instead of avoiding and doing, then later, as you walk through life, you don't have to avoid and you don't have to do. You can just be. Your mind will be in an elevated state whereby whatever it is you are, or what is passing before your eye, the life that you are experiencing, will be experienced very differently because you'll be wandering through the ten thousand states of mind.

Tantric Zen, and people who practice it, of course, make some people feel extremely uncomfortable. Those are the people who have to mind their p's and q's, and they feel extremely threatened by someone—let me give you an example.

I studied for many years in an ashram, in a spiritual community, and I was just innately tantric. The people who were in the community with me were not. They were people who had to mind their p's and q's. Now, I meditated a great deal, probably a lot more than they did because that's what came naturally. I just love to meditate. It's just the best thing to do. It's absolutely fun. And they were real rule-mongers. Yet we were all in the same community. We were all practicing together.

I had no problem with the fact that they liked rules. No problem at all. It didn't matter to me a bit because I saw that the rules they were following were important for their growth and development. Had they practiced tantra, they would have been thrown into an absolute sea of confusion.

They wouldn't have known what to do.

Out of perhaps the 800 people in the community I was in, I think I was the only one with a girlfriend, just about. Had they had a girlfriend or a boyfriend, it would have been a disaster for them. Their attention would have fallen. They would have stopped meditating because they were people who were really into minding their p's and q's. But for me, it wasn't a big deal because it didn't affect my awareness field—because it wasn't a possessive situation. I was in a state of mind in which it was just another part of life. There was no particular charge, one way or the other.

In other words, since my attention was directed towards meditation, I saw the light in all things, and it was just another samsaric experience, an experience of the world that I was passing through. I saw the moments with my girlfriend as part of my inner evolution, my growth and awareness. Then a time came when I left the girl I loved very much because I just saw that's what I needed to do, and I had no problem with that. I didn't feel an absence afterwards because then I entered a phase in my life where that just wasn't of great interest. It didn't seem to matter much one way or the other because everything that I see is part of eternity.

I really respected all my brother and sister monks in the community, and I would have never said anything to them or criticized their practice because I realized that it was important for them. It mattered. And just because it didn't matter to me, didn't mean that it wasn't important for them.

However, I seemed to upset them a great deal because I was able to maintain a very high level of attention, relatively speaking at the time, I guess, in comparison to them, without doing a lot of the things that they did.

Obviously, my vibration was tantric, and it just shook them up that I was able to have a good time doing things that I guess a part of them wanted to do, but they wouldn't allow themselves to do—and that threatened them in some way.

So I wasn't particularly popular. It wasn't vocal. It was just an inner thing, that I would be able to go out and be successful doing a lot of different, very worldly things.

I got a Ph.D., became a college professor, gave lectures, went on television shows. I had a fun life. I still do. And yet, I was able to walk into the meditation hall and meditate as well, if not probably a lot better, than anybody there. Not that it was competitive. That's just how it was because I really liked to meditate and because, of course, I had been meditating in many, many previous lifetimes, and it just came very naturally—as did enlightenment when it came, because of previous enlightenments.

Tantra, then, is for someone who is really broad-minded, and that's the kind of Zen that I teach, which is what I feel Zen is. It is Bodhidharma Zen, your Zen, my Zen. Which doesn't mean I have a problem with Japanese Zen. Most Japanese Zen is minding your p's and q's.

When I go visit my brother monks in Japan and sit down with other Zen masters, and I walk into the monasteries and I meet the abbot, drink tea with him and have discussion or silence, they look at my long hair and they have their shaved heads, and they look at my crazy clothes and my strange expression—but they feel the power that emanates from my dedication to the practice. So they are comfortable with me, yet they're very uncomfortable. They don't quite know what to do, yet they find they have to accept me because I'm one with the practice. I don't feel at all uncomfortable with them and their austere ways of life because that's what works for them.

If you require an austere way of life, if you need to mind your p's and q's all the time, then you should go to another Zen master or Zen teacher, other than this guy here. There are Zen communities in America and around the world where they teach types of Zen that are very, very providential and provincial, simultaneously, and they work.

Tantra is quicker. But for some people it can be spiritually disastrous. Now, I don't really think it's disastrous because all you can do is learn. But some people go into tantra with the idea, sort of an intellectual approach, that now they can just do everything and stay really high. And that doesn't work at all. Instead of ending up in advanced states of mind, they actually can, well, do they really regress? I guess they do in a certain way. But in another way, they progress. They regress in that they might get pulled down into some lower states of mind, but I think all experience is useful. Of course, that's the tantric point of view. They might not feel the same way, if they don't feel that well.

So you have to decide within yourself. If you're very, very liberal, then you should go and find a very liberal Zen teacher. Liberal means that the Zen teacher will break some of the rules, but not all of them—a liberal interpretation of the doctrines of the Soto or Rinzai school. Or if you're very, very conservative and you like that sort of practice, then you should avoid liberal Zen teachers, which are few—liberal Zen masters—and go find a very conservative Zen master and just do traditional Japanese practice, which is not that traditional, actually.

It's fairly recent historically because the original Zen was tantric for many hundreds of years. It's only really in the last 800 years—800 to 1,200 years—that the rules have come into being and conservative Zen has surfaced. Conservative Zen, needless to say, is not particularly popular in Japan at all. Hardly anybody practices Zen any more there because it's just too strict; there are too many rules. It's just like there aren't that many people here who go into the Catholic priesthood any more—too many rules.

So I really think tantric Zen and liberal Zen are more suited for this age that we live in. Liberal Zen is suited for a lot of people because it gives you rules, but in a gentle way. It's not as demanding.

Tantric Zen, on the other hand, is fast—in comparison to conservative Zen or liberal Zen—because it engages you continuously at every moment in the practice of mindfulness, which the other two Zen forms do to an extent. But again, I feel their prohibitions or their intensive attractions are ultimately limitations to enlightenment. And I realize that those are only temporal. Eventually, a person who practices conservative or liberal Zen goes beyond that. So the quick immersion school is Tantric Zen, and then there are more gradual forms. And again, the quick immersion school won't seem rushed for the person it's suited to.

So if you find that you're both conservative and liberal, if you're both drawn to the Himalayas and the snowy regions, and at the same time drawn to the middle of the urban metro environment, if you're interested in working in the world and being successful—in other words, if success is part of your scenario and people are part of your life, yet that's not your whole life; you're comfortable with it, but it's not enough, you also want inner realization and enlightenment and empowerment—or you're a person who just finds that all of this comes naturally, tantra's for you.

If you're a person who just wants to be in the world and doesn't want any knowledge, then I don't know what you're doing with this tape. Shut it off immediately.

If you're an individual who wants nothing to do with the world and wants to renounce everything, live in a monastery exclusively, live in the mountains or whatever and have nothing to do with society, the world, people, household products, Brillo pads, tampons; if you don't want to feel your body and acknowledge that it's there; if you don't want to revel in the temporal part of your self, in your aliveness, you feel you've just got to shut it all off—then that's a way of practice and Tantric Zen is not for you.

Tantric Zen is for the individual who is in love with both the finite and the infinite, who gets a kick out of this weird transitory world and at the same time wants to step beyond it—because they're both the same. In tantra, *samsara* —which is the world, awareness, illusion, all of the ten thousand states of mind—is viewed as the same thing as *nirvana*. And eating a hamburger or a nice salad is meditation—as is *meditation* meditation.

Everything aids everything because all things are a reflection of the Buddha mind or the mind of enlightenment. Even if you're not enlightened, you can engage in the practice, of course.

But I'm suggesting that it's a certain kind of crazy, natural, I feel ultimately very twentieth-century, eclectic mind that does well with tantra. In other words, Zen is for people with strong minds, strong intellects. It's really not for people who just read comic books. You might read comic books, but you should also read some Dostoevsky, if you see what I mean.

In other words, we are in the age of the Zen mind, computer mind.

This is an age of mind, which is why Zen, I think, is probably the best practice for this time. We are intellectual people. We go to high school. We go to college. We use our minds constantly. We are not just out farming. Zen can be practiced by the farmer, but Zen is really suited for people who like to use their minds, with big minds, who think a lot—because it's a practice of mind. And it takes a fairly sophisticated mind to interlock with the teaching.

There are forms of practice that are *bhakti,* or just purely love-oriented, or *karma,* purely service-oriented, that really don't require the developed intellect.

Now, is your intellect developed enough to practice Zen? Well, if you feel comfortable with what I've been saying and you're following me, yes, absolutely. Then I would say that you're intellectual. You may not use your mind a lot. It may not be fully developed, but obviously you have the potential to do so, and Zen develops the mind, not just for enlightenment.

You see, Tantric Zen is also about success in all things because all things are reflections of enlightenment. In Tantric Zen, career, relationships, the type of insurance you have, where you vacation and how—all things are part of your evolution, your awareness, your experience of the suchness of existence.

The emphasis, though, is on meditation in Tantric Zen—the experience of meditation in formal practice, zazen, where you're sitting down and meditating and concentrating. And, of course, in mindfulness the rest of the time—using all of the experiences in life to further your awareness, without a sense of conflict in any experience.

Mind delineates experience, and through the filter of mind, experience becomes something else; it becomes knowledge—in tantra.

(Zazen music begins.)

So how do you practice tantra?

Well, in my opinion, it's best practiced with a teacher because it is being. It is alive. It is in all things. It is a transmission of awareness. It is not simply the attainment of a different state of mind but thousands of states of mind.

In Tantric Zen, you'll develop your mind to an extremely high level. You will address areas of your career, your life, your sexuality, your stillness, your divinity, your humanity. All those things are learned from one who has done that and who does that, who is nothing yet everything, who is human, yet beyond human.

So I would find a teacher of Tantric Zen and study with them because it's a transference of awareness, mind—a sharing of the perception of the beauty of life.

Then you'll practice, of course. Your practice is your life. Your practice is your life and your being and your job and your friends and your loves and your agonies. It leads to illumination.

Tantric Zen leads to illumination and fun right here and now, which is why I like it. It is a combination of all things—beauty, poignancy, craziness, discipline, everything. And if you are both conservative and liberal, you might enjoy it.

So this is Zen Master Rama, wishing you well on your journey—to nothingness and everythingness. Take care.

(Zazen music ends.)

CHAPTER ELEVEN

DEVELOPING WILLPOWER

Good morning. It is around 4:00 a.m. here in Boston, on the 9th of December, 1986. This is a time when most of the world is sleeping, at least in this vicinity. Zen masters, a few others, are up at this hour—a good time to meditate, 4:00 a.m.

The world is still. All the thoughts and impressions and feelings are not transmitting from everyone's conscious minds yet.

There is a doorway that opens at this time of the morning, between the worlds. It is very easy to remember things, see things and know things; to remember who you are, to see where you are and what's taking place—and to know what it is you have to do.

I am here in Boston, and we've had a snowfall. A very light covering of snow has eclipsed the park, as I look out there. It has mostly stopped now; it's just a light frosting. I can see some church spires of the older Boston in the distance and even further, of course, the tall buildings of the new Boston. Boston is in kind of a renaissance period now. Once, perhaps, the most powerful city in America—then it went through a period of decline. But now, thanks to the computer and other related industries, Boston is becoming a very financially powerful city again. And the mood of the people here is upbeat and positive overall.

Yet there's still a bit of the old around—still too conservative, living in the past too much, not in touch with the reality of the moment. There's still a lot of racism, and ... there are problems. Human beings seem to have problems, I've observed. But on the whole, the city is looking very good. Definitely. It's looking quite positive. Its power is up, and that's our subject for this morning—power, specifically willpower—what it is, how it works, how to develop it, why it's important.

Willpower. You have two choices, and only two that I'm aware of. One choice is to be a human being. To be a human being is to be frustrated, unfulfilled, and there are lots of them around. A human being is someone who's bound by emotion, as opposed to reason—a person who is enslaved by their desires, a person who is never really at peace with themselves or fulfilled or happy because they live in the spectrum of the human consciousness, which is endless craving, endless desire. Pleasure is followed by pain, loss by gain, love by the loss of love, joy by sorrow. That is the life of a human being.

There is another possibility. One can be something other than human—human in the sense that I've just defined it. One can become limitless, enlightened, aware, awakened, knowledgeable and powerful in ways that the human beings who traverse this earth cannot yet fathom. Oh, we remember a few people who've been enlightened. We build churches and edifices in their names. We think of them as celestial beings who descended for a short time into our world and brought messages of hope or inspiration. But few people, if any, really feel that they could ever be like that. And, of course, if that's how they feel, that's how it will be.

Life is endless. It goes on forever. We go from one lifetime to another. And a change in lifetimes is not necessarily a change in condition of our awareness. Death is just a rest and then we begin again, but at the same level of attention or awareness that we had when we died. A person who is perceptive realizes that there is an alternative, and you may be that person - there's a good chance. There is another way to lead one's life, other experiences to be had.

Most of the world lives in poor or middle class neighborhoods. A very small percentage lives in wealthy neighborhoods. How did those people who are wealthy get there? They decided to. They willed it, or it was willed to them (Rama laughs)—that's karma. How do you do anything in life? You will it. You decide what it is you want, and you make it happen. That is willpower. Willpower determines success in business, interpersonal relationships, health, whatever it is. All the activities in your life, success and failure in them, is dependent upon your ability to manifest will.

Now, human beings actually have quite a bit of willpower. They don't know too much about it, but they have quite a bit. In Zen we study the will. We learn how to cultivate it and we learn to use it in specific ways, to accumulate will. It is something that you can accumulate, just like money. We use it to direct our actions, and we don't overuse it or abuse it because that's a waste. If you use your will all the time, then it runs out. You deplete yourself and then, when you really need it, it's not there. It's something to be used sparingly.

You have a choice. You can choose the life of an ordinary human being and suffer a lot and not see brightness and beauty in all things. The world is wonderful. It is beautiful, when you're in a correct level of attention. In lower levels of attention, things are dark, gray. Experiences are shallow. Life can be very discouraging and depressing. You get old. Things don't work out the way you thought they would. You become alienated from those around you.

Zen is a study. It's a discipline. It's a way of life. It's an approach to life–an approach. It involves the active use of will to make things happen or not happen. These are the secrets of power.

It's early morning here in Boston. Occasionally a car is driving around the park. But it's still very quiet. Soon they'll all be up, all those human beings, going to their jobs, living their lives—another day of their lives. And you know, they're all unconscious. They don't know what's going on. They don't know why they're born or why they die. Like you. You don't know. You are caught up in a process that you don't understand. A few understand it, the enlightened—persons like myself. We have stepped beyond time and space, and we see a larger picture. Those who wish to elevate their lives and improve their lives come to us, seeking knowledge, seeking empowerment. And if they're good students, we teach them—the teachers of enlightenment.

What is will? It's a decision. It is a decision to be something. We really aren't anything in particular. We can be anything; that's the good news. Everything that you are or conceive of yourself as being is just an idea. It's an illusion. It's a hallucination. You can completely wipe the slate clean and you can dissolve the person you've been and become somebody else. That's the good news. There are ten thousand states of mind, and you can explore and experience them. You can have an uncommonly fine life. But it takes determination. You have to march to the beat of a different drummer. You have to decide.

Listen, no one cares about you. No one cares. You will die and be forgotten. The people who are in your life don't understand what's going on. You are alone. There is only you and your will. Your life can be horrible or it can be incredibly beautiful; it's seldom in between. It can be boring or exciting. Your active use of will, will determine what will happen to you in this and other lives.

Do you wish to become conscious? Do you wish to stretch yourself into the infinite and experience not just this world, but tens of thousands of worlds, and where those worlds come from? Do you want to wake up? If you do, then study Zen, apply yourself to the study. Study with me. Study with a different teacher—someone who's enlightened, someone who's outside of time and space. And we'll teach you, if you really want to know. But you need to really want to know.

You have to assess your life. Ask yourself: what is it that you want? There is a world of deaf, dumb and blind people out there, who are shuffling through their lives, not knowing how wonderful life can be. They have their moments, and they're pretty people, sometimes. Sometimes they're horrible. But in either case, they're very unconscious. You can be conscious, but you will have to will it. You just decide.

One day, you wake up and you decide you want to be different. You want a different life. You are tired of your old life. This is the truth. You *will* a change. You just make it happen with your willpower. You become somebody else, somebody finer, better, more aware. And then you'll move from that personality to someone who's even more aware and more aware, and so on. Or you can just stay in oblivion, going through your days and your life and your experiences, staying with your friends, your family. If that suits you, it's good. But for some people, it's not enough. And that's who I address this tape to.

Now, the path of *will* in Zen is not easy. It's wonderful. It's beautiful beyond compare. You will, in a day, experience more ecstasy and beauty than most people will in a thousand lifetimes. But you pay a price for it. The price is your will. You will it. You dream it. You decide it.

I'm here in Boston because I willed myself here. Boston is upbeat at the moment. It is a nice place to live. Its power is up, and it's an ancient power place. So I came here to make some tapes because I decided I wanted to be in this background and experience it. Life is just a play and you're acting on the stage. And you are determining the backdrop. You are not stuck with where you are or who you are. You can change anything, at any time. You can drop anything in your life if you choose to, if you use your will.

There are realms of light, realms of perfection—beyond everyday experience. You can know them. You can know the secrets of life. The riddles can be answered. But you have to decide to do that, and make that the most important thing in life. It doesn't happen to anyone who's special—you just decide that you want an uncommonly fine life and you *will* it.

You *will* it. You make it happen. It won't just happen. You are on a track right now. Everything is formatted for the rest of your life. The experiences you'll have, the people you'll love, the jobs, the joys, the sorrows, the way you'll die. It is all predestined, unless you will a change. That is what power is all about. That is what Zen is all about—the ability to change destiny.

Everything starts in the beginning, and the beginning is assessment. The beginning is a determination that you want something to be different. You want an uncommonly fine life. You don't want to live in the slums. You want to live in a wonderful place. God exists in the slums. God exists in the ruthless killer. The universe is a mystery. Who can understand it? But the experiences you will have in this and in your future lives, will be determined by you.

I can teach you things, but you have to want to learn them, and you will have to put aside some things in your life—habits, ideas, ways of seeing life. And you will learn new things, and then new things and then new things, forever. You will leave that which is familiar and take a journey. You are going to get on a boat and sail into uncharted waters. Others have gone before you. Or you can stay in the safe, secure oblivion and pain of ignorance, not knowing, and just die. You'll just die, like everyone else, and shuffle into another incarnation that won't be very different.

The world can be filled with brightness and beauty and clarity, poise, control, ecstasy. We are discussing ecstasy, melting in the clear light of reality, the *dharmakaya*. You must decide what it is you want. And then once you've decided, once you've looked it over and decided what you want—you're going to buy a car. You look at the different ones and then there's one that just fits. There is one that will give you a new life. It is not the one you have now. And you just decide to buy it. It's expensive, but you just do it, and it gives you a new life. This is done with will.

Most people are timid. They are so timid, they don't take chances. Naturally, they're bound. They are afraid of the light. They are afraid of their own power. In the land of willpower, anything is possible.

Will. The ability to *will*, of course, comes from meditation, from zazen; sitting each day, once or twice or three times, and meditating. That is *will*. You are willing change by that action. In that meditation, you are finding perfection. You decided to be different, to march to the beat of a different drummer, to not be like the people around you who are placidly headed towards death and oblivion. Your daily practice of meditation will change that, and by doing that every day, you will develop *will*. It is *will* itself just to do that.

I live in worlds (Rama laughs)—I live in worlds that you don't understand. My mind is one with eternity. I experience—what can I say? Everythingness, nothingness. Realms of light are open to me that are closed to you because I decided to will that. I looked around the world and I saw what it was—a horrible, painful place, where the strong victimize the weak. A world of insensitivity, of people who don't care, of egos, and I said, "Yuck! This isn't it. What I seek is beyond this; this is not happy." So I determined to do something different with my life, and I willed it. I willed change. I decided to change everything. That's how life is—we decide.

You've decided to be the way you are now. A lot of it was conditioning. No one asked what you wanted. You were taught a system. You were told that there were only certain options and you had to choose between them, and none of them were very good. I'm suggesting that there are other options that no one ever told you about. These are the things Mom and Dad never explained to you; your teachers didn't know. They weren't enlightened. They weren't luminous beings that stood outside of time and space. They didn't get the big picture.

There are other possibilities, other ways to live. On the surface, it doesn't look too different. You are a person walking around. The body moves through temporal space and time. But the revelations you will have, the states of consciousness that you will live in, the expansion of mind, the clarity, the joy, the purpose—that's *power*. The discipline, self-control, the pure fun of being your higher self—this is what I teach.

I'm a Zen Master. I'm an occult teacher. I teach how to become that—how to be perfect. If you wish to learn these things, I would be happy to teach you. But you have to want to learn them, and you must apply yourself fully. Then I will teach you. Attend my seminars. Listen to what I say and put it into practice because you decided that you want out. This is not enough for you, what these people go through—their suffering, the hoards of the world, the billions—in this or any world. You have decided to march to the beat of a different drummer. *Will* it. Make it happen.

Will is developed in meditation. It is refined. It is within you, but you don't know how to get to it. When you sit down and meditate each day, and you really try, that is the development of will. That is the exercise that develops will. Stopping thought is what you are seeking to will. When you can stop thought, your will becomes complete. Each day, your battlefield is that meditation. You sit down to meditate and you take your 15 minutes or half an hour or hour, or whatever it is, and you have a battle. You have a struggle to silence your mind. And the quieter you can make your mind, the more you've invoked your will. But the very practice of doing this develops will. From there you will then be able to take that will that you're refining and developing in meditation, and bring it into your outer life and will outer changes—changes in lifestyle, changes in personality. You can reshuffle yourself. You can make yourself into anybody you want to be. Whatever you want, you can get, when you understand the secret of will. But wisdom is needed so that you do not use your will abusively because you'll hurt yourself.

Thousands of desires flood the mind, and you can follow them if you choose to. But they don't lead any place. They are dead ends, cul-de-sacs. They won't make you happy. You want to have a beautiful person in your life; you can will it, cause them to come into your life. But it won't fulfill you. You can want a successful career, and you can will it and bring it into your life and make it happen. But it won't fulfill you. It's just something along the way.

You can want to be famous, to be wealthy. You can will these things when you meditate and you learn to refine the power of will. You can do anything. You can perform miracles, but it won't fulfill you. What will fulfill you is the stillness of eternity. What will fulfill you is when you can shut that little mind of yours off and stop your thoughts and merge your being, melt into the universe.

The snow is falling in Boston, and a snowflake hits the pond and it dissolves into it. That is ecstasy; that's release. The burden you are carrying around, the weight, is the burden of self. You seek release from that. You want to let it all go. You want to forget who you are and what you are. You wish to be the whole universe, infinite, endless. By learning to meditate perfectly, which you will do over a course of many, many years of study; by following my instructions, or the instructions of another enlightened teacher and implementing them in your daily life, you will find the way. You will make your life strong and powerful. You will learn to use will in your day-to-day activities to be successful. You will learn how to gain power in life and how to avoid losing it.

Will is a state of mind. You are born alone and you die alone. We live inside our mind. That's all there is. Everything that you experience is not external, it's internal. All your experiences are predicated upon your awareness field. If your awareness is happy and luminous, then no matter where you are, everything is wonderful. You can be in the darkest place and it will be wonderful. If your awareness field is dark and heavy, then you can be in a wonderful place, but it will be dark and heavy.

Nothing is any particular way. It's your state of mind that creates reality—it is reality. So it's necessary to *will* yourself into higher states of mind and attention to experience the wonderful beauties of existence. When faced with opposition, it's necessary to will your way through.

Balance is happiness. Happiness, joy, frivolity, play, light-heartedness is the balance that will requires. Will is guided by wisdom. Wisdom comes from introspection, looking inside yourself, probing, studying the wisdom of the teachers and the masters and bringing that into your mind. Wisdom will guide your will so that you'll use the will you developed in meditation and zazen, this powerful will, correctly. But the balance is the happiness—the pure fun, letting go, enjoying the snowflakes, enjoying the beauty of the day, enjoying a cup of tea in the morning, enjoying the touch of someone you love, enjoying being alone and being untouched, except by the universe itself.

The body comes and goes. This life, my friend, will come and go. It is a fleeting moment, an impulse in an eternal reality. I see the eternal reality. I am one with it. You are not that aware of it yet. But if you use this fleeting lifetime, if you employ it to develop your will to become wise and to achieve a happy balance, not wanting too much, being satisfied with what comes along, not being greedy—self-control creates happiness. Learn to be happy in any and all circumstances, whether you're experiencing pleasure or pain, whether there's loss or gain, whether the world loves you or hates you—learn to be happy. Happiness is not dependent upon the externals. It's a warm puppy. It's a moment.

The three elements are will, which is power; wisdom, which is necessary to guide power, otherwise power can run to extremes and become abusive and self-destructive; and balance, which is happiness. Just living in the moment for the hell of it. Having a wonderful time just breathing. Being. You can decide to live in the wealthy neighborhood. Why? Obviously, it's nicer, it's more beautiful, it's more refined. Oh! everything is perfect. The slums are perfect too. They are perfect slums. But honey, if you can marry somebody who's wealthy or somebody who's poor and the guys are about the same, marry the wealthy guy. I mean, let's be sensible.

Will is developed through the study. You need to study with someone who is enlightened, if you are serious about all this, and aim your life in that direction. You need to be around someone, to go to zazen sessions with someone, who is a master of will. A master of will can teach you how to use will. You watch them and observe them use that will, guided by wisdom, with a happy balance. There are people you will meet in the world who have developed a certain amount of willpower. They have will, but they're not happy. They don't have balance. Or they use their will just for self-gain, for selfish reasons. It is fine to use your will to get on in the world, to pay the bills, to be successful. But if that's the modus operandi, if that's it, then you don't understand too much about the rhythm of life.

The rhythm of life is give and take. It's necessary to put things back in the system. To not do that is to foul your own nest, to use up all the natural resources greedily. To over-consume is the lack of wisdom, and suffering follows the lack of wisdom. You inherit money; you spend it all on frivolous things. Then you're without it. That was the lack of wisdom. Or, you may even have some wisdom and know right things to do. And you may have developed your will. But if you lack balance, if you're not happy with just being, then what's it all for? You'll become ponderous and heavy.

You can get stuck in being wise. You can get stuck in having a developed will. It is very hard to get stuck in being happy—it's too lucid a state of mind. That is why I recommend all three. A system of checks and balances, just as we have in our Constitution—legislative, executive and judicial—they balance each other.

Wisdom; will; and happiness, contentment, a sense of humor—there's a balance there between the three. To become wise, meditate on the third eye, between the eyebrows and a little bit above. Focus on that spot, the *agni chakra*. It leads to the planes of knowledge. Do that. To become balanced, meditate on the heart center in the center of the chest. There you will experience happiness, refinement, sensitivity, beauty, laughter. To become powerful, to develop will, meditate on the navel center, and you will develop will. Don't just meditate on one. One day meditate on one. On another [day] another. Develop those three aspects of your being and you will have a terrific life because *will* must be guided. When it's not guided, it's terrible. Hitler had a lot of will. But he used it for destructive purposes because he lacked wisdom.

We see wise people. We could go to monasteries, you and I. I could take you on a tour and show you monasteries where people practice seriously. And some of them are very wise and they have great willpower, but they're not happy. Isn't it funny? Even though they wear the ochre robes, meditate for hours a day, obviously have great willpower to sustain the types of lives that they lead, they lack balance. They take it all too seriously. They can't be kids. They can't let it hang out.

Then there are those who just indulge in being kids. They are too focused in the heart. They lack power, so it's very easy for them to be taken out by life, to be blown around by the winds of karma. They don't have the will, the power. Nor do they have the wisdom to tell when happiness becomes indulgence, when it becomes too much of a self-love trip. We see a lot of this in the New Age community—these people who are all these sort of happy, bhakti, devotional types who lack wisdom and discrimination, and they lack power. So consequently, they don't advance very far in the world of self-realization, in the world of enlightenment. But if you work on developing wisdom, power and balance, then you will have an uncommonly fine life.

The component parts are simple—to meditate on those qualities by focusing on those doorways that lead to them, those chakras, those energy centers; to find an enlightened teacher and dedicate yourself to the teaching, not the teacher. Devotion to a teacher is not necessary. Devotion to the teaching is. We have seen, unfortunately, in America and in other places, in India, in Tibet, in Japan, great abuses where people are very confused and they think that they're supposed to love and adore a teacher who's enlightened. That adoration is not necessary. What is necessary is respect.

The teacher simply transmits the teaching. The teaching—the real teaching, the highest teaching—is never written down. It's only communicated in person from teacher to student because it's a "transmission of the lamp." It's a transmission of mind. Words are used. But ultimately, the teacher is transmitting pure awareness and consciousness. That is why it's necessary to see a teacher physically, until, of course, you're so developed, the teacher can transmit to you without you being physically present.

The teacher—the enlightened teacher—will reflect those three qualities. They will be powerful, but they will only use their power in proper ways because they will be guided by wisdom. Yet they won't take themselves seriously all the time, nor will they take you seriously, because they have balance. They have perspective. They can laugh, and play with life, and be a child when it's time to be a child. They can be a sage and a wise person when it's necessary to do that. And when it's necessary to just be willful, to use the will to accomplish, to change things, to push things out of your life, to bring things into your life, they use the will. But it requires will to reach wisdom, and it requires will to learn to be balanced. So of the three, the will is the most important.

Just to have balance without willpower—the balance won't last. In a difficult situation, you'll lose your balance because you don't have the will to sustain the balance. Wisdom without willpower is a car without an engine. It doesn't go anyplace. And just to reach wisdom, you need will. So of the three, at least initially, the most important is will, power. Which is why I spend so much time teaching people about power. People want to learn about love. They want to learn about wisdom. That's fine in its time and place. And I teach those things along the way.

You need to learn how to control power, how to accumulate it. Will is assertion, and you begin by learning to will small things. The first thing to will is meditation. Each day practice zazen. Will yourself—whether you like it or not—to sit down, initially once and eventually twice a day, and meditate. That will do more for developing your will than anything else. Will yourself to go and see your teacher. Make it happen. If you have to travel great distances and you need the money to do that, will yourself into a position to get the money to do that. Make it happen. Work a second job, work on weekends, do whatever is necessary. Those moments with your teacher are absolutely important. They are priceless for you. That is when all your circuits come on. That is when your life is most alive. That is when you're with the master of balance, will and wisdom. That is your special time. Make it happen.

Gradually begin to *will* a new life. Continuously evaluate your life and look at the places where you are losing power and gaining power. Gradually *will* those people, places and experiences out of your life that cause you to lose power. *Will* into your life those people, places and experiences that make you feel better, that give you a sense of bodily, psychic, mental and spiritual well-being.

Changes don't happen. We make them happen because we decide to. We decide we want something and we make it happen. Will is the key. Gradually you'll become stronger. As you drop your past, as you change, as you drop your old personality, you'll become more powerful.

Make sure that you study wisdom. Read the spiritual books. Try to understand what the teachers are saying. They are saying it for a reason. You still have multifarious desires. There are many things that you want, and you will use your newfound power to get those things. That is not right in most cases. It is a waste of will. Will is not something that you have an endless supply of. You have to discriminate and learn when to use your will.

You need to learn to be happy. It is something that you *will*. You can be unhappy or happy. Happiness doesn't just happen. You decide to be happy. You decide to take a positive attitude. You decide in a difficult situation to smile instead of frown. You decide to stand up straight instead of slouch. You decide to meditate an extra 15 minutes and sit there, and just smile the whole time to cultivate happiness while focusing on the heart chakra. You decide to take a martial arts class. You decide to work on your computer programming or whatever your career is, more than you need to. You decide to take a day off and go to Disneyland, to go play in the snow, to be silly, to touch nature, to have fun with the simplest things—because otherwise, your *will* will become ponderous and heavy.

You must control your anger and jealousy and possessive nature. Because as you become more powerful and your will increases in strength, you will injure others. When you think an angry thought about someone, it's like hitting them. It will actually hurt them psychically because you now have will. One, you're injuring a sentient being, which is wrong. Secondly, you're using up precious willpower that shouldn't be used for something so ridiculous. That willpower is used at specific moments to reformat your being, to change, to shift, to become a new person, to—in a crisis situation—emerge victoriously because you haven't used up all your will.

Jealousy, anger, fear—these are ridiculous emotions that drain your power. You need to control them by being content, trusting that life knows what is best, accepting with an even mind whatever is presented to you. If your mind rages and your emotions go crazy—being patient and calming the storm. [Leading] a high life, a beautiful life, a life of mindfulness, where, continuously—all day long—you practice mindfulness and refine your being and your life, constantly improving it, constantly becoming more aware. Wisdom must guide the will, and the balance of love and silliness and humor and the appreciation of beauty ennoble the will and the spirit.

This is Zen Master Rama. It is snowing in Boston. It is beautiful. Here, in the snow, it's beautiful. This morning there's an emptiness here. Everyone is asleep and the snow and I are keeping company. The universe is endless. Enlightenment is endless. You have only touched the outer periphery of the endless still center of perfect being. *Will* yourself to go further in. *Will* your fears away. Control yourself and abandon yourself to the ecstasy of the universe.

CHAPTER TWELVE

MANAGING AND INCREASING YOUR ENERGY

Managing and increasing your energy. Everything that we do involves energy, *personal power*. The more energy that we have, the more we can accomplish, whether it's things that you wish to accomplish physically—career-related, athletic things—or whether your goal is to enlighten your mind, to raise your awareness, to become conscious of God, of eternity, of everythingness and nothingness.

Life is wonder. Endless, ceaseless wonder. When you're in a high state of attention, of course, you see that. Now naturally, if your energy level is low, then everything is gray, two-dimensional, boring, frustrating, unhappy.

Happy people, enlightened people, successful people, inspired people—they all share something in common. They've learned how to manage and increase their energy. Angry people, frustrated people, hateful people, unhappy people, dissatisfied people, people that are mean, that seek to injure others—these people all have something in common, the ineffective use of energy. They waste energy, they don't conserve it and they don't know how to increase it. Sometimes they steal it, but what they steal, they use up quickly. They waste it.

The study of Zen is the study of energy, power, knowledge and balance. It's the science of energy conservation and control. In Zen, one uses energy, of course. We use energy to aid others, to see beauty, to discover love where we saw no love at all.

The universe is made up of vibrating, pulsing light. But when our attention level drops, when our energy is low, we don't see that. Instead we see what appears to be a solid material world. Everything is stuck together. People are stuck together. They can't change. Ideas are stuck together. They're irrevocable. We live in structures, houses. We think that the end of the universe is as far as the telescope can see. All this has very little to do with reality. It's a type of reality.

A patient is dying. They're in bed in the hospital. Their sight is fading and they look around them, and they just see grayness. You walk in the room and you're feeling great, and you don't see grayness. The sunlight is streaming in through the window. The flowers are beautiful that are in the vase, the lilies and roses. Awareness is governed by energy.

The primary place where most people lose energy is in their inter-relationships with others. That means that you lose your energy in your interactions with the people you know best. You can also gain energy, if you interact with people in a way that's beneficial. But in most cases, energy is lost in little games of manipulation, in little struggles of will, in the attempts to possess others, to wrap them up, to delude them, to shine them on.

It takes a lot of energy to manipulate someone and keep them on a string—or if you have a lot of energy and people seek it, they try and get to you, get into your life. They try and keep you off balance, keep you from making good decisions that will empower you, keep you from meditating well, keep you from being athletic and building your body up, being successful in your career. Because if you are successful and you meditate deeply and you have a healthy body, then your attention field will become very sharp and you'll look around and see if anyone is in your life for ill reasons.

Oh, let's face it, nobody's perfect, right? We live in a world where everybody wants something. But there's a tremendous difference between a person who uses you and a person who abuses you. A person who uses you is somebody who wants something from you. They may love you, but ultimately they want something from you, whether it's something physical, something sexual or just the fulfillment of their own love by having someone to experience it with. And you use people also, for the same reasons. So reciprocity, a symbiotic relationship, is a relationship in which two people have worked out certain terms: "I'm using you in certain ways; you're using me in certain ways." That's a balanced association. One is aiding the other or allowing usage, if you will.

An imbalanced association, though, is when one or both parties or more—if it happens to be a corporation—when one becomes abusive and takes unfair advantage, tries to block another's enlightenment or success, causes pain to another, injures them in any possible way, shape, manner or form—physically, with energy, emotionally, occultly.

It's necessary to do a very thorough examination of your life and to discover whether the people in your life, no matter how much you love them, are using you or abusing you. If they're using you, no problem. You should expect that, and you should use them. Not abuse—use. Proper energy balancing occurs there—beings helping each other. But if there's someone who's abusing you, then you have to ask them to stop. If they won't, you must eliminate them [from your life]. Otherwise they will keep you in a very low energy state.

Naturally, as we all know, it's possible to take energy from someone else. Just like you can steal money from somebody's wallet, you can take *power* from someone. This is usually done in close, emotional sexual relationships. In sexual contact, there is something that happens—something obviously physical and something subtle and mysterious. The doorways open between people in that deep level of intimacy, intimate contact, and it's very possible for someone to be very abusive at that time with energy. If one party is trusting, it's very easy at that time for the other party to *format* someone. That is to say, to put thoughts in their mind, to jam their consciousness or attention, to lower their energy level or to just take power from them. You can take power from somebody because a person is open on many levels.

That doesn't necessarily have to happen; it does quite frequently, human beings being they way they are—confused, deluded and generally unawakened. So as a person who seeks to increase their energy, which is obviously the reason you got the tape, I address these remarks to you—not to the general public, who may or may not be interested in increasing their energy. You have to be very, very careful about who you have intimate contact with. You have to monitor the situation constantly. It can change.

You can be with someone who is not abusive who becomes abusive. Then you have to confront them, talk to them. Human beings need things explained to them sometimes. And then if they don't change, they probably won't change, so it's time for you to change. Most energy is lost in these types of situations, or just within family structures. The only people who can really drain your power effectively are people you are very close to, you are open to, you love, or people you're afraid of. Fear.

When you're afraid of someone, they can gain power over you, meaning they can drop your energy level. If someone has something you want, if they can wrap you—this is what we call manipulation—they can make you think that they've got something that you have to get from them. They're the exclusive source; they're the only one who can make you happy. And of course, you can never get it yourself.

Now, people come to a teacher to learn Zen or other types of self-discovery, and in a way you go to the teacher to become happy. A teacher who just wants to keep you on a string forever, that is to say, they don't actually teach you how to become independent and strong, but they set themselves up as a god, the god-guru concept, and you worship them and bring them offerings all the time and they tell you what to do constantly; they don't give you challenges to develop your mind, they don't throw you back on yourself. You know, everybody wants a teacher like that, somebody who will tell you everything, tell you what to do, how to live, how to breathe, etcetera. But a teacher like that is very abusive. Those people are actually usually taking their students' energy.

Once in a while, a teacher may make a recommendation. But it's usually after going through the basic Socratic method of trying to get people to figure it out themselves. A good teacher challenges your mind, your intellect and your spirit. They throw you back on yourself all the time. By that I mean they make you do things, work for things. They teach you what they have learned, and the only way to do it is to get out and do it.

It takes many, many years to become proficient in energy conservation, just as it takes many years to get a Ph.D. But it's something that happens. You make progress. You get continually stronger. You see your attention is far different than it ever was before, if you're applying the things that you've been taught. But a lot of people who are involved in self-discovery lose energy to abusive teachers, to abusive friends and to entities, non-physical beings.

Today we see all kinds of *channeling* going on. People go to mediums and they get in touch with these spirits that are outside of the body. And most of these spirits are pretty malevolent and unenlightened, although they often claim to be enlightened teachers who are disincarnate, not in the body. These are low-vibe beings who seek life force. They don't have a body, but they want the experiences that a physical body provides. They want to experience sex, they want to experience food, they want to injure others. Most of them are from very low planes; they're not very evolved, but they can mimic. And today, we see all these people channeling and trying to get in touch with beings and have them speak through them and all this sort of stuff. I mean this isn't new. It's been going on for thousands of years, but right now there's a rash of it.

People think that simply by getting in touch with some being that's outside of the body, it will answer their questions and solve their problems, the same way they think going to some guru gives them all the answers and will solve their problems. This only creates problems. It won't help you a bit.

The person who helps you is the person who aids you in becoming independent and strong. Answering your questions won't do that because then, the next time you need to answer your questions, you just have to go back to the channeled entity, or whatever it is, or the old guru. On the other hand, good teachers don't answer you, they ask you questions. They make you think. They teach you methods of problem solving and analysis, of meditation and intuition.

I'm suggesting that a great deal of energy is lost in this study by people who interact with non-physical beings who want the person's energy, and they get into their attention field. They get into your mind and your body by approaching you in the dream plane, promising you powers, playing on your desires. They get into your consciousness. And they sap your life force. It's a game they play with you. Carried far enough, it becomes demonic possession.

A lot of energy is lost, of course, to false teachers. Wherever dependency is created, energy is lost. In self-discovery, in Zen, you need to become independent and strong. That's the key that unlocks the door of mind, of enlightenment.

There are two sides to increasing energy and controlling it and conserving it. One is avoiding loss. The other is learning how to gain energy. Gaining energy is obviously accomplished by meditating, by right actions, right thoughts, right deeds, by studying with a real teacher—or if you don't have a real teacher, by just studying and following the teachings—by creating happiness in your life, by never giving up and so on.

But my subject today is not so much how you increase it. I really believe that's a natural process, and if you meditate every day that will happen. And you practice. If you follow the study of Buddhism or any type of advanced self-discovery, it will happen. The real problem is not increasing your energy. That's pretty easy, I'm suggesting. The problem is losing it. If you stop the loss and you simply meditate, you'll have more than enough energy, and you'll learn to live strategically. These are things I discuss at my seminars and on other tapes. But the issue that most people don't get—in other words, that's the easy and fun stuff—the issue that they miss is where they lose energy.

If you plug all the holes of drainage and if you simply meditate, the rest will happen automatically for you. But if you miss where you're losing energy, it's a problem. Again, a given is that you're meditating every day; studying with a teacher, if not [then] studying the teachings; learning to have more fun with your time and life and mind; going to places that make you feel good, that increase your energy; participating in activities; following careers—right actions, right career, all that sort of thing. Happy things. Increase your energy. But you need to look for points of depletion.

Now, evolved people need to spend a great deal of time either alone or in areas of low population density. People who meditate, people who are evolved, are very sensitive. And one of the greatest problems that they have is their sensitivity. It's also their greatest boon or help. Because they're sensitive, their consciousness is flexible. They can move quickly towards enlightenment and higher states of mind. But that sensitivity is a double-edged sword. As a sensitive person, when you put yourself around other people, you feel their desires, you feel their angers, you feel their frustrations. And you begin to believe that the thoughts, feelings, desires and frustrations in your own mind are yours.

Even at a Zen seminar, this happens. I'll do a Zen seminar and let's say several hundred people come. I'll be meditating, talking about the *dharma*, about light, teaching strategic methods for having more fun with your life and becoming conscious, awakened. Naturally, all kinds of people come in different states of evolution, in different states of mind. And you'll sit at a seminar, and you may feel other people's thoughts, some of which may not be too good. You'll pick it up. You'll also pick up a tremendous volume of high energy as I meditate with you. When you go home, if you go home to a still place, the thoughts and impressions of those other people will drop away. But the good energy that you've picked up at the seminar will stay with you, and you'll see the next morning, you'll feel changed, enlightened, that is to say, more aware.

I'm suggesting that it's really important that you live in a place that has good energy. Where you sleep, where you *dream,* where you meditate, where you spend a lot of your time is key. You want to do that in a place that is accessible to your career, and you know we live in a world of cities. You have to get in and out of the city and I think that's a fine thing to do. There are lots of fun things to do in cities. But you need to try and get out of the city as much as possible.

If you do live in the city, it's necessary to get out of it on weekends or whenever. You can go for hikes and walks in nature, not simply on a busy ski slope with 10,000 other people on it, but some place more solitary—cross-country skiing perhaps or walking or whatever it is—because only then will you feel the stillness. Then you'll realize that most of the thoughts and desires you have are not yours. You'll just see what's you, in other words.

It's good to take a couple days by yourself and rent a nice cabin in some nice, happy area. Stay a day or two and meditate and take walks in safe areas—areas that feel good to you—to find out who you are again, to remember.

Ideally, you would live in an area that's not necessarily in the middle of the country, out in the woods, because you can isolate yourself there, too, and just get stuck in your own thoughts. Interaction with others is good, but in an area of low population density where you have access to both deeper country and deeper city—a place of balance.

If you thrive on the city energy, then it's necessary, as I said, if you want to effectively increase and manage your energy, to leave the city frequently and to walk in parks, to get away from people. Again, this is addressed only to persons who really want to move into higher levels of mind. Because you're more sensitive than you realize. Find a spot that makes you happy. Select companions who are striving for enlightenment. They'll have their imperfections, certainly, but at least their attention is moving in the right direction. They're accessing the right type of energy.

Preserve time for solitude.

Don't get involved with non-physical beings. This current pastime, this rage, is dangerous. Many of these people who are *channeling* entities and things like this are going to become very sick, physically and mentally. Oh, it is possible to contact higher beings who are not in the body. But the being you really want to contact is you. Or go see a teacher who's in the body, who you can tell more about. You know, these non-physical beings, it's very hard to tell what they're up to. You can't see them. How can you rely on them? It's chancy.

Emotional control is essential for attaining higher levels of mind. It's absolutely necessary to love, of course, but to be able to control yourself. The thing that a teacher looks for in a student is the degree of self-control—not coldness—self-control that someone has. Can you control your anger? Can you control your lust? Can you control your frustrations? Can you control your jealousies? Those are the only people worthy of learning the higher teachings—by worthy, I mean that they're the only ones capable of it. Because in order to really effectively interlock with higher spheres of mind and attention, you must have tremendous balance and control. This comes through conscious decisions to do so. You learn that it's more fun to have control than not to.

Enlightenment doesn't occur by accident. It's a deliberate decision that someone makes again and again, day after day, week after week, month after month, year after year, lifetime after lifetime. It's something that you grow in and develop in. When you could be sloppy, you're not; when you could be indulgent, you're not; when you could be sad, you laugh instead. If you fall down, you pick yourself up and begin again and again and again and again.

Be a perpetual beginner. Each day we start over, each evening, each moment.

Always be inspired. It's that attitude of inspiration and belief that creates energy.

There are dark forces in the world that would have you believe that you can't succeed and that you're a failure and that you're evil and all this nonsense. There are no bad people, there are only bad states of mind, and you dwell in them like houses and you can move out of them like you move out of houses if you so decide. To get into a nicer house, you need a little more money—that's energy. You'll gain that by meditating deeply, by speaking the truth, by learning to be still and by avoiding the crowd—most of the time, not all of the time.

Again, you don't need to be a recluse and stay away from people. But you have to set aside a lot of time for stillness. That's the only place there's real fulfillment, and then when you turn to life and activities in the world and career management and all that stuff, you'll be successful. You'll have a great time because you'll have the energy to do it all. But you can't burn the candle on both ends. You have to recharge. You need to slow it down, and you have to find out whose thoughts are yours and whose are not.

Nature is our friend—trees, squirrels, grass, fields, meadows, oceans—without people. Hike. Walk. Stroll. Bike. Swim. When you have free time, be in a still place and feel eternity, feel God, feel *nirvana*. Have a great time. Just feel it, extend that mind of yours, which you sharpened with the sword of meditation, into eternity. Feel beyond this life, beyond all lifetimes. Be inspired. We live in a world where people aren't. So what? They're all just going to die. What do they know?

Be optimistic always. Always feel that something good is going to happen. It is, if you decide it is and you make it happen. This creates energy, this attitude— belief, sincerity, inspiration, not getting discouraged, right attitude, right mind, right conversation, having a hell of a time.

And don't be a prude. Don't be too strict in your observances, otherwise you're just stuck in it. There is no letter of the law to follow in Zen. It's a free-form experience. There's a lot of etiquette, but there are no rules.

The etiquette is higher consciousness, sensitivity, gentleness, gracefulness, intensity, power, knowledge—feelings that you feel when I talk on these tapes.

That's all I have to teach you are feelings—the words don't matter that much.

But as you listen, *feel* the stillness of my mind, not my mind but of *mind* — *infinite mind,* endless, never beginning and never ending. Live in that stillness and revel in it. Then enter into the activities of the world, without getting overjoyed by success or totally put out by failure.

Whether they love you or hate you, it doesn't much matter. What matters is stillness.

Energy is gained, a great deal of energy, by giving energy. Now this is a curious thing. You'd never think it. Or maybe you would. We assume in life when we take something, that we get it. You go to the bank, and you get a lot of money, and you have it. If you give money away, you don't have it. But in the world of energy, that's not entirely true. When we give energy, we gain energy. Now this is different than having someone manipulate you, take your energy, you know, that sort of thing. We're not talking about that. We're talking about energy that's freely given.

For example, right now I'm making a tape. I'm sitting here in Boston visiting the city for a few days, and I'm taking time to make a tape for you. Whoever listens to this tape—it's for you.

And I'm projecting a tremendous amount of energy into this tape, into the awareness, to inspire you and show you that life can be much brighter and better than perhaps you realize.

MANAGING AND INCREASING YOUR ENERGY

Now when I do this a curious thing happens. I'm giving a lot of energy. I'm giving time. I do this when I teach. But something will come back to me unsought. I just enjoy doing this. I'm not seeking a return, but something does come back—energy—because you're not pulling energy from a limited source, the source of your body. One pulls energy, when you give this type of energy, from *infinite mind,* which is endless energy. Consequently, as you give more you receive more.

Whenever you take the time to inspire someone, to aid them in their inner search, you'll find energy will come back to you—unless, of course, you're ego tripping or you're trying to manipulate them or make them feel that you're powerful and wonderful. Then it's better not to. It's better to keep to yourself. You'll create very painful karmic situations for yourself. You'll lose energy.

The inner laws on this subject are very strict. They were written a long time ago. They're not about to change. You also have to be careful that in giving energy, you do not allow yourself to be excessively drained or used. There can be a sort of a depressive person whom you always try and inspire, and they never change, they just feed on the energy and pull you down in the process. That's not what I mean. That's pouring water through a sieve. None of it collects. It all goes out.

The alternative, of course, is to inspire people very selectively with sincerity and with respect.

We have the opportunity to do this constantly.

You want to increase your energy? Tremendously? Then want, inside your heart, to inspire others. You don't have to get up on a stage and teach. Just want that, and you will find life will occasionally cause you to encounter someone whom you can inspire. And it will lift you tremendously—one of the best ways to increase your energy. Meditate. Inspire others. Spend time by yourself. Spend time away from people. Manage your career properly. Work at something that's constructive, that doesn't injure others, and put your full attention into it.

Self-control is completely necessary for increasing and raising your attention level. One of the places you practice that is at work. You work many, many hours. It's the major activity of your life. Obviously, you can lose a lot of energy or gain a lot of energy from it. When you put your full attention into it and you do a good job, not just for the paycheck but because it's part of your *impeccability,* then you'll find it'll heighten you. Oh, we all become physically tired from working, but if we work with *right intent,* we're inspired. Our mind goes higher. Our level is more expansive.

Work in a place that feels good to you. Again, no place will be perfect, but select the best of that which is available. But it's more of an attitude. In other words, if you see work as part of your Zen, the Zen of working is just to do it, not to worry about it; just to do it as well as you can do it, to feel you'd be doing it without the money. [Then] you'd be doing something, some kind of work, because work perfects you if you do it properly. It's a chance to exercise control, restraint, discipline, creative inspiration. If you're mindful in your work, if you put your best effort into it, then something comes back to you.

Of course, try to feel that you are beyond time and space when you meditate, when you practice zazen.

Go beyond this world, beyond time, beyond life and try to retain that feeling—not a feeling of being spaced out—but cosmic consciousness, in touch with the moment and with eternity.

Throughout the day, remind yourself that you're moving through *eternity.* Be focused. Be centered. Be in the *now.*

Know what's going on in the world. Read a newspaper once in a while. Be precise in your work, in your physical motion, in your movements.

But at the same time, allow your consciousness to spill over and flood

MANAGING AND INCREASING YOUR ENERGY

into eternity, into the endless light of *reality*.

High talk with Zen Master Rama.

So it's about 4:00 a.m. here in Boston. The world is still. Soon everybody will be getting up and going about their tasks.

And there's a beautiful stillness abroad throughout the land and the universe. Feel it and enjoy it. It may not be 4:00 a.m. where you are, but it is here now, always. This moment is always.

You see, the way you increase your energy is by letting go, ultimately.

There's something inside you that knows what it should do, and you fight it all the time.

And when you let go to that part, you become perfect. In every moment, you become perfect—different, different types of perfection.

Perfection is not a final state. It's a state of mind. A child is perfect; it's a perfect child. A teenager is perfect—perfect teenager. The adult is not more perfect. The child might think so, the teenager might think so, but the adult looks back and thinks that the child and the teenager are more perfect.

Perfection is a state of mind. Everything is a state of mind. There are ten thousand states of mind.

Good morning.

CHAPTER THIRTEEN

OVERCOMING FEARS

Hi there! Zen Master Rama here. It's about 2:15 in the morning on Sunday, December 7, 1986. I'm visiting Boston. I'm downtown, looking out the window at the city, watching the cars circling around. The lights of the taller buildings are in the distance.

I came here to make a series of tapes because there's a special energy available in the downtown Back Bay area of Boston. The *power lines* here—the lines of energy that run through the earth—the luminous lines are very clear, particularly around this time of the morning.

This morning I'd like to talk with you about overcoming your fears, whether they're small fears or large fears, fears that you're aware of or subconscious fears, fears that you don't know you have.

What is fear anyway? It's a feeling that we feel in the pit of our stomach, in our body. It's very physical, isn't it? And when we experience that feeling, it really cuts us off from our strength, our power. It cuts us off from knowledge and experience. It's a guillotine that falls and separates.

Fear is an interruption in the normal flow or routine of life. Some fears appear to be more sensible than others, in a way. There are programmed biological fears. The fear of falling is there so that we're careful not to fall, so that we don't suffer bodily harm. Fear of pain is a very good fear, in a sense, in that it helps protect us—until we understand that we don't need to have a fear of something in order to avoid it.

Fear. What are you afraid of? I bet you're afraid of lots of things. You might be afraid of being alone. You might be afraid of dying. You might be afraid of living. You might be afraid of being close to someone.

Everyone is afraid of enlightenment, knowledge, completion. People are afraid of being exposed—the thoughts they think, the actions they partake in—they're afraid that those thoughts and actions will be seen by others and misunderstood or perhaps even understood.

We have lots of fears. We're taught to fear. The operative condition on this particular planet, the central mode which human beings follow, is fear—not love, fear.

Love, of course, is the opposite of fear; or understanding and knowledge are the opposites of fear.

We're taught to fear.

People are kept in line in society because they fear punishment.

It's necessary, it would seem, in a world in which people lack control. One nation doesn't attack and overrun and destroy the other nation because of fear of reprisal. We call it détente. It's fear. The assumption that underlies this mentality is that anarchy is a natural state or one of the natural states of the human condition; that a human being, without given proper restraints, will follow their desires without mitigation; and those desires will usually cause them to injure others, either because of a pure enjoyment of injuring others or because they want something; and another's well-being or happiness will not intervene between a person's lusts and appetites and desires and that which they seek. So if you're walking down the street and somebody wants the money in your handbag or your wallet, they'll attack you and take it away, unless they fear going to jail, being punished, being exposed.

People are taught to fear God. They're taught to fear - everything, just about. It's become such a natural state that no one questions it, or practically no one. Hardly anyone considers that we live in a world that's predicated upon fear. The underlying assumption is that human beings are innately evil and they must be carefully governed and controlled. That's the dichotomy that's set up within the human mind. One side of you is reasonable, the other side is not. One side of you lusts after power, possessions and so on. The other side is reasonable, is moderate and believes in restraint. But the libido, that part of our being that wants to just lash out or plummet itself into orgies of sensual passion, be they orgies of the flesh or blood or destruction or whatever it may be—we don't follow those impulses because we fear.

We might like to eat forever but we don't because we're afraid that we'll get too fat and our clothes won't fit or that people won't like us—we won't be thin enough. Or that we'll get sick and get heart disease; the cholesterol level will go too high. Fear governs. Or it will cost too much or someone will think you're a gross pig (Rama laughs). Or whatever. Fear.

There's the desire for achievement, the desire for excellence, of course. The desire to create, not just to destroy, the desire to experience beauty, love, light, knowledge. But in this world, we see more passion than dispassion. We see more fear than knowledge. Armies rule the world, nuclear weapons. I'm not against armies and nuclear weapons. I'm not for them, but as a social commentator who has seen many worlds come and go, I'm just observing the state of evolution of this particular planet. Fear-net is happening. Consequently, everyone is raised with fear embedded in their consciousness, and the big problem is, of course, fear makes you miserable when you no longer need it.

Granted, some people need it, it seems. That's the only language they understand at their current status of evolution. You can reason with someone who wants to go out and commit heinous crimes, and they may smile and listen and think you're a jerk and then go out and commit heinous crimes. Reason doesn't always work. Love doesn't always work in a practical, pragmatic, immediate sense. It's the only thing that works ultimately. Fear works, definitely. Definitely.

A good friend of mine—I've been telling him to lose weight for years. He had a heart operation, and he lost a lot of weight afterward and then, of course, he gained it back. I've been saying, "Lose the weight. Drop the 15 or 20 pounds." It didn't do any good. I was explaining that he'd look better, feel better. Positive inspiration didn't work. He went in to the doctor because he was having chest pains. The doctor said, "If you don't loose the 15 or 20 pounds, you're gonna die, sir." Lost it in about ten days.

Fear does work, yes. But it's a great limitation when you reach the point where you no longer need it. You know what you want to do. You know where you want to go or what you want to be. You have that knowledge. But yet—in other words, you don't need someone standing over you telling you what you can't do and what will happen if you do that. You've reasoned life out to the point where you know that it's good to have self-control, where you don't wish to injure others for self-gain and so on. [You are] intellectually and spiritually aware, evolved. But fear, which has been embedded in your mind since you were a tiny tot, doesn't go away easily. It's conditioned in. And because we have fear, we fail to fulfill and realize our potential as human beings. So overcoming fear is a critical factor for anyone who wishes to be really happy, or anyone who wishes to become enlightened. Because fear hangs you up.

Attraction and aversion. The reason a person is in a particular state of mind is primarily because of attraction and aversion. Attraction and aversion, like and dislike, cause us to format a mental or intellectual program. The mind is like a computer. It runs programs. It can run one program at a time, many, and most of the software that's written, that runs on the computer of the mind, has been very poorly written. It's primitive. Outdated. It's written in the language of fear. There are many more languages, advanced languages that you can run.

As you study the ways of enlightenment, you'll learn these advanced languages and be able to do things with your mind that you can't conceive of now, feel things that you've never felt, have realizations that you were unaware of.

Life is perfect. It glows.

Everything that you see before you with your physical eyes is an illusion. In other words, you're not seeing it correctly. It seems hard and surface to you. Life is made up of light. It's made up of light. But if you're only looking through the senses, it seems solid and physical.

Nothing is solid, nothing is physical. There is only light. You perceive yourself as being solid and physical, limited to a body. You are made up of light, endless *mind*. But you don't perceive that, that is to say, you don't see life correctly. I mean, the way you see life is correct, certainly. It's a way of seeing; it's a state of mind. But it's a limited state of mind.

You don't see life fully or feel it or experience it, and conversely, you do not see and feel and experience yourself fully and completely and happily because of attractions and aversions, and, of course, memory, a sense of *self*.

These are the components that create *self* —attraction, aversion, memory, longings, cravings, desires and wishes about the future or the present.

But mostly the *self* —the idea of self—that is to say the *state of mind* you're in, the way you perceive yourself, the universe, the world, life, everything that you know or don't know, is dependent upon

> attraction,
>
> aversion
>
> and memory.

And memory is simply a serial account of attractions and aversions that don't exist now except in imagination—imagination holding the past—or that don't exist now except in some possible future that has not occurred, that will never occur.

There is no future. There is only now, a continuous now. But we've become so wrapped up in the past and the future that we don't see the continuous now. There is only now. There is no future. It's an idea that you have. That's what you call the future—an idea.

There's only now.

But we particularize, we cut into consciousness, we cut into states of mind. We take a big hacksaw and we cut up time and space and mind and place and being and non-being. We create a world of ideas, a world filled with beauty and horror, life and death, high and low. This is duality, pairs of apparent opposites.

Attraction and aversion are the principal limitations, if you will, or constrictions of consciousness.

In other words, what you are, in essence, is indescribable. I can't explain it. That's why one meditates—to experience what you really are.

At this point, you're so far away from what you really are, it's ridiculous.

But the good news is that every step you take within to become more aware makes you more conscious, brings you more in touch with that which you really are and lends a rightness and completion and beauty and perfection to everything in your life.

The world glows all the time.

All of the things that you've come to understand aren't. The greatest thinkers in this world see very little compared to the enlightened who are aware not just of a day or a week or a month, but forever. They're aware of forever. Not just a single lifetime but forever. Pain and suffering only occur in temporal time. They don't occur in the world of forever. Frustration and anger, disappointment, injustice, the strong victimizing the weak—these things don't occur in forever. They only occur in limited transient time, which is a state of mind. Everything is a state of mind.

In the study of Zen we classify ten thousand different states of mind, different ways of seeing life. And in Zen, you learn them all. Then, of course, there's something beyond the ten thousand states of mind that we call *nirvana*, which is endless reality. No limitations. The limitless. Not just another state of mind.

Attractions and aversions—take two.

An attraction obviously—something that you want, desire, crave, need, have to have. She's gotta have it. Aversions—something that you don't want to have or experience. (Rama's voice changes with each phrase) "Get it away; ooh! It's gross. It's disgusting. Aaaah! I don't want to come near it. Oh, it hurts! Take it away. I don't want to go through that ever again. I don't like it. It's not beautiful." Aversion.

Fears are aversions, and attractions and aversions lock you into limited states of mind.

Who are you anyway? You are an idea. What distinguishes "you" from that great endless universe out or in there? Just the concept of self. In other words, you think, "I am." You don't just think, "I am." You think, "I am this," and if you think, "I am this," therefore you are not that. You think, "I am not that," therefore you are this. "I like blue better than green. I like girls better than boys. I like Boston better than Cincinnati"—things like that, those sorts of thoughts. Everything you like, every attraction, sets up an immediate aversion.

Oh, there are things that you vibrate with. It's not really attraction or aversion; it's just the way it is. Some vibrations are more similar, some are dissimilar, but we create a sense of self. We get our idea of ourselves through attractions and aversions. Gradually, as you are able to eliminate attractions and aversions, the idea of yourself washes away and with it, so do your limitations.

You have an endless, infinite mind that's filled with bliss. I don't know, pick a good word, ecstasy? All of these words are ridiculous. I mean they don't possibly, they can't possibly, and don't describe the fathomless wonder of what *infinite mind* is like.

What I experience is *infinite mind*.

There are no words that can describe its perfection. All of the experiences that all beings throughout all universes have ever had or will ever have or are having right now cannot possibly equal what I feel in *limitless mind* because they are all limited experiences and transient planes of awareness. But they're unnoticed in enlightenment. Take a match and light it and hold it up during the day to the sun, and you won't see it. It goes away. Its light is insignificant compared to the light of the sun. All the best things you can think of are absolutely nothing compared to enlightenment. That's why it's worth striving for. It's the best. Everything else—hey, it comes and goes, let's face it. Nothing lasts around this planet.

The streets change, the towns change, the cities change, the people change, the things that make you happy today will be gone tomorrow. New things may come, but everything changes all the time. The one constant in this universe is change.

And you need to change. You need to let go and allow the river of life to sweep you along in its currents wherever it will. But you don't keep moving when you hang on or when you push away.

Attraction and aversion create a sense of self. There is no self, in a way of speaking—a self, meaning a fixed idea of who you are. In other words, they're just thoughts. They're not substantial. They don't last.

When you die, all the ideas you had of self will go away, won't they? They don't last. But there is something that lasts, that is forever. It is forever. That which lasts is Forever, with a capital "F."

Forever is not an idea or a concept, it is reality. All of the things here come from Forever. We call Forever *nirvana* in Zen.

You could call it God, truth, Forever, anything you like.

Everything comes forth from Forever and returns to it, in a way of speaking.

And that's your mind.

Your mind is that limitless expanse of endlessness. But in human life, very few people have that awareness and so they suffer because they don't understand.

Fear creates limitation. Fear hangs you up, as does attraction, but our subject today is fear. So it's necessary for a person who wants to be happy and complete and who wishes to move beyond the pleasure and pain of this world into the limitless wonder, the amazing perfection of endless mind—somebody who wants to do that now, here, today and every day, tonight and every night—needs to overcome all fears. All fears have to go—final clearance sale. Everything must go. Fear has to be dissolved.

The student of enlightenment, the student of life who wishes to be happy, has to take on their fears one by one and overcome all of them. It's not at all impossible because fears are learned, and just as they were learned, they can be unlearned. When you were born, the fears were not there. They were taught to you. We call this conditioning, mental conditioning. Mental conditioning can be overcome through meditation, analysis, intuition, feeling, new experiences—by learning, in other words, that there's nothing to be afraid of.

There's pain. There's pleasure. There's life, death and so on, but even the way you perceive these things isn't correct because your mind is in limited states of awareness.

There are limitless states of awareness in which all of the things that you perceive will be different. Frightening, no. Wonderful. Wonderfully different. Wonderfully the same.

So then, the raison d'être for overcoming fear is that it limits you. We live in a world that's on fear-net. And of course, it's on attraction-net also. Desire. But let's stick with fear.

How do you overcome fear? Well, there are different methods, naturally. First, you need reasons for overcoming fear, other than the fact that it feels kind of unpleasant when it seizes you and ruins your life, when it prevents you from doing what you might like to do, from experiencing who you really are.

Fear limits you. You'd like to go to the Virgin Islands or to Hawaii or Japan or Australia or some place exciting for vacation, but you've got no one to go with and you're afraid. So you don't go, and you stay at home because it's all foreign. If you went, you'd have a good time, chances are—if you prepared yourself properly. But you don't go because you are afraid.

You're afraid to get a better job, to start a new career, to meet someone new, to experience something different. You're afraid to go back to something that once was good for you and that you think you've outgrown.

Or there are just paranoid fears—fear of success, fear of failure, fear of fear. There are phobias for everything—fear of computers, fear of music (Rama laughs). There are all kinds of fears, but they're all the same. They're based on falsehood.

There's nothing to be afraid of, ever, ever.

Fear is just an idea in the mind that limits you. It's only an idea. There's pain, there's pleasure, there's life, there's death and the things that happen between life and death. There's enlightenment, there's ignorance but there's nothing to be afraid of, yet we are afraid sometimes.

And you can't become enlightened if you're afraid, nor can you become happy, nor can you just act in a responsible, effective way if you have conscious or subconscious fears.

Step one in overcoming fears is to make a fear list. Take out a piece of paper or sit down at the terminal and type it up. Make a list of all of the things that you are afraid of. It doesn't matter what their order is at this point. Let's just list them all. Think of all the things that you know immediately that you're afraid of. Then start to dig. Think of all of the things that you'd like to do that you're not currently doing. In other words, make a desire list. And if you're not doing those things, chances are the reason is because you are afraid. So it's another way to find out fears.

There are the obvious fears and there are the fears that are not quite as apparent, and then, of course, there are the very deep, subconscious fears. When you were two, your mother told you to be afraid of dogs, and you don't remember that; it's in there somewhere. When you were two, they told you to be afraid of strange men, or whatever it was. Maybe your parents or those who were around you had ridiculous fears. Maybe you should watch out for strange men, but you don't have to be afraid of them. You don't want anything to do with them, but a feeling of fear will not effectively help you. Actually it interferes with seeing and knowing and becoming and acting.

If you're attacked on the street and if you're afraid, aside from a slight adrenaline rush that fear can create, usually you don't fight as well. Everybody experiences some fear. It's a bodily response, and it's a good one. It gets the adrenaline going if you're attacked. But if fear clouds your mind, then your strength is cut in half. It's cut to a tenth, so therefore fear is not useful.

Make a fear list. List them all. Once you've got them all listed, all the ones that you can possibly come up with, then let's rank them, particularly let's say the top ten, the ten things you are most afraid of. Now, we're not talking about positive fears. What I would call a positive fear, again, is that bodily feeling of, "Gee, I'm not going to go sky diving without instruction. I'd be afraid to"—you know, that sort of thing. That is a sensible fear, or it's a sensible thought. We're talking about fears that interfere. In other words, overcoming fear has nothing to do with abandoning common sense. We retain our common sense, but we lose that emotion that is fear. You know not to go out on a ledge of a building and jump off. Fear doesn't have to keep you from doing that. Common sense keeps you from doing that. The feeling of fear, however, will not help you.

So you make a list of the top ten and rank them. Number one, public enemy number one, is your major fear, the big one. Then list them down. After that [number one], it doesn't really matter. Just list them all. Type them up neatly. Put it on your wall in your bedroom or near the medicine cabinet in the bathroom, some place where you go a lot. Put it on the fridge with a magnet. Review it. Look at it on a regular basis, and let's take those fears on, one by one or a few at a time.

Now, there are three approaches—the random approach, starting at the bottom and starting at the top. I would suggest for most people starting at the bottom with the fears that are below number ten and taking them on, because I'm a great believer in little steps. I'm a professional educator. I used to be a university professor. And in my experience in education, I've learned that success in education comes by developing a winning profile.

It's no different in Zen. It's no different with overcoming fears, for most people. There are exceptions. There are other ways to do things, but for most individuals, small successes create a sense of encouragement and they lead to larger successes. Whereas to take on challenges that you will fail at, at least initially, will very often cause an individual to back off and not accomplish anything, or perhaps even to gain a more negative attitude towards the subject or themselves than they had before. So I like the little steps method. Start out with small fears and go after them and successfully conquer them. Well obviously, the way you do it is by doing it.

I mean you can reason through fears and that's helpful. You know that there's nothing in the dark. Well, of course there are things in the dark (Rama laughs), but they're in the light, too. It's just easier to see them in the dark. So it's silly to be afraid of the dark or what's in the dark—it's in the light too. I'd be more afraid of the light, personally. Anyway, you can reason through fears, but that doesn't make them go away. You know that that cat shouldn't make you afraid, but you're afraid. But it never hurts to reason through.

What you need to do, gradually at your own pace, is confront your fears one by one. There's an intelligent way to go about this and most things. Start with those small fears, the fear of the vacation by yourself. Take the vacation by yourself, but first talk to someone who can give you information. Perhaps there's a hotel to stay at in that foreign land where they speak your language, where they have tours available to you, where other people go who go by themselves whom you might meet. And so on.

You have to take on your fears one by one. You need to work at them every day. Oh, that top ten list is there, and you might start with public enemy number one, the fear of enlightenment, the fear of perfection—that's number one on everybody's list. It might be unconscious, but that's the biggest fear. The way you overcome that fear is by meditating, by having mini-enlightenments.

When you sit and meditate and stop all thought and you begin to experience expanded states of mind, you will be afraid. Suddenly you'll find that life is beautiful, life is perfect. And a part of us is threatened. Plato's cave, the light at the end of that cave, makes most people very, very afraid.

There is nothing to be afraid of, and the only way to overcome the fear is by walking down into the light, and then, of course, you see that there was never anything to be afraid of.

Everything is God. Everything is light. It's only when we live in illusions, when there are shadows in our mind and we don't see clearly [that] we feel afraid.

The ultimate way to overcome all fears is by meditating and by acting. When you meditate, you clear your mind. When you still your thoughts and go within, you experience the countless universes of mind. You blend with that eternal light and you see that you are that eternal light. You're not just a transitory being in a body. You are eternal. And then there's nothing to be afraid of. Fear melts away, just as the match held up to the sun—we don't see the light [of the match]. In deep meditation, the fears just melt away because you see that you are something that cannot be created or destroyed or interfered with. That comes from the silence of meditating. It's most beautiful.

The other thing is to go out and do the things that you're afraid of—again, things that won't injure you— in a sensible way, starting perhaps with the easier things and becoming more successful and working your way up. Or maybe you'll just go for it and take public enemy number one or two on, or maybe you'll just have a random approach, intuitively, just taking one on your list for no special reason, but it seemed like a good one to start with—not by ranking.

Meditating will give you the power to overcome fear. It will give you the power to go do those things. As you sit and meditate each day, it makes you stronger. The power of the universe flows through your mind and through your body and through your life. Gradually you will overcome the aversions, one by one or two by two or ten by ten. And your life will be better. There will be peace in your mind and in your life. There will be clarity in your purpose. There will be more laughter because you're not afraid anymore.

And when it comes time to die, you will not be afraid because by meditating, you will have already seen beyond life and death, and you'll see there is nothing to fear. We've all died many times and we don't look any the worse for it, right? Right? Right!

Laughing at fears is one of the best things that you can do—I mean seriously laughing, happily laughing. When you're afraid, instead of just plunging into panic—laugh. Make yourself laugh. Laugh at the fear, at the thought of it, and the fear gets really uptight and leaves. It beats feet.

How to overcome fear? Be around people who are fearless.

If you're afraid of other people—a lot of people are, they don't want to admit it, they're afraid of violence—take a martial arts class. Best way to overcome fear is learn to be proficient in martial arts.

In other words, you have to get out there. You can say, "Well, I'm not afraid of that guy," or "I'm not afraid of some mugger on the street," but when you've taken martial arts classes, if it's physically appropriate for you health-wise and so on, then gradually, little by little, as you learn the arts of self-defense and you interact with others, you'll overcome your fear. I mean, it's no fun to be afraid, even just on a physical level, of those around you. The best way to deter the feeling is by being competent, in my opinion, in martial arts. That's why they were invented. They're not arts of offensive fighting; they're arts of self-defense.

Most martial arts have to do with the mind, ultimately, not simply the ability to knock somebody down—the ability to be unafraid, to walk away from a fight without fear, without having to fight. That's control.

Control is the key in all of this, naturally, to overcoming fear. You will learn that control as you gain control of your time, life and mind through the practice of Zen meditation and through the study of the ten thousand states of mind.

Don't be afraid.

Stop thought, meditate and feel eternity all around you.

OVERCOMING FEARS

Realize that you are alive now. You are as alive as anything else is alive. And your right to be alive is as great as the right of anything else or anyone else.

Fears are just conditioning; they don't exist, per se. They're something that we learn, or that we're taught by people who are afraid or who seek to make us afraid. You weren't born with these fears. We pick them up along the way, or maybe you picked them up in another life. It's time to unload the baggage.

Gradually overcome your fears one by one, through meditation, and by seeing and being with people. I can't express this enough. Be around people who are fearless.

Naturally, be around someone who's enlightened. They're afraid of nothing. They're neither attracted nor repulsed in a deep sense, by anything in the universe.

Be around people who are just brave and courageous, who are able to do the things that you'd like to do. It's catching. You'll say, "Gee, if they can do it, I can do it." Sounds simple, but it works.

Keep that fear list and work on it. When you overcome one,

- cross it off the list
- and have a party.

Go out and do the things you are afraid to do gradually, and gain the power to do that through meditating. In meditation, you will find the strength to become fearless. You will find yourself, which is not a thought or an idea but an endless, limitless reality that knows no fear. That's the real secret in overcoming fear. Good luck.

This is Zen Master Rama in Boston at around 3:00 in the morning saying, "Don't be afraid of the dark (Rama laughs). Don't be afraid of the light. Don't be afraid of what's inside you."

The limitations you see now will go away when you come to know who you really are. You are endless mind, perfection. Think about it.

Chapter Fourteen

Rapid Mental Development

Hi there! Zen Master Rama here. (Zazen music plays in the background.)

Today we're discussing Rapid Mental Development—how to gain the most from your time, life, and mind; how to have an alert poised mind, a happy mind, a relaxed and balanced mind; how to have more fun with your mind and be more successful at work, in school and in meditation, in all places, in all phases of being.

In the background is Zazen from their new *Urban Destruction* album.

For the next 40 minutes or so, let's consider the mind, the ultimate battleground, where all things are real and unreal simultaneously. Going and coming are the same.

Eternity is your friend. It is, of course. (Zazen music ends.)

What do I mean by rapid mental development? Well, rapid mental development is the escalation of consciousness. Mental development is not really IQ, per se. IQ is based upon a series of tests that are given to a person, really not to evaluate their intelligence but their ability to learn certain socially endorsed skills—reading, writing, grammar and so on.

Intelligence is not limited to one's ability to function in a predefined world, in my opinion. Plants are very intelligent; I don't think they'd do very well on an IQ test. So are porpoises.

Intelligence is something that's not just thinking, it's feeling. Ultimately, in my opinion, the highest reflection of intelligence is intelligent life, cooperative life in which all benefit. A life, a planet, a society that destroys its own environment that supports it, I would not consider to be intelligent life. It's like the cancer that ultimately kills itself by destroying the host it feeds on. Symbiosis is certainly a much higher reflection of intelligent life.

So when I speak about rapid mental development, I'm not simply talking about one's ability to score higher on an IQ test. That may or may not be part and parcel of rapid mental development. Rather I'm discussing your ability to become more aware, more intelligent—but not as intelligence is measured or defined by a scholastic system or a society.

As a former university professor, I am well aware of the measurement of intelligence used by our society and our school systems. I think it's a good system in its own way, but it certainly does not reflect all points of view. It's limited. We live in the dark ages—still.

Because again, if an intelligent society can destroy itself in large numbers and if an intelligent society places the largest amount of its revenues into instruments of destruction, it's certainly not an evolved society or an intelligent society. It may be working toward that, and if it survives it might get there, or it may be like the cancer that destroys itself by destroying the thing that it thrives on.

Naturally, there's reincarnation—otherwise life would be pretty dull. Part of rapid mental development is to understand reincarnation, to experience it, to see beyond this lifetime and the patterns of this lifetime. Actually, all of the patterns in this lifetime are resulting from patterns in other lifetimes. And the patterns that you're setting up now, in this lifetime, as you interact with past patterns and create new patterns, will ultimately affect you in your lifetimes to come.

One lifetime is not all there is. Enlightened people know this because they can see beyond the doorway of death. As you meditate and develop your mind through the practice of Zen and other forms of meditation, you will discover, pleasantly, that you too can see beyond this life, that you can see your eternality.

We are made up of light. We are made up of intelligence, light, or whatever we wish to call the basic structural unit of existence, which is intelligence itself.

Rapid mental development simply means becoming more conscious of the intelligence that you already possess. Again, not intelligence simply as it's measured on a standardized IQ test, but the intelligence of being.

Spiritual evolution is the process of becoming aware of everything and yet, at the same time, of making conscious choices—understanding the patternings of life, seeing why life has created this planet, why this planet goes through the changes it does, why the manifold creatures that exist here are present—the zebras, the giraffes—why human beings have a dominant role on this very small theater that is the earth at this time. What will come after this? What has come before? What is and what is not?

Beyond this world there are myriad worlds, thousands of inter-dimensional planes with different types of beings going through other cycles of existence.

Beyond all beings is something that's eternal from which all these life forms spring and to which they will one day return, in a way of speaking.

Unconscious of the existence of the *Tao,* of the eternal truth, beings live supposing themselves to be separate from the universal intelligence—supposing themselves to be powerful or to be weak; thinking that they live their lives and die their deaths, never knowing that behind the curtain of eternity there is something else, something deeper, which is reality itself.

To know this is to know truth, not as a conceptual model but as an experience. When, through the practice of meditation, you can still your mind completely and stop thought and become conscious, that curtain will part and you will see eternity and experience it, but not simply as one sees and experiences something to eat—a transitory experience—you eat something and then it's gone.

The experience of eternity—each time you dip into the well of existence, it changes you. The waters of life change you as you drink them.

Rapid mental development is that process. It's a process of escalating your evolution. Normally a being evolves from lifetime to lifetime. Each lifetime is like a grade in school. In the first grade, you make a certain amount of progress. You learn the ABC's, how to read basic sentences and paragraphs. In the second grade, it's a little more sophisticated, and all the way on through college, etcetera.

So in each incarnation, a being evolves and learns.

Reincarnation is not necessarily linear, though. That is to say, sometimes people actually, in a way, become more immersed in darkness or illusion than they were in previous lifetimes.

Life is a journey, and sometimes there are bright days on the journey and sometimes dark days. But we learn from everything. Everything advances us, even the most difficult experiences, if we're willing to look at them with open eyes, eyes that see not just their immediate temporal effects but the larger patternings of the universe. These experiences teach us and help us grow; perhaps that's why we have them.

Enlightenment is the process of enlarging your mind to contain all of eternity—not simply the human personality structure that you've grown up with, nor the cultural conditions and customs of this planet's peoples and religions.

Enlightenment transcends religion, it transcends the human mind, it transcends life and death and all knowledge and all experience. It cuts through it all, right to nirvana, to eternity.

Rapid mental development is a process of escalating the level of your development. It's like going through many, many years of school in one year. In rapid mental development, you are going to take perhaps a hundred lifetimes, which you would have gone through and experienced and gradually evolved to higher levels of intelligence—as I previously defined intelligence—and do that perhaps in one lifetime. And you will go through all the changes in awareness, all of the different states of mind that you would have experienced in a hundred lifetimes.

Now, of course, someone will say, "Why, what's the rush? We have eternity." Well, there isn't a rush, and there isn't really a sense of rushing for someone who is engaged in rapid mental development. For them, that's a natural progression. They decided they want to go faster because they enjoy it. It's not a sense of speed or rush or competition, but rather of enjoyable evolution. They want to wake up. Some people like to wake up in the morning slowly. The alarm goes on and you shut it off and you go back to sleep for another half an hour, 15 minutes, and then it goes off again and you reset it. And you wake up for a few minutes and you look around, or you might be awake and just lie there in bed, and it's just kind of nice, you don't really need to come to consciousness real quickly.

Some people like to bound out of bed and go out into the world and have experiences. They don't like that hazy, kind of falling back to sleep and waking up and falling back asleep. Sometimes they find when they wake up immediately, if they don't go back to sleep, they have a better day because there's a certain momentum or energy that's present for them when they first awaken. If they follow it, even though they might be a little sleepy, their mind is sharp. They're inspired all day. Whereas, if they go back to sleep and get that extra sleep, they wake up in a very hazy condition. The day just never quite comes together.

So it's possible to wake up very quickly, to become enlightened, more enlightened, very quickly, or you can do it gradually. When you do it gradually, sometimes you wake up in a lifetime and you're fairly awake, but then you go back to sleep again and in your next lifetime you're not quite as awake. You don't quite catch that energy. You might go through a series of lifetimes like that and then suddenly, you wake up a little bit more. Or you can just move in a very straightforward fashion, from level to level and state of mind to state of mind. Naturally it's easier to do that in a given lifetime. In other words, the next lifetime is predicated upon the previous lifetime.

Whatever the sum total of your awareness—of your awareness at death—that will determine your next life. So if, for example, in this life you reach a certain level, that's where you'll begin again, to a certain extent, in your next lifetime. If you are able to really expand your mind and go to very, very high states of attention in this lifetime, then it will be much easier in your next lifetime to pick up where you left off because there is a certain level of inertia that interacts with a person in a new incarnation.

Even people who are enlightened in previous lifetimes, if they choose to return to the world as teachers to aid others in their self-discovery, have a certain degree of difficulty in regaining their enlightenment. Sometimes it comes in childhood; it's very simple. But sometimes it takes many, many years of meditation to reintegrate the personality structure that they gained when they first entered into this world for that enlightenment to emerge and to become complete, for the person to become more conscious and more aware.

Rapid mental development is wakefulness in its deepest sense.

The mind is like a lake, a very, very still lake, a lake with no ripples whatsoever. It reflects something. It reflects the sky; it reflects eternity when it's very still. If ripples appear, lots of them, waves, then the reflection is not clear. Something else is taking place—agitation, waves. We lose the clarity of the perfect reflection. It's a different type of experience.

Thoughts are the waves—desires, emotions, feelings that are turbulent—that slide through the mind and disrupt the reflection of eternity. Your ability to still your mind through the process of meditation and inner reflection and outer change brings a stillness to the mind all the time. Even in the midst of the busiest activities, when everybody is on your case and you've got a thousand decisions to make, and things are going right and things are going wrong—that is to say, according to the way you've structured your life plan, there are agreements and disagreements.

The universe doesn't always agree with your plan, as you may have noticed.

Zen is the study of making the mind still.

As your mind becomes still, a power enters into you. This power transmogrifies your mind. It escalates your evolution and you begin to cycle through many incarnations in one lifetime. You make tremendous quantum leaps and jumps.

This is usually done in the interaction with an enlightened teacher. An enlightened teacher is able to put a tremendous amount of power through a person who seeks knowledge, power and balance, and escalates the evolution of the individual.

Occasionally problems occur, however. Some people come to a teacher for knowledge. Some come for power. A few come for balance. Those who come strictly for power—if they're not balanced and knowledgeable—have tremendous problems because as they study with the teacher and they practice meditation, if they really don't listen to the instructions of the teacher—which are to seek balance and knowledge along with power—they intensify their power level. But they still have all the desires and angers and jealousies of an unevolved person. Consequently, as they become more powerful but not more knowledgeable, they become destructive both to themselves and to others.

If we have an angry child who's bitter and frustrated and we give him a handgun and it's loaded, he may go out and shoot somebody. If, on the other hand, he just has some soft toys to play with, it's not as dangerous a situation. Hopefully, he will learn that happiness comes through self-control and not being angry or jealous and that the only one you really torment is yourself. [With happiness], it's easier to let go and accept and gain new ways of looking at life.

The primary danger of rapid mental development is that a person will seek only power and not knowledge. And in spite of the remonstrances of a teacher, a person sometimes does this. The teacher will say, "Be careful, seek knowledge, seek enlightenment, seek balance and happiness and truth." Power will help you in your life to do that, and to enjoy your life and to help others enjoy their lives.

But to gain power before you have balance and knowledge and discrimination—then, when you become jealous of someone, your jealousy will actually have a power to it, and it's like punching someone psychically. It will hurt them because you have inner power.

When you become angry at someone, your anger will actually have a power. You can hit somebody in a non-physical way and it can injure that being. An ordinary person's thoughts don't have that much power. If they're jealous, if they're angry, if they desire something or someone, they don't have that much power to affect outer things. Oh, there's a power to everyone, and all thoughts have power, but compared to those who have real power—inner power—their thoughts are insignificant.

An enlightened person has real power and when they think a good thought—that is to say if they hold an image of someone growing, changing, developing and being happy, when they think of their friends in a happy way, their students and so on—the tremendous power of attention causes those people to actually lift up into those states. It empowers them. It brings a power into their lives.

People who have power who think negatively of others and seek to hurt them and injure them are practicing a kind of a voodoo, a lower sorcery. But ultimately, those who practice those things hurt themselves the most because as they interact with those negative thoughts and apply power to them, they devastate their own consciousness and their own lives. It boomerangs back on them. It causes them—as they dwell on anger and frustration and jealousy and rage and all these things—as they dwell on these thoughts with power, these thoughts become more and more embedded in their consciousness and pretty soon, that's all they experience. Of course, it's a miserable way to live. They're never happy. They're never satisfied. And while they may cause others a certain amount of pain and discomfort, they create internal hell for themselves.

That is why I recommend that you always seek knowledge and balance along with power.

I don't think you have to wait for knowledge and balance to come before you seek power because to be honest, you need a certain amount of power to gain knowledge and balance. But you really should seek all three simultaneously, and then power is never a problem.

Rapid mental development will take place when you meditate deeply. Everything is dependent in rapid mental development on your ability to stop your thoughts. The longer you can stop your thoughts in zazen, in meditation, the faster you will evolve, the more power you will pick up and the more knowledgeable and balanced you will become.

It's necessary, as you pick up power, to practice thinking positive thoughts because as you develop more power through daily meditation, your positive thoughts will take that power and move it in an upward direction.

Power goes either up or down. It doesn't stay anyplace; it's not stable, it's active.

Your thoughts are the harnesses of power. So it's necessary to consciously think positive thoughts, not just to wait for them to occur, but to introduce them—to work in a positive career, to live a positive life—because the power then will circuit in your life in a positive way.

When you think of others, it's very important—if you think of someone in a jealous way or if you become angry—immediately to pause for a moment and say, "Wait a minute, this isn't the right type of thought to think. This isn't good for that person and it's not good for me. It's going to pull me down and send some negative energy to them."

At that moment, you pause and you correct yourself. Don't feel bad because it happened. It's a habit that you've developed. It's also something that you pick up from others psychically. If you are around a lot of human beings who are filled with jealousy and anger and rage and desire, it filters into your mind.

But you can write a new program. Zen is—part of the process of Zen—is writing new programs to run in the mind, and the way you do that is by debugging the program that's currently running.

Every time you find yourself becoming angry, jealous or frustrated, simply stop and think the opposite thought and hold it in your mind. If you're jealous, then just make a mental note at that point and say, "No I'm not. I don't really feel this way. This is just a habit. I'm really not jealous. I wish the person well." Then take your mind away from that person. In other words, if you can't hold a person in your mind with a good thought, it's better not to think about them at all. This is very important.

Whenever you find yourself becoming angry or jealous, think the opposite, if you can.

Try to see a good quality in the person because then you'll suddenly be thinking a higher thought and that will elevate you. You'll go very high at that point, and the power will work in your life to evolve you.

But if you hold a negative thought, then it will become more powerful and not only will it send bad energy to the person, but it will really crash your consciousness.

All the hard work of meditating that would make you happy and give you a powerful life is sabotaged by these thoughts.

So it's as important, in other words, to monitor your mind constantly, as it is to sit down and practice zazen, to practice meditation.

This is particularly important if you study on a regular basis with an enlightened teacher, if you go to see them and meditate with them, because you're absorbing tremendous power from the teacher.

It's very important to always hold the thought of an enlightened teacher in your mind in a very, very positive way, or not to think of them at all.

Because when you direct negative energy towards someone who is very powerful, it has a terrible bounce-back effect. You shoot a boomerang, you send it out in the air and it comes back and you can catch it. But if you send it out and it hits a tremendous wind current that's blowing back toward you, it can come back and take your hand off.

Enlightened people live in very charged states of attention, with a tremendous power circuiting through them. They only use that power in beneficial ways.

But one who thinks of an enlightened person in a negative way—hates them, gets angry with them because they don't do what they want or they pay more attention to someone else, whatever it may be—I mean the most obscure little jealousies and reasons manifest—if you do that with someone else, it's bad for you, but with an enlightened person as it hits their aura, it just returns very strongly.

The same thing happens when you hold a positive thought of an enlightened person in your mind. If you think of them really well: "This is your friend, this is someone who is helping others, this is someone who's selfless, someone who's humorous, someone who in spite of their own enlightenment and sensitivity is happy to aid others." When you think of someone that way, when that thought touches their aura, it comes back just as quickly but with a positive lift. Suddenly, you'll find you'll feel better. You'll go up.

If you can't think of an enlightened person positively, don't think of them at all. Turn your mind in another direction. The same is ultimately true with anyone and anything, but the more powerful the person, the faster the bounce-back.

There are people who will think of you in negative ways and you'll feel it sometimes, and it actually can be physically painful if they're somewhat powerful. But don't be concerned about that. It won't destroy you. You simply have to inwardly remove yourself from these individuals. You can't be emotionally open to them and share your life with them. But never be afraid of them. Never be afraid to be in the same room with them because whenever you're afraid of someone, immediately you give them an access. They can't kill you, for heaven's sake. They can cause you a little bit of pain, but if you continue to meditate and think positive thoughts and just disassociate yourself from individuals like this inwardly, then you will find that your rapid mental development will continue along at a wonderful pace. They can't stop you if, in your heart, you seek enlightenment, empowerment, balance and knowledge.

You will see, of course, certain effects in your life.

I would never attempt to say what will happen to you and what won't.

We can only say that people who meditate deeply and who practice and who study, find wonderful things happening in their life all the time—whether it's artistic developments, the ability to learn quickly and happily, new skill development, the ability to become more accomplished at careers, and so on and so forth. These are natural outgrowths of rapid mental development

If a person pursues meditation in a deep and honest way, you will find many of these things occurring to you. No one can say at what rate or when or how. It just happens. As you develop the mind you become stronger.

But the most important type of mental development that you will discover, as you pursue Zen—if you pursue it properly, the way I've just outlined it and the ways I discuss it or other advanced teachers discuss the subject; if you pursue it properly with a non-competitive attitude, with a hopeful and helpful attitude, without violence—then you will find that you will become a very benign and powerful being, one who is at peace with himself and the universe.

You will be happy and your mind will meld with the mind of eternity. You will look beyond this transitory world and while enjoying it, enjoy eternity also.

These truths may seem simple and self-apparent and the words are easy to say, but the states of mind that you live in as you progress through rapid mental development are beautiful beyond description.

Everything is internal. The whole quality of your life depends upon your state of mind, and there are very high states of mind that very few people experience unless, of course, they engage in rapid mental development.

They are also quite pragmatic and practical in the sense that you find that they also make you more efficient at living and working in the world.

But the inner beauty and completion—as you experience eternity, not just in its surface form as we see manifested in the forms of the physical universe but in the inner worlds—is beyond description.

This is what creates happiness, peace, and balance—by becoming not simply powerful, but knowledgeable.

Power doesn't make you happy. Actually, power without knowledge and balance is problematic. It's better not to have it in a way, because it tends to drive you down.

Power is something that will automatically follow when you have knowledge. The two are really the same, in a certain sense.

The science of rapid mental development is the science of mind.

It's the science of rapid evolution, of going through hundreds of lifetimes in one incarnation.

It occurs as one is able to gain control of the mind and make it still, initially just during periods of zazen meditation practice, but then throughout the day and throughout the night. As the mind becomes still, you will find that you will experience much more.

It's not that nothing is in the mind and there's no emotion, rather it's as if the flood gates of the universe have been opened, but not just a spew of thoughts and anger and fear and jealousy and confusion come in—rather the lake becomes still and all of eternity is there.

> Endless.
>
> Light.

This is rapid mental development.

Of course, one will see correlations in one's daily life, in one's mind, in one's body and so on, in control.

As you gain control of the mind, you gain control of life and you gain control of your time. Also, as you work at gaining control of your daily life and your time, you'll find that it's easier to gain control of your mind. It all works together.

The most important component of rapid mental development, in my opinion, is silence—to develop stillness in your life. This is the quality that you're seeking. That's when the full power of the mind, in other words, is available. When you're just thinking a lot of silly thoughts and having a lot of worries, when you're not still, you waste tremendous energy and power and you put yourself into very limited states of mind and you slow down your evolutionary process.

So it's necessary to bring about a sense of peace and fulfillment in your life. This brings power and knowledge and stillness of the mind.

Now, how can you do this, when you live a busy life with millions of activities and multifarious noises in the world of, you know, just everything as it is?

I think one of the greatest aids is nature, getting in touch with nature—being out walking in a field, strolling by the ocean—because the stillness of nature is profound and yet subtle.

I think it's a nice idea to have lots and lots of plants in your house, to water them, feed them, put them in nice sunny spots.

Nature and plants understand something about stillness and silence, and as you interact with the green world, without which, of course, we could not exist in this plane, I think you will find a peace will enter your life.

Walking in nature, hiking, not just always playing in competitive sports—that's fun and it has its place—but just taking time to be still.

Practicing arts, arranging flowers, doing some drawing, working on a computer at home—not always running off to the movies or the latest adventure—brings a sense of stillness into your life; realizing that there are a lot of things that you don't need that you probably have and do, that really don't add to your life; finding things that make you still, that make you feel good.

You know, we get so involved with the latest craze or having the latest car or the most high-powered house or whatever it is that we lose touch with what makes us happy.

What makes us happy are not things, but it's meditating. It's being with people who seek light. It's being still and by yourself. Oh, sometimes it's fun to be crazy and to be active. I love it.

But it's really very simple things that make us happy. The simple things are quiet states of mind. But instead we begin to think happiness comes from getting the biggest Christmas present or whatever it might be.

Happiness is self-generated as the mind becomes still. As we become involved with the desires of the world, we lose that centering, that stillness.

What makes people who seek enlightenment happy is to study with their teacher, to practice meditation, to be in solitude, to be with friends of like mind and have an adventure or two, to have very quiet moments, to watch the sunlight filtering in through a window, to walk by the ocean to feel that stillness.

That's what you're seeking in everything, and also the accomplishment of personal success, of doing very well at your job, at bringing about success in your endeavors, having a grace and refined attention in your movements and in your life, creating a sense of balance and beauty—and seeing these as only momentary, fleeting experiences in a momentary, fleeting world in which all things change forever.

Rapid mental development comes through stillness. Look for the things in your life that bring you stillness and happiness, not the things that make you crazy. (Rama laughs.)

Don't follow the crowd. It's too crowded. Look inside yourself and look for that perfect stillness.

As you find things in your life that take you away from that stillness, avoid them. As you find things that add to that stillness, bring them more into your life. It doesn't matter what works or doesn't work for anyone else—it's all individual. Find the things that make your mind still and make you happy and follow them. You will find that rapid mental development will be a natural outgrowth of this.

Don't follow the crowd. The crowd doesn't get there. They just run round and around and around in a crazy race. It never ends.

Follow the things that lead you to stillness. Live in places that are still for you. Pursue activities that bring about stillness, not boredom, but stillness where you can feel more than you've ever felt and be more than you've ever been.

And meditate several times a day, as deeply as you can. It's truly the key that unlocks the door of eternity.

Keep a sense of humor—that keeps you balanced—and you'll do quite well with it all, I'm sure.

Chapter Fifteen

Advanced Meditation Practices

The scene is quite as you'd imagine it to be. I'm here in Big Sur; rented a little cabin. I was just out for a walk along the beach and the surf is crashing along what must be the most beautiful coastline in the world. The moonlight is playing on the water. The mountains are behind me. I've got a little fire going here in the fireplace. Maybe you can hear it crackling in the background. I'm sitting here with a cup of tea. I came up here to have some conversations with you.

Big Sur is a fascinating place. It's one of the true power places in America. And it seems a fit setting at about 12:30 at night, on the 17th of December, almost Christmas, to talk to you about the most important thing—advanced meditation practices.

I've been meditating for a while. I started formally meditating when I was about 18 years old, but really I've been meditating all my life. When I was very young, three, four, five, I used to go into *samadhi*, a very high state of meditation. I'd be outside in the backyard of my parents' home.

And I'd just look up at the sky and go away, dissolve, go beyond this world. Naturally, growing up, I never realized that I was essentially different from other children. Of course, I noticed that I was, but I didn't realize that other people didn't see life the way I did.

I was drawn back to meditation when I was, as I said, around 18. I studied with a number of different teachers. But really, I've never studied with teachers, to be honest. I've spent time with them, tried to help them in ways that I could, be of some assistance, before I became a teacher myself.

But the only thing that's ever interested me in life is eternity. Nothing else makes any sense to me.

The world as we see it is a part of eternity—houses, cars, people, buses, smog. But for me it's always been easier to capture eternity in the falling snow or along the coast where the waves crash and in solitary and lonely places. I never feel lonely in them. Oh, I see eternity in the city. I like the city too. I like its pulse, its energy, so I choose both.

But to be honest, it's the quiet places where it's easiest to feel eternity, far from the maddening crowd. So it's in such a place that I have decided to talk to you about advanced meditation.

Yes, I started to meditate formally at about 18 and I began to go into *samadhi* right away. Samadhi is a very advanced state of meditation. I can remember sitting on a mountaintop in Southern California. I'd been meditating for maybe six months, just on my own. I read a book or two about it. It reminded me of something, and I would sit out there around twilight and focus on my third eye, and everything would become still. Rings of light would appear, and I'd go through them. Then suddenly I would be beyond time and space, beyond life and death. I would dissolve for what, an hour, a lifetime, eternity—there are no words. And I was changed by this experience.

That was many, many years ago. Since then, I have gone through a process of enlightenment.

Thousands and thousands of times I have been cast into the white light of eternity, dissolved, re-formed.

Now there isn't really a difference, essentially, from my point of view, between myself and anything else.

I am that stateless state.

Advanced meditation leads you into the world of enlightenment.

Oh, there's basic meditation. What is basic meditation? Basic meditation is sitting, struggling, feeling love and ecstasy, two times a day; practicing zazen meditation, stopping your thoughts; focusing on a *chakra,* on a candle flame; sitting there trying to calm the inner noise to detach yourself from your mind, trying to stop those thoughts.

But I believe in eternity. As Shakespeare said, "There's a special providence in the fall of a sparrow." Everything happens perfectly. Sometimes we don't understand why we suffer, why we go through experiences. But that's the way of life. It's not necessarily understandable.

The reason we have experiences is because of *karma*. We've done something in this life or a past life. In my own case, I've been a teacher in many, many lifetimes—hundreds, thousands.

I've been enlightened for a long time. And in each incarnation, I come into the world to be of service to beings who seek knowledge, empowerment, enlightenment; who seek to grow, evolve, develop; who want to have more fun with their lives and experience the profundity of being; who want to become more conscious in their short time in an incarnate form. I travel from world to world, teaching as I go, fighting battles with the forces that prevent enlightenment. I'm a teacher.

What do I have to say about advanced meditation? It's a feeling. It's beyond the body and beyond the mind.

I would classify beginning meditation—beginning, intermediate, whatever you'd like to call it—as meditation with thought. As long as there's thought in the mind while you're sitting, practicing zazen, then you're in an early stage of meditation, from my point of view.

When you're sitting and there's no thought at all—no thought, no image,

ADVANCED MEDITATION PRACTICES

no idea, no feeling, no sense of no thought, no sense of self or non-self—now you have entered into the realm of advanced meditation.

Swami Brahmananda, who was a student of a very famous enlightened teacher, Sri Ramakrishna, said that advanced practice begins with samadhi.

Samadhi is meditation without any thought, any focus. To arrive at that point, of course, you begin with simple practice. Each day when you rise in the morning, you meditate because your mind is not filled with impressions.

You sit in front of an object of concentration with the eyes open. You focus on a candle flame, on a *yantra,* on something precise—a little dot, something small—and you just look at it.

You focus on it until there's nothing else in your mind. This develops willpower. After a while, after doing this for ten minutes, 15 minutes, 20 minutes, you close your eyes, then pick one of the chakras.

There are seven primary *chakras* or energy centers that are located in the *subtle physical body,*

- the body of light and energy that is our awareness,
- and that surrounds the physical.

There are seven primary chakras, thousands of lesser chakras.

Chakras are doorways to other worlds. When you focus on them, you step through into something else.

There's a still point in eternity. There's a still point where all things intersect. There's a still point that is beyond life, time, death, pleasure, pain and the senses.

Your experience of the still point is enlightenment. This point is, you could say, everywhere, but

- it's specifically within your *mind*,
- not within your physical brain per se, but
- within your *mind*,
- within your conscious awareness.

Advanced meditation is absorption in the still point.

It's called enlightenment, nirvana, God, truth, call it what you will.

There, there is no activity, other than

> the eternal activities of the universe—
>
> perfect being,
>
> the awareness of all suchness, knowledge.

This is advanced meditation—

being able to detach your mind

- from your physical activities, from your plans, schemes and dreams, from your pains, sufferings, sorrows, thoughts, jealousies, emotions, spiritual ideals, demonic ideas—

being able to let go of all of it

- and focus yourself one-pointedly
- until you are completely absorbed in the still point,
- which is eternity.

Everything you see is eternity. There are ten thousand states of mind, ten thousand windows to look outside of, to view life, death, the world.

Each is real, but they're transient; they don't last.

- You move from window to window in a very large house having different views.
- Life is just made up of views.

You are perception, awareness.

- You are that which views the experience, that is to say,
- the intersection of the view and the perceiver of the view.

In advanced meditation, you're going to step beyond your role as perceiver of the view, perceiver of your life, perceiver of your death.

- That's just a way of looking at things in duality.

Instead, you are going to merge everything into the flux. You're going to go to stillness.

When that happens, the world collapses. There's no time, no space, no viewer, no viewing, no object in view.

Beyond the ten thousand states of mind is the still point. It exists within them all—this is the riddle—yet it's beyond them. It's not affected by them. It gives birth to them.

You came forth from the still point that is reality.

That's where I come from, that world.

There are different worlds, endless worlds, and different beings come from different worlds. Some people are born in Africa, some in Australia, some in America.

Some beings begin in a world, this world or that world.

In my particular case, I come from the stillness—that world. We call it the *dharmakaya,* the clear light of reality.

I know it quite well.

In basic meditation, you sit for 15 minutes, a half an hour, 45 minutes or an hour, depending upon your ability, and you focus—first on something outside and then you close your eyes and focus on the *chakras*. For focusing, I normally recommend selecting one of the three chakras-- either the third eye, between the eyebrows and a little above; the heart center, located directly in the center of the chest; or the navel center, which is about two inches below the navel.

In Zen there are three primary aspects of balance, of focus. Just as we have the legislative and the judicial and the executive, we create a checks and balance system – there's power, knowledge and balance. You need all three to succeed, to reach the still point.

The power chakra is the navel center. The center of balance is the heart chakra; it's the center of our being. There are actually three chakras above and three below. Above is the throat chakra, the third eye and the thousand petal lotus of light, the crown chakra at the top of the head. Below, of course, is the navel center, the power center. The third eye is the center of wisdom, the agni chakra.

There are two lower chakras, which are also power chakras, but it is not advisable for persons who are in the early stages of meditation to meditate, in my opinion, on the two lower chakras. You will unleash powers and forces that will throw you into very powerful altered states of consciousness that might not be pleasant at all. Until you have tremendous control, it is not really a good idea to meditate on these centers all of the time.

The navel center will bring the power of all three of the lower chakras into your being, but with safety.

The throat chakra is the center that really is aesthetic. It gives one an appreciation of beauty.

The thousand petal lotus of light, the crown center, really does not become operative until one is on the verge of enlightenment itself. Then you don't really have to meditate on it. It just is. It lights up—the thousand petals gradually light up. This is all a way of talking, of course, a way of describing something that's impossible to describe.

In basic mediation then, you sit for a period of time. If you're a beginner, 15 minutes; after a while, a half hour then 45 minutes, maybe after a year or two. Then eventually, bring it up to an hour, hopefully twice a day, once [a day] in the beginning. Oh, you might sit longer sometimes. You'll just find yourself doing it. But normally it's not how long you do it—it's better to just sit for an hour and then improve the quality of that meditation. In other words, once you're sitting for an hour—and there's no rush to get to that point, it will happen naturally, you'll just find that it is happening, it's what you're doing—then what you want to do is work on overcoming thought, not increasing the time.

As I said, you begin by focusing on something external, a candle flame, a yantra, something like that, with your eyes open. You should spend at least half your time in a meditation session doing that and then closing the eyes for the second half and focusing on either the third eye, the heart chakra or the navel center. It's a good idea to alternate them. You can alternate one, two or three in an individual meditation session, or I think it's probably better, each time you meditate, to focus on a different one to gain power, balance and knowledge.

That's basic and intermediate meditation.

Naturally, meditation is more than just sitting and focusing. It's also letting go. When you meditate, you focus to clear the mind and to bring the willpower together.

But then, after you've been meditating for a while, as you're sitting in an individual session, perhaps for the first third or half, you focus on something with the eyes open. Then you close the eyes and focus on a chakra, and then toward the end of this session let go. Don't focus at all; just melt into eternity. You've raised enough energy and quieted your mind sufficiently so that you can just become eternity. Try to approach that still point. You don't really try, you just let go and see what happens.

But our life interferes, doesn't it? Our mind. Our thoughts. In other words, meditating is not just a practice of asserting will and learning to develop control of the mind, it's also developing control of one's life and gaining wisdom.

Now we move into advanced practice.

Your mind is turbulent because you're filled with desires, frustrations. You want too many things. You're afraid of too many things. It's necessary to overcome both attraction and repulsion to still the mind. There is lots of mental conditioning—programming—that's been put in there during this life by your parents, teachers, the society. You've been told what is and what is not, what is right and what is wrong.

This has to all be pushed aside.

Then, there are the *samskaras,* the tendencies from your other lifetimes, ways of seeing, habits that are so strong that they affect you now.

These have to be washed away also. They're the operative situations in your life that are created by *karma.*

What you've done causes things to happen. Your situation in life now has been caused by—is predicated upon—your previous actions. If you made a lot of money last year and you didn't spend it, you have it this year. If you didn't work, you may not have much money.

So the way you set your life up and the way you conduct it—the kinds of thoughts you think, feelings that you allow yourself to have, where you focus on life—brings about a mental state. That's *karma.* You can gain power and lose power. That's karma, depending upon, of course, how you handle yourself.

Then there are unforeseen incidents. You're walking down the street and someone comes up with a gun and demands your wallet. That's not necessarily your karma. Someone else is creating karma—bad karma for themselves. You can have good karma, you can be a relative innocent, and bad things can happen to you.

And if it disturbs your mental equilibrium, of course, you won't meditate well.

Meditation is the ability to clear ourselves of all conditioning, be it present life or past; to be able to deal with unexpected situations, both pleasant and unpleasant, and maintain our inner equilibrium; to be able to downplay our desires and our ego which wants attention and wants always to be right and to be noticed.

We must control the tendencies within our being that are destructive—when we want to slam somebody else, hurt them, injure them, push them out of the way.

A reverence for life needs to be developed, in which all things are sacred.

At the same time, we have to create the balance of being happy. In other words, you can't become so "spiritual" that you're not having a good time. You don't want to create a plastic image of what it is to be spiritual and try to become it because you won't be capable of it, and that will frustrate you. Or even if you could do it, if it's not really what you're like, then you'll be miserable.

You need to be yourself, but constantly upgrade that self.

So a lot of self-acceptance is involved in this process. You've got to be able to look at both your dark and your light side, if you will, and not get enamored of or depressed by either.

This is the process of mental analysis—sifting through the selves, sifting through your thoughts, practicing mindfulness, learning to control thought.

During the day when you are thinking and you find yourself dwelling on something negative, actually consciously using your willpower to remove your mind from that which is negative—a jealous thought, an angry thought, a fearful thought—and moving your mind into the flow of something positive.

- Learning not to be attached to others, to other people, to certain types of experiences.
- Allowing the flow of life to guide you wherever it is supposed to and accepting with equanimity, with balance, with poise whatever happens.
- Not trying to force our will on things.
- Allowing our will to work from deep within ourselves, almost unconsciously, to bring about necessary changes.

Advanced meditation, in other words, is not just sitting meditating. It's addressing all these aspects of life—

- to be aware of the designs of others, the dark side of others that seek to interfere with our evolution, and keeping ourselves distant and closed to such beings,
- recognizing that they're part of the universal process too, but not a part that we need to be open to at this time;
- spending time alone, particularly in areas of low population density, away from people, where we can feel the stillness,
- where we don't just pick up—psychically—everybody's thoughts and desires because if you are just picking up everybody's thoughts and desires, after a while you'll

think they're just your own;
- going walking in the woods or on the beach;
- taking weekends and going out into the desert or up into the mountains or to the ocean where there aren't too many people;
- going to the beach, not so much in the summer but in the winter;
- taking short walks in the park, down a happy trail;
- spending time with people who are also on the pathway to enlightenment and avoiding people who aren't—in your free time;
- being happy to deal with anyone in the world of business or whatever is necessary;
- not judging others, always being open to them;
- avoiding the cult mentality, you know, the super-slick, "I'm superior because I meditate, because I'm on the pathway to enlightenment," the subtle ego nonsense, terrible trap;
- just being real even, happy-being you—but finding out that "you" is far different than you have ever imagined;
- going through this process, reaching for it, yearning for it, aching for enlightenment, aching;
- but at the same time being responsible;
- working at your job and bringing it to perfection;
- keeping your house perfectly clean;
- keeping your bills in order;
- finding a teacher and studying with them and devoting yourself completely to the study, but in a balanced way,

not in a fanatical way;

- having a wonderful sense of humor, particularly about yourself and your own situation,
- yet not simply laughing, but working to change and improve things, even though, at times, it seems impossible.

This is advanced meditation.

In other words, advanced meditation is not performed simply when we're sitting down once or twice a day meditating. That's beginning and intermediate meditation.

Advanced meditation means, all day long, all night long, keeping our mind in a specific state or series of states of awareness that engender or lead to enlightenment;

- not being angry when we could be angry; not being hateful when we could be hateful; not being depressed or remorseful;
- lifting ourselves out of these states with our willpower, willing something else, having dreams and believing in them.
- They don't have to come true.
- They are true—just as a dream [is true].
- Life itself is a dream.

In the actual practice of advanced meditation, while you're sitting doing zazen, formally meditating, you won't be doing that much that is outwardly different. You'll be sitting for your hour—certainly it will be an hour at that point—twice a day.

You'll probably start meditating with your eyes open, focusing as a warm-up. Then focus on a chakra, but then you won't spend as much time focusing—

you will just let go and merge.

Not just let go to your thoughts, and sit there and think, or move into sleepy states of awareness—but move into high-powered states of attention that bring you to that still point.

Studying with a teacher. Studying with a teacher doesn't simply mean going to an occasional seminar or lecture or Zen retreat. It means fully applying yourself to what the teacher says, most of which, of course, is not verbal. When you go to see the teacher, you need to be meditating, sitting there in a very precise state of attention.

If you're studying with a real Zen master, a real enlightened person, then the teacher will be moving through thousands of states of mind and sometimes beyond mind.

While you're with the teacher, whether the teacher is talking, doing zazen or taking you out for a bite to eat afterwards, the teacher is always in a state of higher awareness—being sensitive to that, not being flaky and devotional, but just being sensitive and developing the respect that is necessary for the teacher, as the teacher respects you.

We see in a lot of practice this flaky devotionalism where a person feels the necessity of bowing and scraping all the time and sucking up to the teacher and all that sort of nonsense. It's very phony. It's counterproductive to enlightenment and spiritual development.

What's necessary is mutual respect. The teacher respects the student. The student respects the teacher and [develops] a sensitive awareness to what is being taught.

Now as a Zen master, of course, I teach all the time. Most of the teaching I do is not verbal. It's in every movement of my body. It's in my dance. It's in the way I lift a glass of water. It's in my voice tone. It's in every aspect of my life.

Because it isn't my life any more. It's eternity expressing itself in manifold ways.

[Studying with a teacher means] being able to keenly perceive not those outer expressions of enlightenment but the enlightenment itself. Feeling that. Learning from it in a balanced happy way. Again, without over-focus.

A lot of people over-focus on Zen masters and teachers as an excuse to avoid their own life, and that way they fail to take responsibility for themselves. They have this feeling that the teacher will take care of them.

Or some teachers, of course, have said that. They say, "Just devote yourself to me, and I'll take care of it." This is nonsense.

You never devote yourself to a teacher. You devote yourself to the practice.

The teacher is there to teach.

The way Zen masters teach is not just through talking—they teach in a variety of ways. They interact with you in powerful and often surprising ways,

> sometimes shocking ways
>
> that cause you to shift awareness.

The Zen master can see precisely what it will take to cause your awareness to become free. But the Zen master can't do it. If you've done your homework and you've been meditating and putting your life in order and following the teacher's recommendations, then when you interact with the teacher, you're keyed, you're prepared, and then the slightest motion from the teacher can cause you to spin into hundreds of different states of mind, to radically shift in moments. But that only happens for the prepared individual.

So advanced meditation has more to do with the interaction of student and teacher.

It's not that necessary in the beginning. A person just comes, meditates, takes a seminar, comes on a regular basis, applies the general teaching to their lives, works on their lives, feels wonderful improvement, practices zazen once or twice a day, sees tremendous improvement in how they feel, and in their energy level, their ability to concentrate, to accomplish things and so on.

- They just start to become more still.
- That's the measure of your success—how still are you, how satisfied are you? How happy are you with nothing?

But in the advanced practice, in advanced meditation, the relationship between the Zen master and the student becomes very terse.

The Zen master will expect things of the student because the student is now in graduate school, and in graduate school you do the amount of work you did in a year of graduate school that you might have done in three or four years as an undergraduate—which is not rushed or over-pressured, because that's the level that one is ready for—otherwise you shouldn't be in graduate school.

There's a level of professionalism, in other words, of dedication and respect in the world of advanced meditation, particularly in that association.

> It takes tremendous self-restraint on the part of the student not to want to monopolize the teacher's attention, to live a very controlled life and a happy life, and, of course, to be dedicated to the cause.

Advanced meditation has to do with spreading the *dharma*. In the beginning, when you meditate, it's not really necessary to do that. It's just enough for you to learn how to meditate and to have much more fun with your life and to gradually start to clear yourself from the things I mentioned before. If you decide to progress to advanced meditation, then you need to take an active part in the spreading of the dharma. In other words, meditation just can't be for personal gain. You need to consider now, actively, the welfare of others.

This can be done in two ways, essentially.

- One way is by participating in an organic fellowship. That is to say, if you have a Zen master; there are projects that need to be done—office work, working at a seminar, artistic projects, creating a brochure or whatever it may be.
- And if the Zen master sees that that will cause a person to progress, he will ask that person to do a task. Then the task is charged with power and if it's performed properly, it's a *koan*. It's the koan between yourself and the Zen master, and you will make tremendous breakthroughs. If it's not performed properly, of course, then just the opposite can occur.

Everyone in advanced meditation practice should be more involved with the economic support of the spread of the dharma.

We live in a material world, and it's very expensive to teach meditation, extremely expensive to rent halls, to have insurance, publicity, accounting procedures, on and on and on. The costs are phenomenal. Even when one charges seminar fees, it rarely covers the expenses involved. It doesn't even approach it most of the time.

So the advanced student of meditation takes an active part in supporting the work of their teacher, beyond even just participating, attending seminars and giving the normal seminar fee or whatever it is. They happily work more hours or do whatever is necessary to help out more.

And those extra hours they spend—to make more money to support the dharma—is selfless giving.

It's their *zazen,* and it will create powerful changes in their awareness field because they're not just working to make money to buy their own clothes, eat their own food, drive their own car and learn Zen for themselves. If you work an extra ten hours or an extra weekend once in a while, or whatever, or just part of the hours that you're working in your normal work week are dedicated to producing money to spread the dharma, then those hours become hours of tremendous power. That time spent is zazen; it is meditation.

A cautionary note—it's not necessary or proper to give all of your money over to the spreading of the dharma. In other words, you should have whatever you need—a good place to live, transportation, clothes, food, money for entertainment, all those things should be yours.

But beyond that, beyond your own personal needs, beyond your own expenses to study, you should then create money to help spread the dharma.

- This will cause much faster progression.
- Now you're going to do something for the dharma, for a higher cause, for a higher ideal. Part of your time and your life is being directed towards that. That's advanced meditation. It's not just for yourself, in other words.

That's advanced meditation, when we go beyond the self. Such a person will make regular contributions or irregular contributions or whatever. They'll even select a career, perhaps, where they can make more money and work and develop that career. Again, they won't be pie-in-the-sky schemes that never work out. They'll be grounded, whether it's working down at McDonalds on a weekend or doing extra programming or whatever it may be. You don't wait for the perfect job to come along; it doesn't matter what it is.

If you have humility, you're willing to undertake anything to spread the dharma.

Sometimes the teacher will have some people give basic lectures on meditation for those whom that would be helpful. That's another way of spreading the dharma, or just telling people. Again, not pushing people into it, not trying to program them, but [telling] people who are sensitive and aware, who show an interest once exposed to Zen or other forms of self-discovery, who are ready for awakening—by sharing with them your experiences about the stillness and what it's done for your life, what it's like to awaken, even if you've only awakened a little bit. To share that but never to push it, never to be a missionary, and to be completely selfless while you do that—to never think much of yourself, to realize you're only an instrument of eternity, to not get stuck in that terrible trap. You can lose everything if you get stuck in that.

Advanced practice then is, needless to say, sitting and meditating and stopping all thought completely, but there are other elements that become more involved. There's a sense of commitment to the study. It's happy, it's never forced. It's a natural evolutionary process of an evolved being. The association with the teacher becomes more critical. It has to be handled properly, with tremendous respect. A certain amount of time is given in effort to spreading the dharma, whether it's developing funds or working in some way, and it's all done with tremendous integrity. Time is spent all day and all night monitoring your thoughts and constantly keeping them in a high plateau, avoiding places that pull your energy down, avoiding people that pull your energy down, having humility and leading a balanced life, working at that job very hard in a precise way because it will help you develop your attention, participating in sports to develop your body, artistic pursuits to balance your spirit, just plain having fun, dealing effectively—without complaining—with the opposition to enlightenment.

Anyone who seeks enlightenment is going to encounter opposition, whether it's from their society or from non-physical forces or friends or whatever it is, and [you are] being strong enough to go through that and win. That's advanced practice.

There's much more to advanced practice, needless to say. These are the elements of style.

Advanced practice really, beyond all this, is the entrance into the ten thousand states of mind. Most people exist in five or six of these states in their whole lifetime.

Gradually you will go through all of them with your Zen master. He will lead you from plane to plane, level to level. And then, once you've mastered the ten thousand states of mind, then it's *parinirvana*, the absorption into the stillness forever—to go beyond this life while in this life and at the same time being normal, happy, effective in the daily world, fearless, having humility, a wonderful sense of humor, and just plain being satisfied and happy with your life.

Again, there's no fanaticism in any of this. There's intensity.

You have to make it happen. Don't sit around and wait for this to occur. You've got to sit down at those daily meditations and work on them. Don't just sit there and expect it to happen. You have to put your *will* into it. You have to put your will into creating money to spread the dharma or participating in it and doing it in a good consciousness. It's easy not to. You have to put your will into perfecting your daily life, into monitoring your thoughts.

You have to put your *will* into your association with the Zen master which is, as far as I'm concerned, the most key and most misunderstood part of the advanced meditation process.

As a Zen master, of course, I only work closely with people who are prepared for that.

Most people come to seminars, and I do as much as I can for them there. I use energy applied in different ways—koans, meditation, thousands of things to shift the awareness of all those who come to see me, on many physical and non-physical levels. This creates powerful change, particularly if the person follows some of the recommendations and implements them in their daily life.

But I select people to work with more closely when they are prepared to, and I see that. They don't have to tell me. I know. Then I will give them a task of some type, and that task becomes the koan between us.

I highly respect those who support the dharma economically, who have that level of commitment. These individuals receive my highest respect because we share something in common—a belief in truth.

That individual is exceptional. They're stepping beyond. They're doing something extra. I recognize that, and while I will not necessary acknowledge it outwardly, which would only add to their ego, we understand—I understand what you do. If you don't do that, that's fine. There is no right or wrong in any of this.

I understand you. I can *see*. I understand your sufferings, your difficulties, your higher and lower tendencies, and there's something beyond all of that nonsense. That's what I'm trying to tell you about. There's a wonderful glitter that you can follow in life.

It's the joy, it's the ecstasy.

Nothing is here in this world that's of any interest at all.

There's no point in being, if you will, straight, a responsible member of society. Who cares? All the responsible members of society are just stuck in being responsible members of society. Nor is there any point in being an irresponsible member of society. All those people are just stuck in being irresponsible members of society. Both are very defined descriptions of selfhood.

What matters is the spiritual adventure as you move into those higher planes of consciousness. It's ecstasy. It's perfection.

- All the experiences in all the worlds of all beings who have ever been or will ever be, all their joys will never equal the perfection of one moment of absorption into the stillness of nirvana, the ecstasy of enlightenment.

So always follow the glitter. Follow those inner impulses. But at the same time, it's essential to be grounded because that helps you do that. Otherwise it's my experience that people who practice, who don't work, who don't participate in society, who don't have jobs, who don't have friends and so on, these individuals think they're being very spiritual and they're just being very stuck in irresponsibility and cultism and all kinds of nonsense. That has nothing to do with Zen mind or enlightenment.

Enlightenment requires discipline, balance, knowledge, power, happiness and a sense of responsibility—being able to make sacrifices and do things with your life that you would not have done otherwise, aiding others, meditating well so you can become a good instrument of eternity. You could have a mediocre meditation today, but you're not going to because you must be at your best because today you might run into someone who you might talk to about the dharma, and you have to be at your best.

[Enlightenment requires] doing your best at your job, when you could just do a mediocre job, bringing it to perfection, not because of the money, but because that brings perfection into your attention field. Any area you slough off in your life will reflect in your meditation.

[Enlightenment requires] being happy when you could be depressed; pushing jealousy and fear out of your mind and anger, when you could just indulge in it; not feeling sorry for yourself.

This is advanced meditation, approaching these goals. This is advanced practice, and it's the most wonderful, beautiful thing.

All of it on the surface may sound kind of austere. In other words, it sounds like, "God, I've got to do all this stuff?" But each time you do one of these things, a curious thing happens—you smile more and your mind becomes more still. And when you do sit down to practice zazen meditation, it's easier.

You're in a higher state of mind.

But there's a part of us that resists all of this, naturally, and wants to make it sound as if it's much too religious. You know, it's sort of this arbitrary thing that we have to do with our life and we can't have any fun. This is nonsense.

This is the real fun. Each time you do this, it refines your attention. You perceive the beauty and perfection of life. It's wonderful.

But it should never be forced. I say "will it" and work at it, but that's because you've selected to do this because you enjoy it. But never force it. If you're forcing it, there's something wrong.

There is a difference between *willing* and *forcing*.

- When you *will it,* that simply means you're not being lazy. You're applying your full power and intensity to something, and, of course, you immediately feel great—just doing that raises your power level and you feel terrific. You never feel good if you don't do something perfectly.

- But *forcing it* means that you are not just willing something, you're trying to do something that's inappropriate or you are doing something that's appropriate in an inappropriate way. You're not being intelligent here. This you should avoid.

There's a beautiful flow to the study of Zen.

Sometimes we have to be hard on ourselves, naturally. We've got to get on our case—if we're being sloppy, lazy, indulgent; we're hanging around in mental states that we don't belong in; we're not working effectively and efficiently; we're just being selfish; we're not working for others; we're not contributing to the spread of the dharma, and all that stuff.

All of this should make you happy.

If it's not making you happier, then you're not practicing correctly.

You're not listening to the Zen master, what he's saying outwardly, but even more importantly, what he's saying inwardly.

Peace, sublime peace, ecstasy, love—all these things are there for you. But you have to reach for them; they don't come by themselves. We live in a world that's dominated by war, hate, violence and suspicion. Those are the things that come naturally in this world. So you have to will something else and not allow yourself to be discouraged when it doesn't work out quite as quickly as you thought it should or in the way that you suspected it would.

This is advanced practice. The person who, in spite of their failures, in spite of their imperfections, in spite of the times that they've been literally knocked down by it all, they're willing to get up with a smile and start again.

Having the right attitude is advanced practice, feeling that you are always a beginner in Zen. They refer to it as "beginner's mind"—being a perpetual beginner is what they're saying. The beginners are the most excited. I feel I'm a beginner, always. Because it's true.

So advanced practice is not simply meditating a couple times a day, but it's living your meditation 24 hours a day, doing more for others, contributing with your love, with your effort, supporting the spread of the dharma. Believing in it, getting excited about it, being excited about the fact that new people are discovering meditation and that it's awakening them, not being selfish and feeling those people will take more of the teacher's attention and you won't get it. That's nonsense. With that attitude, you won't get it, that's for sure. Because the teacher sees that attitude and will have very little to do with you because you're selfish and stuck on yourself and you're not seeing things properly. You're in a very illusory state of mind.

People who use their mental powers to block the enlightenment of others, who see somebody doing well and they attack them and knock them down—the teacher has nothing to do with people like this. These people lack control. What can you teach someone who lacks control? They can't control their anger and hostility.

The teacher is only interested in persons who have control, who can control these feelings. Everybody feels some jealousy, some anger, some hostility—at least until you're enlightened. Then there's no one to feel any more. Not that there's nothing to feel. There's everything to feel. There's just no one to feel. So to feel these things is not bad or wrong, don't feel guilty. But to allow them to become dominant expressions of your way of life is definitely off the wall. You can't let it happen. If you do, you're a beginner.

Advanced practice occurs when you gain control of your time, life and mind in a happy, productive, sincere way. You don't take yourself completely seriously, you work very hard, you meditate impeccably, you work hard to support the spreading of the dharma and you're mindful all day long. You practice mindfulness; you monitor those thoughts, emotions and feelings.

You're creative and you follow the glitter, the shiny stuff, the beauty. You never get so stuck in being responsible and mindful that you can't let it all go to run off with the Zen master or to run off chasing your private dream if it leads to the shiny worlds, the worlds of beauty.

Some people are so solemn. They take their practice so seriously, that when the moment comes to let go of it, they can't. They get so stuck in the catechism that they forget that the point of the catechism was to lead you some place. It wasn't an end in itself.

Some people just chase the glittery stuff and they have no substance to their life whatsoever, and no balance and no wisdom. And actually all they really want is power. But they pretend that what they're interested in is enlightenment.

Complicated? Yes and no. Depends. This is advanced practice or an introduction to it. Advanced meditation. It's not something that you just do. Oh, advanced meditation, yes, sit and stop your thoughts for an hour. Merge with eternity. Reach the stillness between the turning worlds. The way you learn that is by sitting with the Zen master, and as he moves into those states of attention you feel that and follow him. He generates tremendous energy during meditation practice or when he's doing anything, and if you're there in his physical presence, you will feel that. You're taught inwardly in other words. It's a psychic teaching. The rest of the time just work on it and have fun with it.

It's the most exciting study there is. It's the only thing I know of in life that makes you feel consistently better, no matter what's happening outside—whether it's success or failure, whether they love you or hate you, you're consistently happy. In the beginning you're not consistently happy, you're consistently up and down. But at least there's up! Before there was only down. Eventually you reach a level of stability where you just don't let yourself go down, or if you do, you quickly bring yourself back up to an even higher place than before.

Eternity is everywhere. It stretches endlessly in all directions, never beginning and never ending. Merge with it. Embrace it. Let go of your ideas and your concepts of what Zen is, what Zen masters are, who you are and what life is and what death is. Be free and disciplined.

Advanced practice. As one Zen master sees it.

Chapter Sixteen

THE ZEN OF SPORTS AND ATHLETICS

(Zazen music plays in the background.)

Zen Master Rama here. Today—sports! Athletics. The agony of victory, the thrill of defeat. In the background, Zazen. "LA Digital Mindscape" from their *Urban Destruction* album.

Zen of sports and athletics. How to make the body and soul one. Running those miles, shooting those arrows, working out, getting strong, getting stronger.

That point of intersection when there's no separation between the dancer and the dance. Between the ball and the player.

Sports! Teamwork. One unit, one mind, one body out there on the court.

Preparation of the mind. All athletics, and success in sports and athletics, from the Zen point of view, comes from the mind. If your mind isn't disciplined, integrated, free and one-pointed, how can you possibly do well in athletics? No matter what kind of shape your body is in, if your mind is out of shape, there's disharmony in the being. So in Zen we strive to bring both the mind and the body into perfect condition and integrate the two, so that there is no intrinsic difference between 'em. That's right—Zen.

Sports and athletics are zazen, they're meditation—moving meditation. As

THE ZEN OF SPORTS AND ATHLETICS   315

you are running down that field or shooting that basket, putting that golf ball, taking down your opponent in martial arts or just competing with yourself, there are moments of timelessness and ecstasy and challenge and emptiness.

Zen is the way of emptiness—and fullness! So for the next little while, we're going to discuss the Zen of sports and athletics, emptiness and fullness, beginning and ending.

Sports. (Rama laughs.)

(Zazen music ends.)

Like all things, sports and athletics mean different things to different people. In America and many countries of the world today, sports and athletics mean that on Sunday afternoon you get together with your friends, with a lot of beer and pretzels, and you sit around in front of the TV and watch a lot of people knock each other down, shoot the baskets, shoot the moon. For the individual players, those super athletes everyone watches, it means what? Money? The chance to do advertisements? That's Western sports. Oh, there are exceptions, of course.

Today I'd like to take you to the world of the Zen mind, in which all things are equal and nothing is the same. Zen, of course, has had a certain influence on sports, at least in the Far East, in Japan. The samurais, the warriors, were very interested in Zen because they admired the tremendous precision that the Zen masters had, and, of course, their lack of fear of pain and their absolute lack of fear of death. The samurais lived with death constantly. They wore a short dagger along with their other weapons on their belt, and that was to take their own life if need be. At any moment they might have to do that—that was part of their code—rather than live with dishonor and disgrace. They lived with death all the time, as we all do. It's just most of us aren't too aware of it. We don't think about it. They did.

Zen, of course, and Buddhism have really produced, strangely enough, martial arts. Because of the Buddhist injunction against the use of weapons, we've found that the martial arts have developed, and today they are popularized by movies like *The Karate Kid* and Bruce Lee and Chuck Norris and other people who we see up on the screen demonstrating these arts. We've all seen Ninja movies, and we all love to watch their acrobatics and the incredible things they can do. But of course missing from most of this, although we certainly get a little bit of it in *The Karate Kid,* is the sense of the discipline and the state of mind involved in martial arts. The same is true of Zen in archery or any other aspect.

Today I would like to talk a little bit about these things, and I'd like to use a particular example or two. I myself have participated in a number of different types of athletics and sports throughout the course of my life and still do—swimming, martial arts, running, yoga, shooting and many other types of pursuits—hiking, Frisbee, soccer, what the Europeans call football, and on and on, dance.

Let's start with Frisbee, a popular game played with a very slim disc. Now the theory of Zen is non-competition. But that's not really true at all. People who practice Zen are very, very competitive, highly competitive. But they are competing against *emptiness,* not against an opponent. And they see their opponent—if there is one, or their object, if it's the Frisbee in the case of Frisbee, if it's a basketball, if it's a football—as emptiness. What one seeks to do is blend one's self with that emptiness in order to gain control over it.

So there's definitely a sense of competition in Zen. You're competing with your *thoughts* and trying to overcome them. You're competing with unnecessary *emotions* and trying to will them down, as you would any opponent in any match. But there's also a sense of *blending,* of stepping out of your body and mind and gaining access to powers and abilities that are (Rama imitates a television announcer) "far beyond the minds of mortal men."

(Back to normal voice.) Naturally, people who go into advanced states of mind through the practice of Zen have access to powers that most people are completely unaware of. The very advanced practitioners of martial arts never had to raise a hand. They could knock an opponent down without physically touching them, just with *chi,* with energy, with pure power. We don't see too many of them anymore.

It is possible to exert a power over all things, all beings. And one who studies the art of *mind control* —which is Zen—gains control of their time, life, mind, body, spirit, and of certain powers that are very useful. But we begin with *intent,* always.

The Frisbee is the disc—round, shiny, comes in different colors, in different weights. But what is the intent? Is the intent to impress others? To become famous? To be on the cover of *Frisbee Magazine?* Or is the intent to throw the disc perfectly?

Perfection. Now, what is perfection? Well, of course, different people see perfection in different ways. From the Zen mind, perfection is not being there. If you have the sense of participation in sports or athletics, if you have the sense of being a player, then you're not really in the Zen mind. In Zen mind, in enlightened states of mind, there is no sense of self in the play.

The reason you trip, make a mistake, miss the ball, don't throw the Frisbee properly, fall down when you're skiing—aside from just lack of experience, which one gets through practice—is because your mind is not *centered.* No matter how good an athlete you are, you can strike out if your mind isn't centered.

Naturally, first one must become a good athlete, and to do so can even be a Zen practice. Each time you practice—each time you throw the Frisbee, hit the golf ball, run down the field, throw your opponent, swim those extra laps, each time you're practicing—you can practice in an ordinary state of mind or in a Zen state of mind. In a Zen state of mind, you do not worry, you don't give your thoughts to your opponent, you don't give your power or thoughts to success or failure. You don't care about the crowd that's watching you or the fact that no one is watching you. There is only one thought, one feeling, and that is *becoming one* with the play, with the move, with the action, with the sequence, with the team.

Power comes from the *navel center*. There are seven primary chakras or energy centers in our bodies. You probably have heard of people meditating on their navel. One doesn't actually meditate on the navel. The chakra is located about two or three inches below the navel, and at that point there's an energy access sphere. By concentrating for many hours in meditation upon that sphere, if you meditate for an hour or so a day and you focus on that sphere, you will release a tremendous power that will enter your body, and in moments of intensive competitive play, when you're practicing the arts of sports and athletics, that power—we call it the *chi*—will flow smoothly through your body and through your mind and through your spirit and direct the play perfectly.

However, in order to succeed on the athletic field, it is necessary to succeed in daily life. Your spirit and your life and your body must be perfectly trimmed for the *chi* to flow properly. Naturally, step one is working out and building your body up, gaining reflexes and learning as much about the sport that you have undertaken as possible.

When I began to play Frisbee, a long, long time ago, I would play with my friends for many, many hours, and we used to do very difficult things. We would stand in front of lines of trees that were parallel, with tiny spaces in between them, and we would spend hours just throwing the Frisbees back and forth between these tight little spots. There might be two rows of parallel trees that were several hundred yards long and we would have to throw through all the spaces in them perfectly, and we would just practice again and again and again. Why would anybody do anything so crazy? Because we liked it, because we enjoyed the feeling of bringing about synchronization of our body movements and our minds. Because it's fun to be outside, it's good to move your body and there's just a joy in sports and athletics.

There's a joy in moving the body—when you seek perfection. In other words, physical perfection, working out, adds to your spiritual perfection if that's your *intent*. There are lots of people who work out and aren't at all powerful in terms of their mind or their spirits. That's because they're just working out for vanity or because they've got excess energy or whatever. But if you decide, if your intent is that your athletics and your sports are not simply athletics and sports, but they are tools or devices to reach higher levels of mind, to bring you into a state of empowerment and knowledge, then your workout sessions become meditations. Then you can spend hours and hours working out the most ridiculous little moves and enjoying it completely because each time you move that body and you get closer to perfection, there is something similar happening inside your mind.

You're using the practice of mind and body to make the mind stronger and the body stronger. In order to make those moves perfectly, you have to engage your *attention,* you have to pull your mind out of its mundane thoughts and awareness and bring it into the body movement. The more completely you concentrate—which is the key word here, at least in the beginning—the more completely you concentrate on the practice, the stronger your mind becomes.

It is also necessary to meditate, to practice zazen, for an hour or two a day broken up into a couple of sessions. You need to learn the art of meditation. It's easiest to master the mind exclusively, initially. That is to say, while a certain degree of mental mastery will come as you practice sports and athletics, if you use your mind completely and interface it with your moves, you will also gain much, much more from pure meditation.

People who practice martial arts have learned a little meditation. But if, in addition, you meditate for an added hour or two a day and learn to shape and develop your mind, then you will find that when you practice—whatever type of sports or athletics you're engaged in—you will in all probability reach much higher levels of efficiency in your practice because your mind is strong and focused.

In other words, it's easier to develop the mind independently through meditation than it is just through athletic practice. As you sit and practice meditation, your mind will become awesomely powerful. If, at the same time, you're also working out at different times of the day, working on your body, and you put the two together—a strong mind and a strong body—it will be unbelievable.

You have to become a master of self-discipline, and this is done through practice. And you have to learn to live with athletic injuries. In Frisbee, of course, it's usually the finger injury unless you're running after one and jumping crazily and showing off and you land on your ear, which teaches you, don't be a show off. Keep your mind on business. Keep your mind on perfection. Watch what you're doing. Follow through. In Frisbee, the finger injury is a powerful injury because when you throw the Frisbee and release it, very often you can scrape the skin, particularly if you are throwing very hard. In running and in many sports, it's the knees and the ankles. It can be the elbows in tennis. It can be the back; it can be anything and everything sometimes.

One of the advantages of practicing meditation, of course, is that it's quite possible—if you are a very good meditator—to speed up the healing process by directing energy to the part of the body that's injured. Now, all of this has to do with the release of the *chi*. The chi is the central energy or power that we use in physical expression, and when the chi is flowing smoothly and properly in our lives, we can be very adept athletically. If the chi is blocked—if it isn't flowing properly or if it's being wasted by useless activities in our lives, by useless emotions that drain us, by associations with individuals that drain us, by purposeless activities, by boredom and so on—then we don't have enough chi, enough power when it comes time to perform.

Any good athlete is always in a state of perpetual training, as is the Zen student. The Zen student sees themselves as an athlete. Their competitive sport is enlightenment. They're not competitive with anyone else, only with enlightenment do we compete.

So in the game of Frisbee what you do is, you throw the disk, usually to someone else—unless you just want to run after it all the time—and they throw it back. It's a non-competitive game. Oh, any game can become competitive. You can try and out-throw the person you're throwing to, but you're missing the point. The point of Frisbee is perfect communication. Perfect communication. That person at the other end of the field is receiving an impression or a vibration from you. You're yin, they're yang. You're throwing the Frisbee to them. They catch it, hopefully. They throw it back to you; hopefully you catch it. The more perfectly you can throw and refine the process of Frisbee, the more perfectly you can throw that disk, the more perfectly they can catch that disk, the tighter your energy is and the more you become one with *nothingness,* the nothingness of the Frisbee, the nothingness of the play.

Your ego interferes, your sense of self, your worries, your tensions, your doubts, your limited ideas about what you can do and not do. When you can let go of your *mind,* the Frisbee will go perfectly on its own. The Frisbee will take its own path. But if you interfere by trying to direct the Frisbee, even if it looks perfect, it's not.

In other words, you can simulate perfection, but it's not the same. Someone can do a copy of a Rembrandt, but it's not a Rembrandt. It doesn't have the vibration or the power, even though to the uninitiated, it may look like one—but it doesn't feel like one. You can hit a perfect home run, but it's not perfect. If you're honest, you'll know when it's perfect because if it's perfect, you didn't hit it. At that critical moment of connection, there was no sense of you being there. Suddenly you found yourself on home plate. You don't even know how it happened. That's perfect play. There's no self involved.

So in the Zen of sports and athletics, we seek to bring discipline and control into our physical movements, but at the same time to eliminate the *self,* the messy old self that gets in the way of perfect play. The *emptiness* of play, or we could call it the *fullness,* is when there is no self present. There is no one playing; there is only play itself taking place, perfect fluid motion.

The same thing occurs in team play. If a team is playing, if the members have synchronized their energy and they have all subordinated their egos and their selves to success of the team, then we have a functioning unit. The same is true in an army, in a business office. If we have a lot of hotshots who want a lot of attention, we don't have success. We have a lot of hotshots and mavericks who want attention. That may be fine if you work all by yourself, except that you won't be happy or play really that well. But in the team spirit, we all plunge our individuality into a pool and we become one, and the play is perfect.

In the West, we think of sports and athletics as individual achievement—the thrill of victory, the agony of defeat. In other words, it all revolves around you and the ego. The whole reason you're doing it, is so you can be a winner. You can beat someone else. You can be the hero. (Rama imitates a woman's excited voice) "Oh Bob, you're so wonderful!" (Back to normal voice.) This has nothing to do with the Zen of sports and athletics. It's inefficient and you don't play that well. You might be a hotshot; you might do OK for a while, but you could have done much better, and you could have been a lot happier with your play and with your life.

It's necessary then to undertake the "discipline of spirit." It's not for everyone—the path of self-discovery. But if you are serious about sports and athletics, if that is your life, then you need to begin the discipline of spirit, and that's what the Zen master shows you, the discipline of mind. With the power of mind, almost anything can be accomplished. And just as you developed your body, now you have to develop your mind. If you've been engaging in the discipline of mind and neglecting sports and athletics, then it's time.

I recommend, literally for everyone—unless there's some medical reason or other personal reason—who practices mind control, who practices Zen, to engage in the study of some type of sports or athletics, particularly

THE ZEN OF SPORTS AND ATHLETICS   323

martial arts, be it from Tai Chi on to karate, whatever it is, where you are using your body and working out very hard—again, within the normal limitations of your body's abilities and under sound medical advice. You're not undertaking a sport that you're not physically prepared for. Always check with your doctor first, naturally. But then, if you get the green light and if your body is capable of it, go for it because it will do much to enhance your study of Zen.

There are moments of mindlessness in meditation. When I meditate, I stop all thought, and the world as you know it goes away and I enter into other realms. There are feelings and scenes that cannot be described in words. And the universe spills through me; it dances through me. This happens to anyone who can enter into the Zen mind, into enlightened states of consciousness. We are no longer our selves. We become the universe and the universal powers flow through us.

A person who practices sports and athletics, who is able to stop their thoughts during the play and allow the universe to spill through them, is capable of great magic. And as I said, sports and athletics can be a path in Zen. They can be a way to develop your consciousness and your mind, in concordance with daily practice of zazen meditation. To just practice sports exclusively is not enough. It's necessary to set aside time for meditation sessions in which there is no physical movement at all. You need to learn to move with your spirit, not just with your body, to move into other realms of mind. Then, when the spirit is free and the body is well developed, magic occurs. You are able to let go and become the play.

You see, everything has a *nothingness*. This may be hard to follow, but try, meditate on this. Everything has a nothingness—a Frisbee, a football, a baseball, a team, an opponent. Everything has a nothingness. In other words, there's a physical form that you perceive with your senses—eyes, touch, smell, feel and so on. But on the other side of sound and sight, on the other side of the physical reality, there is another world, and in that world, everything is something else. When you can journey into that world, when you can take your mind into the other side of reality and see there and be there, it's another dimension you can walk into. There the ball is quite different; the player, the opponent is quite different. The play is quite different. I can't possibly describe what it's like. You have to make that journey yourself, as have I, and as I continue to. But let us say that it's the nothingness.

We see the *something-ness* of something, a football, a Frisbee. The Frisbee is a round disk; that's the something-ness. You touch it, you feel it, you throw it. But it has another side; it has a nothing-ness, which you cannot perceive with your physical mind or your physical senses.

But there is a part of you, there's a place within your mind that understands this, if you can get to it. When you stop your thoughts completely, you enter into the nothing-ness of your mind, and at that point you can perceive the nothing-ness of the Frisbee or of anything. When you unite the nothing-ness of your mind with the nothing-ness of the Frisbee, then the Frisbee is not a Frisbee, and you are not you. Then there is perfect play, and that is the goal—if we wish to call it that—of Zen, in reference to sports and athletics. It's not to win; it's not to lose. It's to realize the nothing-ness of things and of yourself.

Your athletic and sports training can be an adjunct or a tool to that. You're always trying to pierce the veil, to break through, to break through the Frisbee so that it doesn't exist, to break through the football so it doesn't exist, to break through your opponent so they don't exist. But to do that, you must transform yourself. It's not the opponent that will change, or the Frisbee. They will change in relation to your change, but you must change.

You must change. And it is only by taking the disciplined will and directing it both inwardly and outwardly to the development of your sports and athletics, into the development of your meditation practice, and by straightening out your life and putting it in complete order so that the energy of your life supports you, that you will be able to do this.

Your life either takes your energy or gives you energy, and you need to set up your life so that it gives you energy. If your relationships are draining you and not empowering you, you must sever them if you wish the *chi* to flow properly. If your career is draining you and not adding to you, then you have to drop it and develop another one that adds to you. The way you spend your time, the place you live, the way you dress, the way you think of yourself—you must constantly raise yourself to higher and higher levels of energy efficiency, and of course, then happiness will be a result of this.

The reason one enters into lower mental states—depression, delusion, frustration, anger, hostility, trivial emotions that waste tremendous amounts of energy—is because you don't have enough power or *chi* flowing through you.

Chi is developed through meditation. Through studying with one who has a great deal of it, one who is a master of the chi, a teacher of enlightenment—and by taking their structured recommendations and placing those that seem sensible to you into your daily life so that you can turn your life into a field of power and energy to draw from—you can develop your mind through zazen meditation and the practice of mindfulness to be efficient and sharp and clear. You can unlock the power of the will, learn balance and gain the knowledge and wisdom necessary to govern the power that you are unleashing to succeed in sports and athletics. And of course, you've got to get out there and play, and throw that Frisbee or throw that ball, throw that opponent or throw yourself. That's what you're really trying to do—throw yourself. You're trying to realize your own emptiness. When you realize your own emptiness, that will be something, won't it?

There are two types of athletes, good athletes. There are athletes who power up. They work hard and they use their *will* to a certain extent to accomplish something. I can remember when I was first learning to play a little bit of tennis, I was out knocking the ball around and this guy who was pretty good came by. He was a powerful man, and he took that tennis ball and he smashed it over to me a few times. I was almost knocked over, not by the ball, but by the energy that was coming out of this guy. It was very aggressive; it was real tough, masculine energy (Rama imitates a tough guy)—"That's right guys, I'm tougher than you." (Back to normal voice.) A guy like this will be playing tennis, and some days he'll be really good and some days he won't because that's not a reliable source of energy. If he had learned—he was doing well, he was very good—but if he had learned to be completely impassive, he would have been unpredictable.

In other words, people who use the mind and aggressive energy to blow their opponent away and intimidate them, can be figured out. Anybody you can figure out you can defeat, and you can figure out anybody unless they're enlightened. You can't figure out someone who's enlightened and in enlightened states of mind because they don't make any sense—because they don't operate from the plane of mind.

Success in anything depends upon being smart, not just being strong. And winners are people who are smart. They work hard, but they use their minds, not just their bodies. When you can be completely impassive in play—in other words, you're not trying to push it out, nor are you holding it back, and you are impassive and the whole universe is shining through your eyes—then you become fluid and completely unpredictable and no one knows, including yourself, what you will do next, how you will hit the ball, where you will run, what you will do, how you will move, how you did what you just did. You couldn't even explain it.

When I play in sports or when I dance, which for me is a kind of sport, dancing on the stage in public, the things I do out in the desert, when I teach mysticism—I can't explain, even to myself, how I do what I do.

There's a moment when I come up to the end of the diving board, and that moment is reflected in *every* second in my life. I've lived my life a certain way, I've given some things up. I've done some things perhaps that I didn't initially want to do. But I have lived my life a certain way, and everything in my life points to that point when I come up to the end of the diving board.

If I've made one mistake, if I haven't done one thing right,

> if I wasn't deliberate,
>
> if I wasn't happy when I needed to be happy,
>
> if I didn't mourn when I needed to mourn,
>
> if I wasn't poignant when I needed to be poignant,
>
> if I didn't work when I needed to work,

then when I come up to that diving board, if I'm not exactly at the pinnacle of my personal power, how can the dive be? How hot can it be?

It is the same thing in everyone's life. If I've led my life totally deliberately and not omitted one thing that was necessary, nor done things that were unnecessary, then when I come to the end of that diving board, I don't have to worry about how the dive is going to be. I'm not concerned. I can just fall off the board, and it will be perfect. I won't even remember what happened.

The diving board is not just a physical diving board. It's a diving board inside our minds. When I dance, when I play soccer, whatever it is, when the critical moment comes for the move, I can do things that are extraordinary from the normal, rational point of view because my life has been lived deliberately. My life is tight, my spirit is impeccable, I'm happy and free and I've mastered the mind so that at that moment I go off the diving board, as I said, I enter into the nothingness of things.

When I dive,

> *I dive into a different dimensional plane.*

As I go off that board, I'm not in this world anymore. Someone might see the body, but my spirit has left the body and gone elsewhere. It's gone everywhere or nowhere. And then what will happen? I can't say; I won't know about it until it's over. I won't know what the dance was like until it's all over. I won't know what the Frisbee throw was like until it connects perfectly with that other person. If the ego comes up, it'll block it. If fears come up, they will block it. So you have to conquer these things in your daily life and in your practice. And you need to go off that diving board with all the power in your possession from leading a perfect life. That's the Zen mind—perfect life—and then you're free.

Then, at that point, you don't have to try. There's no exertion, there's no sense of difficulty, of being up against anything. At that point, there's one perfect motion that you're not even aware of because you're not even around. You've gone into the other world. And suddenly, to the surprise of everyone except you—because you weren't even observing—the play is perfect. But in order to do that, you must lead your life deliberately—happily, in a balanced way, not fanatically—but very, very deliberately.

If you address every aspect of your life, from balancing your checkbook to the way you do your shopping, the way your clothes are in the closets, the way you work out, the way you sing, the way you think, the way you feel—if you address everything in your life properly, which you learn to do through the practice of Zen over a period of years, and you learn to meditate perfectly and you work out fully, then you will have those magic moments in every aspect of your life.

(Zazen music begins in the background.)

So this is Zen Master Rama talking about willpower and how you cannot divorce any aspect of your life from your play, as you can't divorce your play from your life because it's all one. Life is a play; we play in the world of life. If you bring the power of mind into play, into sports and athletics, and you bring the power sports and athletics into your daily life, then you've got teamwork, right? Teamwork. Everything is one. You can connect with the *emptiness* of all things. All things are empty. There's nothing in some worlds; in some worlds there's everythingness—balance between all of those worlds.

Life is a play, it's a motion, and if you're conscious of it, you can direct the play—by letting go. If you're not conscious of it, you try and direct things, and of course they don't come out quite as well. But in order to let go and not direct, you have to direct everything in your life to the point where you go off that diving board into *nothingness,* which is where, as I'm sure you know, we all start from.

So this is Zen Master Rama wishing you well. Get out there on that field and give 'em hell, tiger. Give 'em heaven, too.

(Zazen music ends.)

CHAPTER SEVENTEEN

HOW TO BE A SUCCESSFUL STUDENT

(Zazen music plays in the background, and Rama speaks to the beat of the music.)

Zen Master Rama here. Our topic today is how to be a successful student. So for the next 45 minutes, let's all become students—students of life, students of death, students of eternity, students of our minds, students of all the beauty and horror that passes before our eyes, students of the eyes, students of that which is real, students of that which is unreal, students in college, in graduate school, professional school, computer school, students of Zen Buddhism, music students, architectural students, law students, medical students, elementary school students, students of life. Yes.

(Zazen music ends.)

I've been a student really all my life. We all start as students. We come into a world naked, knowing nothing save that we came, and we look around at the landscape, at the terrain. We feel a body, we breathe, we experience heat and cold, pleasure and pain, love and anger, solitude, the company of others. And we learn. We learn customs, languages. We're given a sense of right and wrong, which may be right or wrong. And we watch everyone; everyone is a model for behavior. We begin to make judgments. We choose and select a personality. Most of it is really picked up from others.

We're conditioned. We're told, "This is a beautiful thing. This is not beautiful. This is a happy thing. This is a sad thing." As little children we are conditioned. We're taught, we're sent to school, shipped on yellow buses or we walk miles, and just the journey, if you remember correctly, is quite educational. Suddenly we're away from the family and we're around our friends. Each one is different, and yet they're all the same.

There are girls and boys and books, and raincoats when it rains, and we sit in classes. We spend years and years and years sitting in classes every day. Monday through Friday we're in a class, all day long, being taught. And of course, most of what we're learning has very little to do with what the teacher says. Because actually we could absorb what the teacher says in a much shorter period of time, just in a couple of hours, I would say, without any problem whatsoever, [perhaps] a day. But this is an opportunity or a chance for us to learn something else, something different.

We learn how to be, how to interact with others, and we decide who we are. Are we reclusive? Are we outgoing? Are we successful? Are we going to be a failure? Exactly what is it that we want to be? We cast a role for ourselves and we step into it. And most people will play out that role that they start way back there in those first few years of life and school for the rest of their stay on this earth.

We're taught how to live. We're given tasks, but no one ever really teaches us how to be a successful student. Oh, occasionally there are courses at some universities where they teach you a little speed-reading. They talk about how to do research, how to look up a bibliography, things like that. But no one ever teaches us how to be a successful student. Some people just pick it up; some imitate others who have been successful students—perhaps their parents or someone around them. Or maybe they had a teacher who they watched very closely, and they keyed to the teacher's awareness, the consciousness of the teacher, and they gained a sense from that of how to be a successful student. But it's really, by and large, something that we're not taught.

I've been a student for a long, long time. I was a student through this life, in elementary school, high school and college. I graduated from college with high honors. I'm a member of Phi Beta Kappa, the National Honorary Society. I received an outstanding fellowship, competitive fellowship, to graduate school where I got a master's and a doctorate. I taught in a few universities for a while, until I decided to do something else with my life, to teach something else. I've studied the arts of self-discovery for a long, long time in this life for many, many years, meditating for thousands and thousands of hours, studying with different teachers before my own enlightenment returned from other lives or wherever it comes from. And I've always loved being a student. It's my absolutely—it's my favorite thing. Being a student—it's the happiest of all things to be a student.

Some people, when they grow up, look back with fond memories upon the happy years they had as a student, now that they're out in the work world, which I always think is pretty absurd. I've never stopped being a student. Going out and working and not being in a school environment has little or nothing to do with being a student. Now, of course most people think of that time of their life as being a student because that's all they did. That was their job title, "student." You had the books and the paraphernalia and a lot of free time to screw it up, (Rama laughs) which is what most people did, except for a few of us who just worked all the time, and we really got a charge out of it. But then again, you had the opportunity to learn something else—how to party (Rama laughs), or whatever it was. But as a professional educator, as a former university professor and as one who now teaches a slightly different subject—and that's enlightenment—I'd like to talk with you for a while about how to be a successful student in anything.

Success as a student is completely dependent upon a certain attitude that you gain in living. I've learned a few tricks, I suppose you might call them, along the way, which have enabled me to be a highly successful student. I had basically straight A's all through college and graduate school. I won a number of outstanding, as I said, competitive fellowships and scholarships, and all that sort of thing. But the real success, of course, was enlightenment. I mean, how many people out of millions and millions become enlightened? In this case, for me it was a return. I'd been enlightened in other lifetimes. I've been an enlightened teacher. But still, there was a time when it happened for the first time, and I remember it quite well. So I know a little bit about being a student and I'm still a student.

I'm fascinated by everything—shopping malls, nature, human beings and their strange idiosyncrasies, the latest daily newspaper, the powers and forces that live in the deserts and mountains, the endless far-flung worlds, poetry, music, art, computer science, medicine, law, architecture, on and on. I'm fascinated by life, and I learn constantly.

Enlightenment does not mean that you stop being a student. Being a student is a state of mind, like everything. Enlightenment simply means that you no longer have a fixed personality form. You are everything and everywhere. And yet you're still walking around, paying taxes (Rama laughs), being in a body, dealing with all the hassle that everybody deals with. The only difference is you're not limited to any structural world or dimensional plane. Your inner form has been dissolved in the clear light of reality so many times that there isn't any difference anymore, and yet you're still here—if you're still here. Not that you're here, But it doesn't preclude being a student. You don't have to be one; you can be anything at that point, but I personally like being a student.

What is it to be a student, albeit a successful student? A student is someone who looks at life with curiosity. There's a sense of eagerness and particularly, I might add, a sense of newness. You see, when you're a student you're always learning something. Therefore, you have to be new at it. There's always something new to learn. You're learning a new language, you're learning a new type of mathematics, you're learning a new way to meditate. You're learning how to ski for the first time. You're learning martial arts. You're learning how to sail, how to dance, whatever it might be.

You're a student of an art. There has to be a sense of anticipation, coupled with newness, hope, confidence. There's always a degree of a—or a lack of—surety. You're not exactly sure what it's going to be like. That's what makes it fun. But what makes it most interesting is not simply what you're learning, but how well you do with it. Now this is a secret, if you're a very successful student, that you learn—otherwise I couldn't say that you were a very successful student.

For example, when I was in college, I remember, I had a lot of classes with professors I liked very much. But there were a couple that I suppose everybody gets, where the teacher obviously was not very excited about what they were doing and they would literally read from the book to us or from notes that were 15 years old, and everybody would fall asleep. There was always a subject or two that wasn't your favorite. The real trick was how to get an A in that particular class—how to ace it. The ones that you like are easier.

But when there's an area that you're not crazy about, what do you do? Well, there are different approaches. One thing that always got me through was just the pure fun of learning how to do my best and succeed in the situation. In other words, the subject that I got a kick out of wasn't necessarily medieval history. The subject that I got a kick out of was how I could do well in medieval history. That's what I studied. Needless to say, as a consequence, I would learn a great deal of medieval history. It would be inevitable.

So in order to be a successful student, you cannot really be dependent upon subject material. Because some of the things that you study in life, you like, and some you don't. And if you only do well in the things that you like and you don't do well in the things that you don't enjoy, you'll never be successful. Your success will come and go depending upon like and dislike.

I was a yoga teacher for many years. I taught hatha yoga, pranayama breathing, how to stand on your head, how to do all those exercises.

HOW TO BE A SUCCESSFUL STUDENT

Before I became a yoga teacher, of course, I was a student of yoga and there were some positions that came very, very easily; some were very hard. There were some people in the class who the first or second time they came in, gosh, they were standing on their head, and it took me six months. Finally I just kept trying and trying on my own, and one day managed to do it when I got very determined. Whereas all of these other very seemingly naturally gifted people only practiced for a short time and gave up. Nor did they become teachers. In other words, people who excel at a subject don't necessarily have a natural inclination for it – sometimes [they do]. People who excel at something have a natural inclination for being a student. The particular subject doesn't matter.

I could study anything and be successful at it because I enjoy the process of studying, of being a student. That's why I get a kick out of whatever happens to me in life. Whether they write good articles about me or bad articles about me, whether people love me or hate me, whether they understand me or misunderstand me, it doesn't really matter, essentially, because my life is not totally wrapped up in those matters. My life is wrapped up in being a student of this world.

Of course, now I'm a teacher and as a teacher you not only have to be a student of the things that you teach, you have to be a student of how you teach, and naturally you also have to be a student of those you teach because you have to understand them and study them in order to impart information and other things that they need to learn. So you have to study others, you have to study various methods and ways of transmitting information—just the art of teaching, plus the subject itself.

So boy, you're an endless student as a teacher, if you're a good teacher. You're always learning more about your own field. Because if you're not excited about what you're teaching, if you're not a student perpetually of the subject you teach, then no one's going to benefit. No one's going to be charmed by what you're doing. Because you're not on fire, you're not excited about it.

If I wasn't more excited about sitting down and meditating today and doing zazen than I ever have been, then I shouldn't be teaching it. If I'm not more excited about the seminar that I'm going to be doing next, then I shouldn't do it. There needs to be, in other words, a sense of challenge. You need to challenge your mind, challenge your body, challenge your psyche, your spirit, to be a successful student.

As a student of yoga, when I would hit those exercises that were particularly difficult, I would just keep trying and eventually will would prevail. Or, I remember one exercise—it was very difficult for me to do. It's actually very difficult for most people. The natural attitude that I would have evolved would have been, "OK, here's this really hard exercise, it is absolutely a monster to do. I don't like this exercise because it's so hard."

I found myself thinking that one day as I was lying on the floor on a blanket, up in the mountains in Southern California, when I was around 19 years old. I was doing this yoga exercise and I was trying really hard, thinking how much I didn't like this exercise, when it dawned on me that of course I should decide to like this exercise more than any of the others. I decided that from that day forward, the exercise that was giving me such difficulty, which is what they call a full locust, would become my absolute favorite exercise. And every day when I did it, I said to myself, "This is my favorite exercise," and I began to like it. I began to like how hard it was to do, how hard I had to struggle to perform this exercise. I learned to enjoy the feeling of struggle, of using all of my energy and all of my willpower—just to enjoy that feeling.

Most people enjoy the feeling of complacency. They've learned to like the feeling of sitting down in front of the television set, of lying on the beach in the sunshine, of driving around in their car without anything to do, of talking endlessly for hours with others about trivial subjects—in other words, no demand. A successful student decides that they enjoy the world of demand, the world of willpower, the world of work, more than the world of trivial pursuit. If you're out there playing Trivial Pursuit, it means that you've got nothing going on in your life. And Trivial Pursuit is more than a board game (Rama laughs). It's the way that most people live. Their lives are trivial pursuits.

Go to the dry cleaners, pick up the laundry, run down to the store, do some shopping, figure out who you want to spend time with. Or if you're married, figure out how to get away from somebody. Watch your kids grow up, watch yourself get older, work at the job that you're not really enthusiastic about, get wrapped up in the world of money, and on and on and on. The human condition. Get angry when it doesn't work out the way you want it to. Take it out on somebody else; you know, all the usual nonsense. What a dull way to live. Trivial pursuits.

Students don't have the liberty of time. As a student you're always busy. There's absolutely no way on earth that you can be bored. Because there's no end to the amount of studying that you can do. You can never really have enough time to prepare for your classes. If you're studying Zen Buddhism, you never really have enough time because you're going to die. You wish to become enlightened in this life, and you may do it. And if you don't become fully enlightened, if your enlightenment is not completely integrated, certainly, if you practice, you can reach very high, enlightened states of mind.

Becoming enlightened is—it's not special, but it's unusual. I try to make this clear at seminars, but I don't know if it always comes through. Sometimes I tease about, you know, "Don't hold your breath until you become enlightened," which of course is a pun because when you're enlightened, very often you don't breathe for long periods of time (Rama laughs), when you're in deep meditation.

Very few people become enlightened in any given lifetime. By that I mean that, of the four or five billion people on the planet Earth, there might be, what, a few dozen who are enlightened, maybe a dozen who are fully enlightened, maybe a hundred who are partially enlightened and then maybe thousands and thousands, several thousand anyway, maybe ten thousand, who live in enlightened states of mind.

Now, as a student of Zen working with an enlightened teacher, of course, the probability of your becoming one of those, say, ten thousand persons who live in enlightened states of mind out of the five or so billion on Earth, is very good. That in itself is remarkable, since there are very few enlightened teachers, and if you happen to work with one, and if you do a good job, if you really apply yourself over the years as a student, it is more likely than unlikely that you will be one of those few people, one of those ten thousand who lives in enlightened states of mind, just purely on a numerical basis. And then, there's a step beyond that. I would say it's a kind of a partial enlightenment, and you may be one of those who goes forward to that.

Then of course, there will be some people who will reach a full enlightenment and you could even be one of them. You never know. It's not really a big issue. You see, being a student is not all about graduating and becoming something and getting a title. We're with the Wizard of Oz and he's handing the Scarecrow a diploma. That is about the size of it, when they give you your diplomas, right? The piece of paper does represent something, though—it represents that you won't be in school anymore, and you've got to go get a job. So—it represents more than that, certainly. It represents a lot of hard work, (Rama laughs) which is all gone (Rama laughs). Everything is transitory here.

As a student of enlightenment, your attitude should not be to become enlightened. But it should be to learn. In other words, when you are studying for a Ph.D., let's say there are a number of areas that you have to study and become very competent in, and then you'll take comprehensive examinations and perhaps do a dissertation or an experiment or whatever it is that your program has. You have to learn about these different areas. You have to become an expert. Now, needless to say, you won't be an expert just to get a doctorate. You learn enough to teach these things on a basic level, and then after you complete your doctorate, that's when you really begin. The doctorate just gives you exposure to the subject and then you have to continue beyond that. There's no end to what you can learn about anything.

So, in the school of enlightenment there's a lot to learn. But the proper attitude, if you want to be a successful student, is not to be concerned about graduating, not to be concerned about becoming enlightened. Obviously, one is doing it for that reason. You go to school to get a degree, but that shouldn't be the only reason because otherwise you'll be miserable for many years until the day comes when they hand you the piece of paper.

Optimally, you hope that you will go—this is the right attitude according to Rama—optimally you hope to go as far as you possibly can and do not put a limitation on that, since you don't even know what the word enlightenment means. It's just a word, until you've experienced it. You really don't know what it is. You may have had some enlightening experiences, but most people's enlightening experiences, from the point of view of someone who's truly enlightened, are just basic beyond belief.

So if you enjoy experiences in enlightened consciousness, if you enjoy meditating and learning to stop your thoughts, which is the hardest thing, that's why you need to enjoy meditation the most. It's like my yoga exercise—you learn to like it because it's the hardest thing, the struggle. If you like learning about being selfless, being kind, being dedicated, being honest, not being a virtuoso performer but learning how to work with some concordance in a group, at times being separate, sole, alone in eternity, in the beauties of eternity—that's the right attitude. People who are too concerned about graduating would be better off to keep their mind on their work and not on their graduation day. They're much more apt to graduate more quickly.

I think a healthy attitude is this—you never know. You never know if you will be one of those ten thousand people who enter into enlightened states of mind. You never know whether you'll be one of those hundred or thousand or whatever persons. The number really doesn't matter, but let's say there are less who become partially enlightened, and to become partially enlightened, to experience that much of the totality of yourself, is amazing. I speak of it as partial, but it's a very deep absorption in *samadhi,* a very high level of realization.

It could be your destiny in this lifetime, or perhaps in a future life, to become fully enlightened. If that is to happen, it will happen. But the only way any of it occurs is if you enjoy the study and if you're happy just to learn, just to progress, because every time you step up to a higher level of consciousness, every time you unlearn some type of conditioning, every time you meditate more perfectly, every time you are able to will things in your life to become things, to get unstuck from the personality that you are now and just merge with life, [then] you feel better. You've progressed.

Being a successful student then is an attitude, and the right attitude is enjoying the study. That's the first step. You have to have a sense of commitment. You are going to undertake something. You've decided to go to college or to computer school. You thought about it and what ultimately made you do it was a feeling. That's why we do anything. We can say, "Well, I decided I wanted to make more money," or "I didn't like the job I had," or "I wanted to get out of the house and get away to school." Well, all these things may or may not be true, but the real reason we do anything, of course, is not what most people would call a rational decision.

We all think things out, but then we follow a feeling. If the feeling coincides with the rational decision, then we can say we made a rational decision. But as we all know, very often the more important things we do in life have nothing to do with the rational. The rational is a very limited way to look at things. That's just an equation and equations are fine on paper, but they don't always work in daily life or living in the school of experience, in the bardo of existence.

What is necessary then is to have fun, to have a good time with your life, and you do that by following feelings, and some feelings cause you misery and some cause you to feel good. Some bind you and some bring you to freedom. So the student selects freedom and they select happiness. It's a choice that you make. You reflect and decide, yes, I want to study computer science. I want to study Zen and meditation. I want to study mysticism and the powers of the deserts and the mountains, whatever it might be. I want to study law or medicine or become a musician or a dancer. I want to study martial arts, skiing, sailing, scuba diving, whatever it might be—sky diving, flying a plane, flying through the astral planes.

You follow a feeling and you need to meditate on that feeling and feel it and walk around with it for a while before you do it. Once you've decided, once you have decided, "Yes, I'm going to study a particular subject," great. Then the next step is to find a teacher, unless it's a self-taught subject, in which case you're the teacher or your books are the teachers, or whatever it is you're working with. The teacher is the all-important component, and one of the things that you learn early on as a successful student is that you don't take classes, you take teachers.

In other words, three people, ten people, a thousand people can teach the same thing, and very few will do it well. There are lots of dentists and only a few good ones. Most are average, some are terrible, and that's how it is with everything. It's how it is with carpenters, sculptors, with students, the vast majority are mediocre. There are some who are just downright awful, and a few who are superb, who excel. It is the same with teachers.

As a college student and a student in graduate school, I never took a class because of the title. There were certain classes, of course, that were required, but I would go individually, before signing up for a class at the end of the semester when you would sign up for classes for the next semester. I would make it a point to meet every teacher, and just come in and spend a minute or two with them during their office hours and say, "Hi, I'm thinking about taking your class next semester. I wanted to meet you and ask you what's it all about. What books will we be reading?" I would find out in that minute or two enough to tell me whether I wanted to work with the teacher or not.

Now most students won't do this. They just sign up from the list in the book, and yet then they will sit with that teacher month after month experiencing that teacher's consciousness, their vibration, listening to them and ultimately being bound by the teacher's grade.

One doesn't pick easy teachers. Easy teachers can be disastrous because they're so easy, you're so bored that you don't do well. You pick good teachers. Some of the teachers I picked were hard; they had reputations for never giving anyone an A, which I found to be untrue. Those were obviously the people who didn't get A's who spread those rumors, who didn't work too hard.

Selecting a teacher is a very important thing, and the more time you spend with a teacher, the more important it is. If it's a teacher you're going to have in a classroom for one semester, it's important. Once in a while there's nothing you can do. Only one teacher is teaching a section of a particular course and there's no way around it and you have to take it that semester. Then, you have to take it. It's still worthwhile going in and making an initial contact, I think, with a teacher.

If it's a subject you're going to be spending much more time in, if the subject is enlightenment, if the subject is martial arts or something where you're working with a master of the art, a mentor, someone who you will be involved with, not just for a month or two but for a long period of time, who will really oversee your study for many years—then you have to be very selective.

As I said—most teachers are mediocre. Most people who profess to teach about enlightenment are terrible, in my opinion. They're mediocre. They're not terrible, but that's how I view them because my standards are different. Then there are some who are even worse and there are a few who are very good. I found the same thing as a college professor. Most of my colleagues were boring, so their students thought anyway. They were great scholars, but that's a little different.

To become a college professor, you don't have to be a good teacher. Your Ph.D. indicates that you're a scholar and you enjoy libraries and writing papers. You may be very good at doing all that, but that doesn't mean you're a good teacher. No one ever asks you if you're a teacher.

High school teachers take some courses about teaching; that doesn't ensure that they're good teachers. It ensures that they passed courses in teaching. Being a good teacher is another matter, as is being a good student. Put a good student and a good teacher together and you've got an unbeatable combination because the teacher likes teaching and the student likes learning, and they lived happily ever after, right? Well, I don't know about that, but you need to be very careful in selecting a teacher.

If it's a basic meditation course, it doesn't much matter. But if you are working on your enlightenment, then you will work with someone for years and years and years. And you need to feel, one, obviously that the person is qualified or the most qualified of all the people you've met, and [two] you need to respect them. You don't have to like them, but you need to respect the way they teach. If you don't respect a teacher, you can't possibly gain anything from it. Some teachers are funny, some are not. Some are strict, some are more liberal, but you can respect any of them if you understand what they're doing, that is to say, if they're worthy of respect—if they're masters of their art.

A master of an art is someone, I suppose, who's been mastered by the art. They've become so one with what they teach that you can't tell the teacher from the subject. The teacher is the subject; that's what their whole life is about. They're so wrapped up in it. I had college professors like that. They were so wrapped up in their subject that that's all they could talk about. I would say such a person is a master of their subject, or that they've been mastered by it. Their life and their subject are one.

That's how I define a master. A Zen master is someone whose life is so one with enlightenment and self-discovery that they can never be separated from that. They've been essentially mastered by Zen. No one ever masters a subject; I mean, that's a strange concept. The subject masters you.

So you need to selectively pick a teacher, one that you respect, and also, of course, one who's capable, one who can do what they say. In the world of enlightenment it's not just someone who can talk with wonderful poetic figures about enlightenment, but someone who has the personal power to bring you into altered states of awareness, someone who has an advanced knowledge of other planes of consciousness, who can see beyond the physical world.

Now, there are people who profess to do that, but very few actually can. Someone who can literally perform miracles, not just outwardly but inwardly, who can shift your awareness around like you would move a child's toy. Just by moving one finger, they can change the way you feel, just as a good martial arts teacher can take one finger and put you on the floor, if they're a real master. So the master of the study of attention can just move one finger and shift the way you feel, or they can do much more.

Now, no teacher does it for you and unfortunately, some people have this idea that teachers of enlightenment or other subjects are supposed to watch over you and make sure that you do the work, or somehow magically make it happen. In Zen, and in other forms of self-discovery, we do have a transference that occurs where psychically, information—blocks of attention—are transferred to the student, which is a little different than in some other subjects. But that transference can only take place with the student who spends hours and hours working on their daily life as their teacher suggests – [working] on their meditation with a very enthusiastic, positive, hopeful, optimistic and fun attitude. Such students prepare themselves, and then you can transfer something to them.

We call it the transmission of the lamp in Zen. That's when we take enlightened states of mind, and literally you can transfer—just like you can hand somebody flowers—enlightened attention to someone. But you can only hand them, so to speak, as much as they can hold. If a person has a little glass, you can only fill it with a certain amount of water. If they have a swimming pool, you can fill it up. Someday you'll become endless, and then what's to fill up? (Rama laughs.)

Enlightenment is something that's inside you; it's not outside. This is a hard concept, I realize, but it's in your mind, not your brain—but it's in you. There's a place inside you. Let's say there are thousands and thousands of roads inside you. But there's one particular road—it's really there, this is not a figure of speech—and if you walk down that road, bam! Enlightenment is there. But we have to walk down thousands and thousands of roads, sometimes over and over again because we forget that we were on them a while ago, in order to find the road that is enlightenment. All things are part of enlightenment, it's true, yet there's one particular road. There's one particular pair of shoes that will fit Cinderella better than any others, and it's inside you.

The teacher shows you and aids you, both externally and internally, to get a sense of how to find that road and how to eliminate the roads that are not useful. But in order to be a successful student, you have to have a good teacher. Once you find the teacher, you have to really apply yourself and if you're very basic, you just sit there and learn and listen. As you become more advanced, you help the teacher to a certain extent in their work because there's a level of commitment, not so much to the teacher, but to the subject. You're in love with the subject, obviously even more so is the teacher. So the two of you just enjoy it.

There was a time in my life when I was going to become a botanist because I love the world of plants. I used to go out foraging with some of my botany teachers and we'd walk in the woods and things like that, and we just enjoyed so much being out in the woods. We shared something. I admired and respected my teachers, and one teacher I was walking around the woods with was a great teacher, not only a scholar but also a teacher and a gentleman. We would tromp around the woods, and he'd show me some weird fern or some strange vine, and we had a great old time. I also admired the way the teacher taught in the classroom. But what inspired me the most was the subject itself. There was a sense of shared camaraderie about the subject.

If you study with a teacher of enlightenment, if you enjoy enlightenment, if you enjoy meditating and the way you feel after you meditate; if you like learning about yourself, learning to utilize your mind in millions of new ways, overcoming fear, sorrow, anger, hatred, all of the things that make you unhappy; if you like transcending the limited self and merging with eternity, finding that there are tens of thousands of selves that you can be, countless worlds to explore; if you like all that stuff, the study of consciousness, then, if you find a good teacher, you've found someone who likes it even more than you do. So you share a common interest.

As a beginning student, you'll just sit there and listen and practice what the teacher says. If you don't do your homework, there's no progress—if you don't meditate on a daily basis and if you don't really look forward to that time. You make it the best time of your day, and then you have to be mindful all day long and practice thought control and all of the different things that are part of the subject of enlightenment.

If you do that enthusiastically and you feel good about it, then you will respect yourself because you're applying yourself properly, and you'll feel good. You're doing a good job. You're trying your best, and then you try a little harder. You'll respect your student—as a teacher—because they're doing a good job, and of course, you respect your teacher because you're so lucky to have one who's actually any good when there are so few who are. If you've found somebody like that, then do a good job for them.

This is the attitude of success, in other words. There are no technical secrets to being a good student other than hard work, working cleverly—meaning not working on things that waste your time, not spending your time with people who don't work well. If you hang around with a lot of bad students, you just pick up their habits. If you hang around with good students, then you do well.

When I was an undergraduate, I used to spend my time with other students who really liked the subject. We would sit next to each other in class. It was easy to figure out who was doing well, who really liked it, and I would sit with them sometimes. Sometimes I enjoyed sitting by myself, but most of the time we'd sit together and listen and take notes or do whatever. And then we would sometimes study together, not necessarily talking together.

At the university I went to, they had an honor society for people who were in the honor's program, and we would all spend our time studying together. Everyone else was partying and running around and having a wonderful time. We were partying and sitting still and having a wonderful time studying on Saturday night, Friday night. Oh, once in a while we'd go to a dance or have a great time, but we spent an inordinate amount of time studying—a lot more than your average student because that's what we got a kick out of. It reinforced tremendously that sense of scholarship to be with other people who were doing the same thing. Sometimes—I spent most of my time actually—studying alone in my little apartment because I always found I could assimilate more that way.

It was fun sometimes to work with other students who were doing well. Certainly I didn't spend time with people who weren't good students. Oh, I had friends and associates who I would go to a movie with, for whom studying was not the keystone of their life—not many, but a few. In other words, one is not an effete snob about the matter. That's just how it worked out. Our common interest was studying, so naturally I didn't want to spend time with people who were just running out to bars and partying all the time because I wouldn't have seen them very much. We wouldn't have something in common. What we [the study group] had in common was we really liked to work and excel at being students. It was fun. Everyone had figured that out.

Naturally, when you get to graduate school, the only people who are there are people like that. If it's a good graduate program, you're just dealing with the top ten percent of the class. There's an attitude of professionalism, sometimes boredom as far as I'm concerned, from a lot of graduate students. They're much too enamored of themselves and their study. It's one thing to work hard, it's another thing to take it all too seriously.

So as a student of enlightenment, it's good to find some people who really like their teacher and really like the study and spend time together. You don't form an exclusive club—how boring, how self-defeating. Rather, you enjoy spending time with each other because you're really excited about your meditations, what the teacher has to say. The subject itself, in other words, is exciting you. That's the trick, whether you're out in the woods with your botany teacher and looking at a fern, whether you're out in the desert with your enlightenment teacher looking at astral beings, whether you're sitting in the class, working on your own—you need to love learning. That's the secret of being a successful student.

You need to create a stillness in your life, otherwise you can never know if you love learning or not. You really need to separate yourself from the mainstream of humanity. Most successful students live alone or if they can't afford to live alone, they have their own room in a house they share with other successful students, and there's a sense of quietness to your life, a tremendous order, an overall cleanliness in everything that you do. Because without that stillness, the mind cannot turn inward or outward in a directed way.

A lot of people aren't successful students because they don't know how to study. Studying involves quiet. Your mind can't be running all over the place. You need a quiet place that feels good to study.

I remember in college there were so many people who used to study in the library, and I could never understand it because the library is the worst place to study—better a room in a noisy dorm, where at least you can put on some earplugs. The library was just filled with people who were goofing off, who were falling asleep. There was such a sleepy energy there that you wouldn't get anything done. The best thing to do was go in, get your books and go off by yourself someplace where the energy is clean. You need a place to meditate, to study, where the energy is clean.

So it's very important to choose an apartment, a house, a dormitory room, a rented room. The size doesn't matter. What matters is that you took the time to pick a proper room to do your working in and then you cleaned it up and you decorated it in a fastidious way that inspired you. If you don't have a clean working environment, you won't do well in most cases. There's the occasional bumbling genius who does well in a very cluttered environment; but they're few, to be honest. And of course, in the study of Zen, we feel the outer environment is simply a reflection of our inner state of consciousness. If your environment is a mess, probably your consciousness is a mess. By cleaning up our environment, it helps one clean up the mind.

So you select a good place where you like the energy, to study and work. Of those places that are available, you fix it up, you get all excited. This is the place you're going to meditate; this is the place you're going to study. You fix it up and you make it special. You get excited about it. You find the best teacher you can find and you begin and you learn, and you don't worry about graduating.

You don't worry about becoming enlightened. You share a common interest with those who study. Anyone who studies, if they just study a little bit or if they are great scholars, they're all the same, they're all students.

Sometimes you have the opportunity to help a student. You can't really do anyone's work for them, but sometimes you can get them excited about the subject. Excitement can be catching; that's what a teacher does. But you don't want to spend so much time doing that, that you neglect your own studies.

In the world of enlightenment, we see a lot of people who decide to go out and teach meditation, and they become so wrapped up in it that they stop progressing themselves and they really don't have that much new to teach. The most important thing is that you yourself should be progressing. There should be a greater level of accomplishment in your discipline, constantly. Without that level of accomplishment, what is there to teach? What is there to learn from a person who doesn't have that? Of course, there are people who put out they have that, but they don't. So the student must discriminate. You know yourself what your level of accomplishment is, unless of course you're completely insane and deluded, which happens sometimes.

People enter into those states of consciousness where they think they've become enlightened or this or that or the other thing, and in fact they have not. The best thing to do, if you've gone through one of those phases, is to be sensible, laugh at yourself for how foolish you were, realize that you're a beginner. Because even enlightened people think of themselves—and great teachers and scholars think of themselves—as beginners. They probably think of themselves as beginners more than others do—perpetual beginners who begin again each moment because their subject is endless.

The study of enlightenment in life is an endless subject. No one knows it all. An enlightened person doesn't know it all. They've just gone beyond knowledge into another realm that we can't even describe in words. But no one knows it all. Enlightenment simply means walking beyond this and all worlds into nirvana, which is beyond knowledge and ignorance. It's something else. But there's always more to learn. There's always more to become. That's what makes life so exciting.

Being a successful student is an attitude. Oh, I could talk for hours about study methods and this's and that's. But we don't really have hours on this particular tape. So I've hopefully transmitted that which is most important with a couple of little anecdotes and some feelings. And that's that success in studying has a lot to do, everything to do, with your attitude. It's a feeling that you don't necessarily have but you walk into—you make it happen. That feeling is love for being a successful student—not successful in the sense that other people think that you're successful, only in your own eye. It's a state of mind, in other words, which exists inside you, that you need to find.

Successful means that you work hard and do well and enjoy it. I'm not talking about success as a reputation that others hear. Who cares what others think? If they're successful, then they understand that what you're doing is no big deal—it's what you do when you work hard. If they're not successful, then do you want the admiration of those who don't understand anyway? It's kind of pointless.

Success is a personal matter. It means that you enjoy working very hard. You like the feeling of progressing. You like the feeling of expanding. You like the feeling of learning. It's a nice world to live in. It's very hopeful because there is always something new in it. You're never bored. There's no trivial pursuit. There's too much to learn, there's too much to be, there's too much to become.

(Zazen music begins in the background.)

A little bit of *Urban Destruction* in the background, from Zazen.

Being a successful student means having an attitude of success, which is—you need to like what you're doing, not just the accomplishment, the pot of gold at the end of the rainbow, but the rainbow itself.

CHAPTER EIGHTEEN

WINNING

Good morning, good afternoon, good evening. It depends on what time of day you're listening to this. Here it's about 1:15 in the morning. I'm in Big Sur, sitting by the fireplace, burning some Monterey pine. It's cloudy tonight. The ocean is overcast. A storm is coming in. It's very warm, though. It's December, almost Christmas time, and it's probably 60 degrees out tonight. Beautiful days—sunny, clear this time of year. The fog doesn't really come till the spring and summer here, and then it's only right along the coastline. But when the fog is there, if you happen to be there, you don't see too well. You can drive away from the fog, go back from the coast a half an hour, and it's completely sunny. And then come into the coast and you can't see more than a few feet ahead of yourself when the fog is very thick.

Today our subject is winning—the Zen of winning. Now that may seem to some like a contradictory term, which is appropriate. A lot of people perceive Zen as non-competitive. It's interesting, I built an advertising campaign around "Gaining the Competitive Edge through the Practice of Zen," and I got a few angry letters from ardent Zen practitioners—who seem to be terribly stuck in their practice—who said that the ad misrepresented Zen. How could Zen help you gain the competitive edge? Evidently, they've all read *Zen Mind, Beginner's Mind*, which is a fine book, and they've read that there should be no competition in Zen. But of course there's competition in Zen. Let's not be ridiculous. There's competition in everything in life. Zen gives you the competitive edge to be a winner.

Naturally, being a winner in Zen is very different than being a winner in a sense of competition as most people play the game in the world. Being a winner in Zen means competing and winning in the world of enlightenment, in the world of career, in the world of sports, in the world of personal aesthetic achievement. Winning is doing what you want to do, essentially.

Of course, part of Zen has to do with understanding precisely what it is you want to do. And a lot of people don't know. They think they know because they've been brought up with certain ideas and expectations of what they should do. Zen is very competitive. All self-discovery is competitive. We're not competing against anyone else who practices. That's an absurd idea.

There's enough room in eternity for everyone to be enlightened. We gain or lose nothing by the success of others. But we're definitely competing. We're competing against our imperfections, we're competing against the fog, illusion. We're only alive for a certain period of time in any given lifetime and we're competing against time. It's a race to see if we can wake up before we go to sleep again. That's the challenge—Zen challenges your mind.

Most people lead boring and complacent lives. By the time they're 30 or 40, they think there's nothing new under the sun. They've seen it all and done it all. The universe is endless, endless perfection. There are endless possibilities. Gaining the competitive edge, winning, is what Zen is all about—being able to do what it is you want to do and, of course, understanding—knowing—the still center of perfect being. That's winning, in my estimation. I'm sure one could choose other terms to express it, that perhaps might be less offensive to Zen practitioners who are stuck in their practice, but perhaps that's not my intent. I like common American usage, personally.

See, one of the problems with Zen or any practice is that it's a practice. That's why people don't win. The reason people don't win is they get stuck in ideas, habits, ways of seeing mostly—life, ourselves, the universe, what we do, what we don't do—and these ways of seeing block our natural energy and creativity. We have very fixed ideas about how we should approach things.

Perhaps we have been successful in something before, and now we assume we should approach the project or endeavor, the meditation, the career, the relationship, whatever it may be—sports, athletics, school—we assume we should approach it in the same way. And it's the doggonedest thing. Even if we were successful before, we won't be successful again. We might be successful in a certain sense, in that we may be able to replicate the results. Last semester you got all A's. This semester you used the same approach, and you got all A's again. But if you use the same approach, it means you're in the same state of mind, and so from the Zen point of view, you've lost.

Some will be quick to say, "Well, you know there's no winning and losing; that's just a state of mind in duality." But duality is part of reality, and there is definitely winning and losing. If you don't think so, talk to someone who's gone to the racetrack and lost, and talk to somebody who's gone and won. Talk to somebody who's beaten cancer, talk to somebody who hasn't. There is definitely winning and losing. It's a state of mind, yes; it's a way of looking at things. And I think it's a very honest and accurate way.

It seems to me that a lot of people use ideas of non-duality as an escape from reality. In other words, it is very easy to say there's no winning and losing, and justify the fact that you didn't do a very good job, that you didn't bring something to perfection. I like the idea of winning and losing. It's clean; it's sharp, like Zen. You won or you lost. I mean, it's one or the other. Only you can decide. It's based upon your inner predilection, your determination. It's a feeling. Winning and losing are feelings; something in us knows if we've won or lost.

Never subject yourself to the standards of others who define winning and losing in certain ways that may not be applicable to you. In other words, someone says that you're a winner or a loser; that means nothing, that's someone else's idea. Someone's in the fog and they can't see well. A boat may pass them, but they don't even know it's there. They may hear the rush of the wind and think it's a flock of birds. So it doesn't pay to listen much to what human beings have to say in their evaluation of you, since they don't evaluate themselves very properly. Because from the point of view of enlightenment, everyone is enshrouded in the fog. Once in a while the fog clears a little bit and you see a little better, but then it rolls back in again. Only the enlightened are outside of the fog.

So winning—I believe in winning. I like it. It's clean. I definitely don't believe in losing. It's a bad attitude. It's not necessary to lose, but it does happen once in a while. And honestly admitting that you lost and not trying to rationalize it or push it off, is an important step in self-assessment and mindfulness. Then understanding why you lost so that you can prevent that from happening again, is progress.

Winning, of course, is based to a certain extent upon *personal power*. To a large extent, if you have enough personal power you tend to win. If you don't, you tend to lose.

So the strategy of winning, from the Zen point of view, is gaining personal power. The real challenges, the places you need to win, are not necessarily on the sports field or in the office or in relationships or in running for election, or whatever. The Zen of winning has very little to do with that. It has everything to do with that, ultimately. But there are no techniques to learn that will cause you to win an election or to win on the job. I mean, there are techniques to learn that cause that to happen, of course. But they're not what you would suppose. In other words, you need power, balance and wisdom to win and to learn from your losses.

It is in Zen practice that you gain power, balance and wisdom, and the battles that you fight are within your own mind. That's where the real victories and defeats are.

Winning, the Zen of winning, is gaining control of your time, life and mind. Having the competitive edge to be able to succeed is having control of your time, life and mind. It might seem indirect. In other words, in order to win you're going to go work on a lot of things that don't seem at the moment directly applicable to your success in any given endeavor or project. But if you win, if you succeed in these small things, then you will find that any project that you approach—within reasonable limitations—you will be successful in. Most people put the cart before the horse, which is an interesting way to go through life. They approach everything directly. But in Zen we approach everything backwards or inside out. So it seems. It's not. Actually it's quite direct and very specific.

The description of the world that most people have—how you win, how you succeed, how you become happy—is very limited. They're in the fog. Once in a while a genuine insight comes through, but most of the time not.

So winning, then, is an approach to life, and the place it starts is not on the playing field or in the business organization. Nor is it competitive; we're not trying to win something from someone else. We're trying to do our best to bring perfection into whatever we turn our attention to. That's winning.

We live in a competitive society. To pretend that's not there is ridiculous. That's how the whole planet is set up. If you're not competitive, you don't succeed, you don't survive. It's part of the system here in this world. Zen is the acceptance of reality, many realities. In other words, there are as many reasons to win as to lose, so you might as well win. If you can marry a handsome man or a beautiful woman and you have two choices and both people are equally nice or obnoxious as the case may be, you might as well marry the wealthy one. That's what we call common sense, and Zen is definitely not devoid of it.

If you want to succeed in Zen, if that's winning for you—enlightenment is the game that you're playing, and there are many battles, many tournaments on different levels—then you should study with a winner. You have to find someone who has already succeeded, who is indeed enlightened. They can show you the way.

If you want to succeed in business, whatever it may be—school—always associate with winners, people who have understood something. You'll notice that they all share something in common—tremendous attention to detail in their personal lives and associations, a level of self-respect and integrity that seems to go beyond the bounds of necessity. That's why they win. In other words, there's the flash in the pan, which is a moment of lightning in the sky; lights everything up. The sudden illumination, the sudden success, and that's a part of the universal reality, but continued lightning, continued success, is dependent upon tremendous attention to detail.

Everything starts within your mind. Obviously, the way you conduct your life, physical choices you make, drain your power or give you power. If your power is low, then you stay in lower levels of mind and you don't see opportunities. You don't see problems coming. If you have more personal power and you're in higher states of mind, then naturally you see these things and you can adhere to them or avoid them.

Personal power is really the issue.

And it's only through tremendous attention to detail and searing self-honesty that you will be able to gain personal power.

Searing.

Self-honesty is not putting yourself down or feeling sorry for yourself. Self-honesty is looking at things as they are and then being compelled to make changes, honestly.

How do you become a winner? What is the Zen of winning? Well, the

Zen of winning starts out, of course, as all Zen practice does, with a central idea or reality, if you prefer, of *nothing*.

Everything is nothing. The way of *nothingness* is the way of Zen, or we could say the way of *everythingness* is the way of Zen. It's just a term. The contemplation of nothingness or everythingness is where everything starts.

There's a *still center* to the universe. Within that still center are all things, all achievements, all losses, all gains, all states of mind. Everything and nothing exist there. When you place yourself in harmony with that, that is to say, when you become aware, consciously, of the still center of being, you've won.

All that stands between you and that, are your uncontrolled thoughts, uncontrolled desires, attachments, aversions, your conceptions, your sense of a past, ideations of the future, your sense of self, tendencies from this and other lives.

When all those things are erased, there is nothing but eternity.

It's impossible to distinguish you from the still center of perfect being. So winning and gaining power has to do with addressing these subjects with patience, with clarity, with tremendous willpower.

Willpower, of course, is winning—gaining willpower and using it correctly and not abusing it, because when you abuse willpower, you waste it. There really is not an infinite supply of it at your disposal.

There is an infinite supply of it in the universe, but not necessarily at anybody's disposal.

As I suggested, winning begins with *nothingness;* matching yourself against nothingness. That's your only real opponent—nothingness. You're fighting against nothingness all the time. And the way you fight against nothingness is by creating a series of shields that you call personality, life history, feelings, ideas, ways of seeing. These are your shields against nothingness. You fight nothingness all the time.

Thought control is the ability to direct mind and attention anywhere. Your ability to win is dependent upon the power of your concentration. Winning is a state of mind.

First of all, you need to conceive of yourself as a winner, not a loser. And as I said, it's very helpful to associate with people who are successful in meditation, in enlightenment, in business, in sports, in cultural activities, in personal happiness—whatever the arena is, you pick it.

You need to model a new image of yourself as a winner—as a hero—not in an egotistical sense, but in a pragmatic and realistic sense.

We are nothing, we are made up of nothing.

There is no self.

We are whatever we decide we are.

If you decide that you're a winner, and if you hold that image in your mind strongly enough, you will become a winner.

Most people are taught from an early age on, to conceive of themselves as losers.

They're taught that there are a very special few who are eminently successful in life.

And unless you were raised among people who had that image of themselves—if your parents considered themselves to be winners and passed that conditioning on to you, then it will be easier for you.

But in most cases, that's not what it's like. Most people's parents don't conceive of themselves as being winners. They may be satisfied, they may feel that they did OK in life, or they may feel that they're inadequate, that they have failed, that they haven't done as well as they could have.

It's necessary to conceive—or hold in the mind—an image, and that image has to be backed up with reality.

You need to approach each task in your life, no matter how simple or how complex, with power.

And I feel it is better first to start winning on a small basis. That is to say, to pick and choose things initially, life tasks for yourself which are challenging, but which are not impossible to succeed at.

- You need to develop the profile of a winner.
- In other words, you need a string of successes behind you to buoy that self-image.
- Otherwise you have a terribly negative attitude about yourself, and it's very unlikely you're going to succeed at anything.

So you begin by learning something. Maybe you can't type, so you learn how to type and you do well at it. Maybe you've never practiced martial arts so you study karate or judo or aikido, and you gradually become better and better at it. Maybe you've never skied and you learn how. You've never meditated and you practice meditation, and you become better and better at it.

You go to school and you don't take the most difficult subjects to start with, or you don't go to the most difficult school, and you do well. Then go to a more difficult school.

In other words, you can raise the level of challenge, but first you have to develop a winning profile.

Naturally, as I've discussed on other tapes in this series and at the seminars, you need to continually examine your life, inner and outer, and see where you're losing and gaining power.

If you're losing power in your relationships with others, then you have to try and remedy that, and if you can't, you need to sever the relationship—if your primary goal is winning.

In your thoughts, you need to be selective.

Thoughts are powerful, powerful vehicles of attention and you have to only think positive thoughts about yourself and your endeavors, and think well of the endeavors of others.

When you hold positive thoughts and images in your mind all day long, all night long, you raise your power level and you create a vibratory energy around those thoughts. Those thoughts are more likely to manifest.

> In other words, whatever you think, you become.

If you think of thoughts of success and back them up with the hard work necessary to accomplish that success, then you'll be a winner.

If, on the other hand, you cherish doubts, negative thoughts, "Oh I can't," "Oh, it probably won't work out," "Oh, why bother?"—then you won't be a winner at all.

There's a tremendous amount of psychic transference that occurs.

People we are emotionally open to and close to affect us more than most people realize. So if you are emotionally open to people who conceive of themselves as losers, they are filled with self-doubts and anxieties, uncontrolled and unmitigated desires and angers and hates and jealousies, then you'll pick up a lot of that and you'll find yourself experiencing the mental states of others. If, on the other hand, you associate with people who are much more progressive, you'll pick that up. You won't steal anything from them; they will retain it, of course. But you're just sharing the positive energy and avoiding the negative energy.

You may say, "Well, I love so-and-so, how can I let go of them?" You don't have to. You do whatever you choose, but you must realize the result. What you think, you become. And your thoughts are affected strongly by those you are emotionally open to.

Winning begins in the home. It begins with your thoughts and your actions. You need to create a body of success—a strong physical body, a body you feel good about, that looks good and feels good within the range of age that you have. It's most important to engage in regular physical exercise, to maintain a high energy level, for most people. And it's important to feel good about the way you look, to care for your clothes and your appearance. It's all part of generating a winning image.

Naturally, real winning and losing all takes place at the meditation table. This is where the battles are, and, of course, in daily thought.

Winning is stopping all thought for protracted periods of time. Losing is sitting there and being subjected to all kinds of ridiculous thoughts.

Every time you sit down to meditate, you have to sit down with a resolve to win. You're going to win at zazen.

When you go to a Zen seminar, you need to have the resolve that you're going to use that seminar and not just sit there and think a lot of negative thoughts, or perhaps even pick up the negative thoughts of others and let them stay in your mind—their angers, their hostilities and their problems. You're going to sit there and will your mind to be happy, quiet and still, and learn from your teacher.

A lot of winning has to do with being happy and satisfied.

A lot of people miss this part. You need to feel good about your life. Winning is a great idea, but you can get stuck in it too. It's just another idea. It's another way of looking at life, an idea form.

But you need to renew yourself and your spirit, which you do of course in meditation, and you also do it *just by being happy with what is.*

Remember, winning is not winning or losing as the world defines it. You could lose the race, but win.

Winning means giving your very best effort to whatever you do—that's winning.

And if someone else runs faster than you or makes more money than you or is more adept in anything, that doesn't mean you've lost.

You're not measuring yourself in winning and losing against anyone else—only against yourself and your tendencies not to win, not to succeed, not to do all that you are capable of doing or be all that you are capable of being.

No discussion of winning and losing would be complete without considering not only the obstacles within yourself that you need to overcome and win, over—the mental conditioning, the ideas, the insecurities, doubts and so on, which gradually you have to root out one by one and replace with positive thoughts—

> but you must consider that there is definitely opposition from other human beings and also non-physical forces that don't want you to succeed.

People whom you love and whom even love you to a certain extent will try to block your success. They're threatened by it, particularly if it's spiritual success or inner success.

Human beings fear light and knowledge and power, and there's a weird quirky sort of thing that happens with people. When you log on to the truth and you start to become it, it threatens them because they live with countless falsehoods in their life.

If they recognize that you are achieving some level of self-awareness and becoming honest and true, then they have to look at their own lives and see that they're not doing the same.

A lot of people would rather not do that because they don't want to go through the struggle of change. Even though it will make them happy and feel wonderful, they don't want to. That's their conditioning because they think of themselves as losers subconsciously.

So people will try and block you. Some will do it just for pure hostility. But most are just afraid themselves. When we see a hero, on the one hand, we applaud them; on the other hand, there's something in a lot of people that wants to tear the hero down, that wants to see that the President is at fault, that wants the enlightened person to make mistakes, to fall—that's only the part of a being that is afraid of truth and light and knowledge and power.

So there are those who will seek to block you.

There are also non-physical forces, call them demons or entities or what you will. They exist—astral beings who try to do the same thing for the same reasons. So in order to win in the world of enlightenment, it's necessary to be able to will away these forces, to see that they're insubstantial.

Everything is voidness. Everything is emptiness.

And when you see the essential voidness and emptiness of all your opponents, they will have no power over you—when you see that they are only idea forms of the infinite mind.

This realization will come about in the deepest practice of meditation. When you stop all thought, when you win in meditation, the battle is won, the war is over and everything is still and peaceful.

You will come to see the eternal voidness of all things, the emptiness or completeness or fullness of all life and you will see that nothing is, really.

All the manifest forms of existence are but illusions. They're momentary displays of consciousness, flashes of lightning in the sky. They're there for a moment and then they're gone.

That's all life is.

Winning, then, has to do with gaining personal power through the practice of meditation and mindfulness, thought control; not draining your energy on ridiculous things or people; having a sense of mortality; realizing that you don't have endless energy and you need to conserve it and gain it; gaining a winning profile, conceiving of yourself as a winner, not a loser; being observant of those who would block and interfere with you and with your success and, of course, avoiding a sense of competition within your own being. [It's a] tremendous waste of energy to try to block anyone else. That same energy could be applied to furthering your own success.

What a foolish person who tries to block the success of another. They really interfere with their own success more.

How much better to use all of your energy just to be all you can be.

At the same time, it is necessary to be aware of those and disassociate oneself from those who would interfere with your success in enlightenment, in your career, in your life. They're not worth it.

The main thing that blocks you are your associations with others.

That's the main reason people fail, is they become attached to others who hold them back. Letting go of others and going forward may seem like a lonely and impossible task, but I assure you it's not.

Naturally, if someone is in the same state of mind and doesn't seek to block your success, then of course you have a friend and the two of you can strengthen each other. Such friends are rare, and if you find such a friend, value them.

There is no beginning and there is no end to life. Life is endless reality. There is reality after reality, spinning on endlessly into the cosmos, billions and billions of manifest universes. And underlying all of this is the unmanifest, the absolute reality. Both are existence, and then there's something beyond both the unmanifest and the manifest. We call it nirvana, beyond winning and losing. My idea is that as long as you're in the relative worlds, you should be realistic and know there is winning and losing here.

In nirvana there's no winning or losing. There's no one there to win or lose. But as long as you're in this world, there's definitely winning and losing.

Only the completely enlightened are beyond winning and losing.

Yet strangely enough, they had to win to get to the point of being beyond winning and losing. It seems contradictory. The rocket has to have enough thrust to get beyond the gravitational pull of the earth, then they can shut off the engines and coast. The thrust isn't necessary.

It is necessary to win in zazen, in meditation, in mindfulness, to be with a teacher who has already succeeded and learn from them, to win in your association with that teacher—meaning to do a good job, to bring perfection into everything in your life so you can go beyond all of this transitory nonsense and merge with the eternal. We would call that winning from the relative view, from the ten thousand states of mind. We'd say that's winning, from that point of view, those points of view.

But absorption in nirvana, there's no winning or losing. At that point, we've gone beyond space and time and condition and dimension and mind. There, there's no winning or losing.

I think it's very important to view life in terms of winning and losing until complete enlightenment has occurred. After that, there are no views, there is no mind, there is no self. There is only reality, and that's but a vague word to define that which is impossible, and I wish you well on your journey towards that goal, if we can call it that.

The absorption in nirvana, in perfection, is all that matters.

In all of the strategies in your life, in all of the winnings, they're only there to strengthen you and empower you for your final assault on the impenetrable cliffs of forever, which will one day give way. The windy cliffs of forever. The white light of eternity. The *dharmakaya*, the clear light of reality, in which all things are knowledge and perfection.

So I'm up here at Big Sur on the coast of California. It's around 2:00 in the morning. The world is sleeping and dreaming. Tomorrow it will awaken and everyone will spin off in a million and one directions, and so it will be forever—winning and losing, success and failure, pleasure and pain, loss and gain. That's the way it is in the *maya*, in the illusory worlds.

Even in the enlightened worlds—that are still worlds—there's winning and losing.

But beyond all of this, there's another condition and that's what I would direct your attention to.

Strangely enough, as I said, you need to become a winner to go beyond winning and losing.

But beyond all of this, my friend, there is something else.

Perfection. Not as just an ideation—as a living reality. It is a reality.

Think of that sometimes, dwell on that idea. Even though it may just be an idea for you, hold that idea in your mind. Don't worry about when it will happen, or how, or why. That isn't important. All that's important is that it exists; it is.

The universe is perfection, but there are just different ways to look at it from different stages of attention.

There are different views that the universe provides for itself to view itself.

But beyond all views, there's nirvana—shining, clear, perfect, void, full—and that is all that matters.

So it's necessary to go through all of the daily tasks and bring perfection to them, to learn to be perfect in your meditation, to win in all your endeavors so that one day you will be complete again as you once were in that perfection that is nirvana—that absolute absorption beyond time, space and condition, yet right here and now.

So this is Zen Master Rama from the windy cliffs of forever, of Big Sur, wishing you well on your journey and telling you that you can win. You can be a winner. It takes work, effort, but it's definitely worth it.

It is much nicer to live in a perfect mind, free from pain and agony of the thought forms that dominate most individuals—the jealousies, the deceptions, the hates, the revenge plots. What a terrible way to live. How painful to be unenlightened. Buddha called it "the nightmare of the day."

Anything but enlightenment is pure pain; it's the lack of enlightenment. There are joys, of course, and they should be enjoyed. And there are sorrows, and they should be passed over briefly. But enlightenment is reality. Meditate on that truth. Feel it, grow into it, become it, do whatever is necessary. It's all that is worthwhile.

So from the world of Big Sur, where the waves crash and the seals are all in the water by the rocks barking, or it's cloudy and moody and desolate in the wintertime around Christmas, I wish you well.

Also By the Author

BOOKS

Surfing the Himalayas

Snowboarding to Nirvana

Lifetimes: True Accounts of Reincarnation

Total Relaxation: The Complete Program for Overcoming Stress, Tension, Worry, and Fatigue

The Bridge Is Flowing But The River Is Not

The Lakshmi Series

The Wheel of Dharma

Insights: Talks On The Nature of Existence

Rama Live In LA

Talks and Workshops

The Last Incarnation

A Workshop With Rama

On The Road With Rama

Psychic Development

Zen Tapes

Tantric Buddhism

The Enlightenment Cycle

Insights: Tantric Buddhist Reflections on Life

MUSIC

Atlantis Rising

Breathless

Canyons of Light

Cayman Blue

Ecstasy

Enlightenment

Light Saber

Mandala of Light

Mystery School

Occult Dancer

Retrograde Planet

Samadhi

Samurai

Surfing the Himalayas

Tantra (2 vols)

Techno Zen Master

Urban Destruction

Zen Master

Zen Tapes: Talks on the Essence of Zen and Enlightenment

2002, 2020 © The Frederick P. Lenz Foundation for American Buddhism (the Foundation). All rights reserved. This product is published under exclusive license from the Foundation.

ALL RIGHTS RESERVED

No part of this publication may be reproduced, distributed, stored in a retrieval system, or transmitted in any form or by any means, including photocopying, recording, scanning, or by any information storage and retrieval system, or other electronic or mechanical methods, or otherwise, except as permitted under Section 107 or 108 of the 1976 International Copyright Act, without the prior written permission of the publisher, except in brief quotations embodied in critical articles and reviews, and certain other noncommercial uses permitted by copyright law.

Published 2002 by The Frederick P. Lenz Foundation for American Buddhism

Published 2020 by Living Flow
www.livingflow.com
Boulder, CO 80302 USA

Paperback ISBN 978-1-947811-25-6
Ebook . . . ISBN 978-1-947811-26-4

Publisher's Code r31-v11

Cover art & design by Meg Popovic
Interior dragon art by Janis Wilkins
Back cover photo by Greg Gorman

www.ingramcontent.com/pod-product-compliance
Lightning Source LLC
La Vergne TN
LVHW020925090426
835512LV00020B/3202